Violence and Trauma Without Borders

Jun Sung Hong
Jennifer M. Bondy • Anthony A. Peguero
Editors

Violence and Trauma Without Borders

Perspectives of Immigrants, Migrants, and Refugees

palgrave
macmillan

Editors
Jun Sung Hong
School of Social Work
Wayne State University
Detroit, MI, USA

Jennifer M. Bondy
School of Social Transformation
Arizona State University
Tempe, AZ, USA

Anthony A. Peguero
School of Criminology and Criminal Justice
Arizona State University
Tempe, AZ, USA

ISBN 978-3-032-29220-9 ISBN 978-3-032-29221-6 (eBook)
https://doi.org/10.1007/978-3-032-29221-6

This Palgrave Macmillan imprint is published by the registered company Springer Nature Switzerland AG.
The registered company address is: Gewerbestrasse 11, 6330 Cham, Switzerland

Foreword

Next year marks my twentieth year researching the immigration–crime nexus. Early on, I recognized a striking gap between what the evidence shows—that immigration and crime do not go hand-in-hand—and what much of the public believes: that immigration brings crime. In 2011, I created a course at the University of California, Irvine, designed to bust some of the most persistent myths about immigration, including the idea that it is a major driver of crime in the United States. More recently, with my academic partner-in-crime Graham Ousey, I conducted a meta-analysis of the immigration–crime literature, reviewing over 50 studies with more than 540 findings. Most recently, Graham and I published our book, *Immigration and Crime: Taking Stock*. As the title suggests, we provide a comprehensive survey of the field, leaving no stone unturned. All this is to say: I know the research base about as well as anyone can (this will be important in a moment, when I explain why this volume is sorely needed). Over nearly two decades, through dozens of studies and books and countless hours in the classroom, I have read, taught, and regularly cited the work of all three editors of *Violence and Trauma Without Borders: Perspectives of Immigrants, Migrants, and Refugees*. This editorial team has the diverse intellectual background and deep research experience needed to produce such a critical volume.

Violence and Trauma Without Borders examines the many forms of violence and trauma experienced by immigrants, migrants, and refugees—from violence within the home to broader societal harms and everything in between. The book encompasses the realities and experiences of immigrants across races, ethnicities, religions, and backgrounds, spanning generations, young and old. Its chapters address the challenges and unintended consequences that stem from forced migration, such as those during Russia's invasion of Ukraine, from global crises like the COVID-19 pandemic, and from systems of "crimmigration" that impose harsh, exclusionary policies on immigrants. Readers will encounter urgent topics such as child maltreatment, elder abuse, anti-Asian hate, domestic violence, and the trafficking of women and children. Along the way, contributors identify and define problems, dispel misconceptions, take intersectional perspectives, assess victimization risks and protective factors, and propose solutions aimed at minimizing harm.

Addressing such broad and complex issues is no small task, but this editorial team is more than up to it. Their intellectual backgrounds span sociology, social work, education, cultural studies, and criminology. Collectively, they bring more than 45 years of research experience on immigrant incorporation, socialization, and victimization. Their contributions over this time have earned them major awards, high-profile appointments, and recognition from national organizations. Couple this with a long list of intellectually diverse and accomplished contributors to the volume, and one realizes the reader is in good hands.

Returning to my earlier point about knowing the state of research: A quick survey of the academic literature reveals an overwhelming obsession with immigrant criminality, mirrored in the media, on social platforms, and in public discourse. This singular focus obscures an important but neglected reality: Immigrants themselves are often victims of violence and trauma—experiences that demand scholarly attention and practical responses. *Violence and Trauma Without Borders* brings these overlooked realities into view, compelling readers to confront them as essential social facts.

Irvine, CA Charis E. Kubrin

Acknowledgments

First and foremost, we wish to express our deepest gratitude to Elizabeth Graber, Chandralekha MahamelRaja, Samantha Scheidt, Ben Ingraham, Roberta Mistretta, and the staff members at Palgrave Macmillan for their expressed interest in our book proposal and for rendering invaluable assistance from the conception to the final stage of this edited book.

Secondly, we are extremely grateful to several people who provided assistance: Drs. John Doering-White (University of South Carolina), Yuri Jang (University of Southern California), Matthew M. Rivas-Koehl (Child Trends), Jonathan Ibarra (University of California, Santa Barbara), Rose M. Kim (Borough of Manhattan Community College), and Kay Varela (Arizona State University), who assisted us with this book. We deeply appreciated their insights and sound advice, which significantly enhanced the quality of this book.

We are thankful to the many immigrant rights activists who continue to fight for and advocate for equity and social justice on behalf of millions of immigrants, migrants, and refugees who sacrifice everything and undertake perilous and life-threatening journeys every year to cross the border.

Special thanks go to our mentors, colleagues, and students with whom we have had the pleasure of working closely over the years.

And most importantly, we are indebted to our family, whose unconditional love and support have sustained us and kept us going.

Contents

Editors and Contributors

About the Editors

Jun Sung Hong, Ph.D., is an associate professor in the School of Social Work at Wayne State University in Detroit, Michigan, USA, and a visiting professor in the Department of Social Welfare at Ewha Womans (Women's) University in Seoul, South Korea. He explores the antecedents and psychosocial outcomes of various forms of youth violence (i.e., bullying, polyvictimization, school shootings), risk-taking behaviors, and delinquency using primary and secondary data. He focuses on violence and victimization experienced by racial/ethnic minorities, immigrants, LGBTQ+, juvenile justice–involved, economically disenfranchised, and urban children, adolescents, and young adults. He has also collaborated with scholars in South Korea, Taiwan, Sweden, Scotland, Switzerland, Spain, Brazil, Germany, China, Hong Kong, Ukraine, Serbia, Iran, India, Belgium, and Indonesia on research projects. His research has been published in several major peer-reviewed journals and edited books. He co-authored a book entitled *School Bullying: Youth Vulnerability, Marginalization, and Victimization* with Dr. Anthony A. Peguero, which was published by Springer Press in 2020. He is also the leading editor of the *Handbook of School Violence, Bullying, and Safety*, which was published by Edward Elgar Publishing, Ltd. in 2024. He was also the lead editor of the book *Bullying: Global Case Studies in Policy and Prevention for Young People*, which features chapters on bullying in 110 countries and societies. This book was also published by Edward Elgar Publishing, Ltd. in 2026.

Jennifer M. Bondy, Ph.D., is an associate professor in the School of Social Transformation and an affiliate faculty member in the Mary Lou Fulton College for Teaching and Learning Innovation at Arizona State University. Her research focuses on the factors that promote and impede the successful integration of the children of immigrants into US schools. Dr. Bondy's most recent line of scholarship focuses on the intersections of teacher education and documentation status disparities. Her research has been published in major peer-refereed journals, and she co-authored a book entitled *Immigration and School Safety* (2021) with Dr. Anthony A. Peguero at Arizona State University. Dr. Bondy is currently the lead co-editor on a special issue, "Educational Equity: Disrupting White Supremacy and Colonialism in Schools," in the *Journal of Curriculum and Pedagogy*.

Anthony A. Peguero, Ph.D., is a foundation professor of Sociology and Criminology in the T. Denny Sanford School of Social and Family Dynamics and the School of Criminology and Criminal Justice at Arizona State University. His research interests involve youth violence, the intersection of the educational and juvenile justice systems, socialization and marginalization, and the adaptation of child immigrants. Dr. Peguero is also currently a member of the *National Academies of Sciences, Engineering, and Medicine*, Committee on "The Impact of Active Shooter Drills on Student Health and Wellbeing." He is also the Director of the *Laboratory for the Study of Youth Inequality and Justice* (YIJ). Dr. Peguero is also a member of the *Racial Democracy, Crime, and Justice Network* (RDCJN) and co-founder of *Latina/o/x Criminology* (LC), which holds the goals of advancing research on the intersection of race, crime, and justice. He is also the 2025–2026 vice president-elect of the American Society of Criminology (ASC), 2023–2024 president of the *Academy of Criminal Justice Sciences* (ACJS), 2023–2024 vice president of the *Society for the Study of Social Problems* (SSSP), and 2024–2025 vice president of the *Southern Sociological Society* (SSS).

Contributors

Fahmida Afroz School of Social Work, University of Georgia, Athens, GA, USA

Hassan Arab College of Social Science, Department of Sociology and Social Work, Kuwait University, Safat, Kuwait City, Kuwait

Miguel A. Arana Gevirtz School of Education, University of California, Santa Barbara, CA, USA

Haleigh Armstrong College of Education, Counseling Psychology, University of Texas, Austin, TX, USA

Dante' D. Bryant School of Social Work, University of North Carolina, Charlotte, NC, USA
Department of Africana Studies, University of North Carolina, Charlotte, NC, USA

Kateryna Buchko Faculty of Social Sciences, University of Stirling, Stirling, Scotland, UK
Department of Pedagogy, Ukraine and Social Work, Ukrainian Catholic University, Lviv, Ukraine

Anna Burlaka Grimsley High School, Greensboro, NC, USA

Viktor Burlaka Department of Social Work, University of North Carolina, Greensboro, NC, USA
American University Kyiv, Kyiv, Ukraine

Alison Cerezo Department of Counseling, Clinical, and School Psychology, University of California, Santa Barbara, CA, USA

Miya Chang Center for Multicultural Studies, Daegu Catholic University, Daegu, South Korea

Mijin Choi School of Social Work, Texas State University, San Marcos, TX, USA

Irena L. C. Connon Faculty of Social Sciences, University of Stirling, Stirling, Scotland, UK

Lena Dominelli Faculty of Social Sciences, University of Stirling, Stirling, Scotland, UK

Fernando Estrada Department of Specialized Programs in Professional Psychology, Loyola Marymount University, Los Angeles, CA, USA

Holly Feen-Calligan College of Education, Wayne State University, Detroit, MI, USA

Gabrielle Y. Garza Department of Communication, University of Utah, Salt Lake City, UT, USA

Leandra H. Hernández Department of Communication, University of Utah, Salt Lake City, UT, USA

Janice Iwama Department of Justice, Law and Criminology, American University, Washington, DC, USA

Arash Javanbakht Department of Psychiatry and Behavioral Neurosciences, Wayne State University School of Medicine, Detroit, MI, USA

Ashlee Jensen College of Health and Human Services, University of North Carolina Wilmington, Wilmington, NC, USA

Karime Jiménez-Limas School of Nursing, Johns Hopkins University, Baltimore, MD, USA

Rose M. Kim Social Sciences, Human Services and Criminal Justice, Borough of Manhattan Community College, New York, NY, USA

Hermeet K. Kohli Department of Social Work, University of North Carolina, Greensboro, NC, USA

Charis E. Kubrin Department of Criminology, Law and Society, School of Social Ecology, University of California, Irvine, CA, USA

Sarah Lindstrom-Johnson T. Denny Sanford School of Social and Family Dynamics, Arizona State University, Tempe, AZ, USA

Angelica Lopez T. Denny Sanford School of Social and Family Dynamics, Arizona State University, Tempe, AZ, USA

Ragini S. Malhotra Department of Sociology, University of Southern Maine, Portland, ME, USA

Daniel E. Martínez College of Social and Behavioral Sciences, School of Sociology, University of Arizona, Tucson, AZ, USA

Marissa Medina Department of Communication, University of Utah, Salt Lake City, UT, USA

David Okech School of Social Work, University of Georgia, Athens, GA, USA

Valeriia Peshkova Private Practice in Odesa, Odesa, Ukraine

Luis A. Romero Department of Sociology & Anthropology, Texas Christian University, Fort Worth, TX, USA

Bushra Sabri School of Nursing, Johns Hopkins University, Baltimore, MD, USA

Kay S. Varela School of Criminology and Criminal Justice, Arizona State University, Tempe, AZ, USA

James Diego Vigil School of Social Ecology, Department of Criminology, Law and Society, University of California, Irvine, CA, USA

Dexter R. Voisin Jack, Joseph and Morton Mandel School of Applied Social Sciences, Case Western Reserve University, Cleveland, OH, USA

CHAPTER 1

An Overview of Trafficking of Women and Children in the United States

Fahmida Afroz and David Okech

Introduction

Trafficking of Women and Children: Statistics and Contributing Factors

Exploitation of women and children through trafficking is a severe form of human rights violation (Greenbaum, 2014). However, generating credible estimates on the scope and magnitude of the problem remains a challenge (Zhang, 2022); a recent report from the International Labor Organization (ILO) revealed that approximately 27.6 million people worldwide are victims of forced labor. Women and girls comprise 11.8 million, while over 3.3 million are children (ILO, 2022). Victims are often trafficked into commercial sexual exploitation and forced labor (Greenbaum, 2014). Women and children subjected to sexual exploitation are coerced through threats into pornography, live or online sex shows, or the sex trade (Kotrla, 2010; Miller-Perrin & Wurtele, 2017). Meanwhile, child and adolescent victims of labor exploitation are forced

F. Afroz (✉) • D. Okech
School of Social Work, University of Georgia, Athens, GA, USA
e-mail: fahmida@uga.edu; dokech@uga.edu

J. S. Hong et al. (eds.), *Violence and Trauma Without Borders*,
https://doi.org/10.1007/978-3-032-29221-6_1

into begging, peddling, domestic servitude, and bonded labor, particularly in the agricultural and service industries (Greenbaum, 2016).

There is a misconception that human trafficking does not occur within the United States, yet it is a widespread issue across the country (Fordyce, 2012). Although the accurate number of trafficked victims in the United States remains unknown, the National Human Trafficking Hotline documented 10,360 incidents of trafficking in the year 2021 (National Human Trafficking Hotline, 2022). Additionally, between 2015 and 2020, the US Department of Homeland Security (DHS) received 6,171 reports through its tip line regarding suspected human trafficking and child sexual exploitation (Department of Homeland Security [DHS], 2022). Further, in the fiscal year (FY) 2022, DHS initiated 1,373 human trafficking investigations, which indicates an increase from 1,111 cases reported in fiscal year 2021 (United States Department of State [US DOS], 2023). Similarly, the Department of Justice (DOJ) launched 668 human trafficking investigations in fiscal year 2022, which marks an increase from 599 cases reported in the previous year (US DOS, 2023).

The prevalence of domestic minor sex trafficking (DMST) in the United States has been rising (Jordan et al., 2013). The number of American youths at risk of sexual exploitation ranges between 244,000 and 325,000, with approximately 199,000 cases of minor sexual exploitation occurring annually in the United States (Estes & Weiner, 2001). Additionally, an estimated 293,000 youths are vulnerable to becoming victims of domestic minor sex trafficking (DMST) (Estes & Weiner, 2001). Beyond domestic exploitation, an estimated 15,000 to 50,000 individuals are trafficked into the United States each year from different countries (US DOS, 2004). While the average age of female victims of DMST is between 12 and 14 years, the average age of boys and transgender youths at risk of DMST is 11 to 13 years (Jordan et al., 2013). Many of the child victims of DMST are homeless, runaway, or throwaway youths, and within 48 hours of running away, they are recruited into prostitution (Jordan et al., 2013). In the United States, sex trafficking commonly takes place through street prostitution, massage parlors, and brothels. In contrast, labor trafficking is prevalent in industries such as domestic service, agriculture, manufacturing, janitorial work, hospitality, construction, healthcare, elder care, and even strip clubs (US DOS, 2011). Additionally, foreign victims are more frequently subjected to labor trafficking, whereas domestic residents are more often exploited through sex trafficking (Banks & Kyckelhahn, 2011).

Children trafficked into the United States from other countries are exploited for both sexual and labor purposes (Gozdziak & Bump, 2008). Those trafficked for labor are often forced into domestic servitude or work in sectors such as salons and agriculture (Bronstein et al., 2010; Smolenski & Ingerman, 2017). Several environmental and structural factors contribute to the trafficking of children from low-income countries to the United States. One key factor among these includes the separation of children from their families and communities due to changes in national economic policies, war, civil unrest, or natural disasters like drought (Smolenski & Ingerman, 2017). For example, a change in government agricultural policy might force families to abandon farming and migrate to urban areas. In these transitions, adults may move to cities for work, leaving children behind, or children may be pushed into street-based work, such as peddling, to support their families (Smolenski & Ingerman, 2017). These children, left unsupervised and without stable support systems, often face heightened risks of exploitation (Smolenski & Ingerman, 2017).

In other cases, forced migration caused by political instability, armed conflict, or environmental crises leads to family and community separation, especially making children vulnerable to trafficking (Capaldi, 2014). Unaccompanied children who lack parental care and protection are often targeted by traffickers (Capaldi, 2014). Sometimes, families driven by poverty and desperation encourage their children to seek work opportunities in the United States and entrust them to intermediaries who promise safe housing, schooling, and paid employment (Smolenski & Ingerman, 2017). Unfortunately, the reality is often starkly different (Smolenski & Ingerman, 2017). Many of these children end up living in poor conditions without access to education, family, or community, and are forced to work without pay (International Committee of the Red Cross [ICRC], 2004). Some are even subjected to sexual abuse and coerced into the commercial sex trade (Bales et al., 2004).

Several factors increase youths' vulnerability to trafficking, including political, social, economic, family, and individual influences. Family-related factors that contribute to the risk of child trafficking include parental substance abuse, lack of caregivers, a history of involvement with child welfare services, and placements in foster care or group homes (Jaeckl & Laughon, 2021). Additionally, family and social networks involved in trafficking or the sex trade further elevate the risk of children being trafficked (Klatt et al., 2014; Miller-Perrin & Wurtele, 2017). Other forms of family factors, such as physical, mental, and sexual abuse, also increase the likelihood of trafficking victimization of children. To escape these abusive situations, many youths run away from home, which eventually makes them vulnerable to trafficking (Wilson & Widom, 2010).

A study involving 913 adolescents found a higher prevalence of family violence, emotional abuse, sexual abuse, physical abuse, emotional and physical neglect, and foster care placement among these adolescents (Reid et al., 2018). The study also highlighted health risk behaviors, with a significant percentage of these adolescents having a history of substance abuse, suicidal thoughts or attempts, involvement in relationships with criminal individuals, and chronic running away (Reid et al., 2018). Literature also indicates a link between substance abuse and abusive experiences in youth, as such experiences can contribute to drug addiction. Furthermore, substance abuse often leads youths into risky behaviors, such as engaging in prostitution to source money for their drug use, which consequently increases their vulnerability to trafficking (Miller-Perrin & Wurtele, 2017).

Social factors that increase the risk of trafficking for women and children include violence, government corruption, discrimination, armed conflict, political instability, unemployment, and lack of access to education (Fouladvand & Ward, 2019; Miller-Perrin & Wurtele, 2017). Conflict in countries creates opportunities for human traffickers to traffic people (Rahman, 2011). For example, during the civil war in the Ivory Coast, many children were recruited as child soldiers by both government forces and rebel groups (Sabine, 2008). Girls recruited by militias were often tasked with domestic duties such as cooking, but they were also subjected to sexual exploitation (Sabine, 2008). Armed conflict and deeply rooted cultural norms marginalize women and consequently exacerbate their economic dependence (Abioro & Akinyemi, 2020). Additionally, limited access to education and employment opportunities keeps many women trapped in poverty and perpetuates a cycle of exploitation (Sanders, 2025). Further, failure of government policies and responses addressing these systemic issues due to corruption, weak enforcement, and inadequate resources enhances the risk of trafficking of women and children (Abioro & Akinyemi, 2020).

Sociocultural elements such as gender inequality and devaluation of women and girls also play a significant role in making individuals vulnerable to trafficking (Miller-Perrin & Wurtele, 2017; US DOS, 2005). Economic factors contributing to trafficking risk include extreme poverty, economic deprivation, limited job opportunities, and wealth disparities

(Mo, 2018). Additionally, the combined pressures of economic hardship, the desire to escape poverty, discriminatory environments, and the search for employment opportunities often push individuals to pursue risky occupational choices, which increases their susceptibility to trafficking (Miller-Perrin & Wurtele, 2017; Mo, 2018).

Traffickers often target children and women in vulnerable situations and exploit their weaknesses through deception, false promises of assistance, and financial incentives (Reid et al., 2018). In many cases, traffickers establish friendships with their victims and offer them gifts such as food, clothing, and jewelry, or even have sex in exchange for favors (Albanese, 2007). Once the victims are entrapped in trafficking, they endure ongoing abuse, control, neglect, and threats. A study examining 43 cases of minor sex trafficking victims revealed that traffickers use various techniques to entrap their victims. These strategies include promises of a better life, spending money on grooming, offering drugs, establishing romantic or sexual relationships, and building trust or friendship (Reid, 2016; Roe-Sepowitz, 2019).

How Gender Plays a Role in Trafficking Vulnerability of Women and Children

Gender inequality is widely recognized as one of the root causes of human trafficking, particularly affecting women and children (Crawford, 2019; Hounmenou, 2016). Structural inequalities such as limited employment opportunities, discrimination, and restricted access to education exacerbate trafficking risks (Weatherburn, 2015). In societies where these vulnerabilities persist, women often experience cultural subordination, which increases their risk of exploitation (Weatherburn, 2015). Furthermore, poverty exacerbates the effects of gender inequality, as women from poverty-stricken families are particularly susceptible to the risk of trafficking (Crawford, 2019). In some cases, families facing extreme poverty may resort to giving away their daughters for commercial exploitation as a desperate means of survival (Crawford, 2019).

The intersection of gender inequality and poverty further exacerbates women's and children's trafficking vulnerability. This issue is reinforced by social norms and cultural traditions perpetuating discrimination (Crawford, 2019). Women's disadvantaged status, which has been shaped by prevailing gender stereotypes and devalued social roles, continues to place young girls at greater risk of trafficking and commercial sexual exploitation (D'Cunha, 2002). For instance, in Cambodia, the widespread trafficking of girls into brothels and karaoke bars in Thailand is linked to gender-related risk factors, including harmful cultural and societal norms, the feminization of poverty, and religious beliefs that view females as being born from bad karma. Additional contributing factors also include early marriage, divorce, gender-based violence, and disparities in educational attainment (Crawford, 2019).

Traditional practices in many societies prioritize boys' education over girls', based on the perception that investing in girls' education is a waste of resources. This belief results in significantly lower school enrollment rates for girls than boys (United Nations International Children's Emergency Fund [UNICEF], 2006). In Southeast Asia and other regions, girls are less likely to achieve literacy, attend primary school, or progress to secondary education. Even when they do access education, they frequently encounter discriminatory attitudes and biases that further entrench gender inequality and limit their potential (UNICEF, 2006). These systemic issues make girls particularly vulnerable to exploitation and trafficking (Wakgari, 2014). Beyond education, gender-based discrimination also extends to employment opportunities. The gendered division of labor restricts women's involvement in public and productive sectors, which, as a result, limits their economic independence and reinforces their vulnerability to exploitation (Crawford, 2019).

Moreover, gender inequality and the early objectification of women and girls contribute to their vulnerability to trafficking. From a young age, they may internalize the belief that their primary value lies in being sexual objects, increasing their susceptibility to exploitation in the commercial sex industry (Franchino-Olsen, 2021; Konstantopoulos et al., 2013). Cultural norms in many societies further normalize gender-based violence against women, which leads to the perpetuation of a cycle of abuse, thus increasing their likelihood of being trafficked (Chong, 2017).

Research has also shown a strong link between poverty, injustice, and social inequality (Barner et al., 2014). Individuals experiencing social inequality are less likely to possess social capital, which is crucial for building supportive networks and achieving stability (Barner et al., 2014). Furthermore, violence against women and sexual victimization are more prevalent in areas with high rates of unemployment and poverty (Martin et al., 2006; Vyas & Heise, 2016). The lack of social capital, combined with systemic gender inequality, further exacerbates women's vulnerability to trafficking (MacKinnon, 2011). These factors push many women to migrate internally and internationally for better economic opportunities (Piper, 2005). While poverty is often cited as a key driver of migration, gender inequality is critical in encouraging women to leave their home countries in search of adequate income to support their families (Benería et al., 2012). The feminization of poverty, migration, and trafficking is deeply interconnected, as gender discrimination restricts women's access to fair wages and economic opportunities in their home countries, thereby increasing their susceptibility to exploitation, particularly sexual exploitation (Noyori-Corbett & Moxley, 2016).

Human trafficking is closely associated with gender inequality, with key contributing factors including gender-based violence and stereotypical gender roles (Meriläinen & Vos, 2015). The majority of individuals negatively affected by gender inequalities are women, which heightens their vulnerability to trafficking (Voronova & Radjenovic, 2016). Additionally, the intersection of violence against women, the feminization of poverty, globalization, and exploitative capitalist market forces exacerbates women's and children's susceptibility to trafficking (Jones & Kingshott, 2016). In the United States, the patriarchal structure of society further compounds this risk. Jones and Kingshott (2016) argue that male dominance within the US criminal justice system, where men overwhelmingly hold key positions such as legislators, judges, and law enforcement officials, results in anti-trafficking efforts that fail to achieve meaningful impact. This systemic bias reinforces male authority and perpetuates the structures that allow trafficking to persist.

Gender inequality plays a significant role in shaping vulnerability to human trafficking, with women facing a heightened risk due to systemic disparities. The literature consistently reports that women are more susceptible to trafficking, particularly in societies where their rights and freedoms are more restricted compared to men. A recent study examined the relationship between trafficking and gender inequality and found that countries with higher levels of gender inequality also had higher rates of human trafficking (Ariail et al., 2024). These findings underscore that human trafficking is not only a human rights violation but also a profoundly gendered issue disproportionately affecting women and girls. Addressing gender inequality is crucial in combating trafficking, and adopting a gender-sensitive approach in assisting survivors can help mitigate stigma and stereotypes in the recovery process (Querol & Lerner, 2024).

Like girls, boys are also trafficked across the world (Tien, 2012). There is a prevailing notion within traditional masculinity that men and boys are not vulnerable to exploitation, especially sexual exploitation, which hinders the recognition and understanding of their victimization in human trafficking (Barron & Frost, 2018; Todres, 2010). However, evidence indicates the prevalence of trafficking victimization among men and boys, both in the commercial sex trade and forced labor sectors (Barron & Frost, 2018; Todres, 2010). A recent study found that the number of boys involved in child sex trafficking was nearly equal to that of girls (Greenbaum, 2014). A legal report further revealed that in Afghanistan, which is often considered one of the worst places for girls, boys are more vulnerable to being trafficked than girls (Tien, 2012). Men and boy victims of trafficking are prevalent in the United States as well (Jones, 2010). In the United States, young boys are primarily trafficked into the child pornography industry and labor trafficking (Barron & Frost, 2018; Jones, 2010). Besides child pornography, the demand for cheap labor, combined with the migration of men from impoverished countries to the United States for employment, has contributed to the labor trafficking of men and boys within the country (Jones, 2010). These victims of labor trafficking include not only foreign nationals but also US citizens, legal residents, and lawful visitors (Jones, 2010).

Gender is often portrayed in trafficking literature primarily through a focus on females (Hebert, 2016). Such framing has resulted in an over-concentration of scholarship in certain areas, while leaving substantial gaps in our understanding of the intersecting structural forces that drive migration, create conditions for exploitation, and leave many victims unrecognized or unprotected by existing anti-trafficking laws and policies (Hebert, 2016). In reality, both males and females experience gender-based pressure shaped by broader structural factors such as race, ethnicity, nationality, and class (Hebert, 2016). These intersecting factors often influence their decisions to migrate within or across national borders (Hebert, 2016). As a result, they are frequently concentrated in sectors that are prone to labor exploitation, such as construction, mining, logging, fishing, and military contracting (Hebert, 2016).

Impact of Trafficking on Women and Children

There is ample evidence from research that trafficking victimization causes harmful consequences for the individuals who experience victimization. Such negative consequences can last for an extended period (Kulig & Cullen, 2021). It has been reported that trafficking experience at a young age can have far-reaching effects (Warria, 2020). A study examined the impact of trafficking on the behavior of children and reported withdrawal behavior among the affected children (Nnebedum & Ogugua, 2022). The respondents reported experiencing sexual and verbal abuse while trafficked. Additionally, this study also indicated that child trafficking leads to various negative outcomes, such as poor physical and psychological health, poor performance in school, low self-esteem, depression, and distrust (Nnebedum & Ogugua, 2022).

Another study examined the association between exploitation age and social health issues and revealed that individuals who experienced sex trafficking as minors and adults reported having problems with a romantic partner, family, school, and housing. The findings of this study indicated that experiencing trafficking may significantly affect the social life of a victim (Krushas & Kulig, 2023). Another study that examined the relationship between stigmatization and health outcomes among child sex trafficking survivors mentioned that victims of child sex trafficking suffer from social isolation, difficulty reintegrating into the community, sexually transmitted infections, reproductive health issues, seizures, malnutrition, untreated injuries, depression, anxiety, PTSD, eating disorders, and substance misuse (Wallace et al., 2022). Likewise, a recent study that examined the prevalence of mental disorders among sex-trafficked children reported higher rates of ADHD, bipolar disorder, and PTSD found in the sample of trafficked youth in comparison to other high-risk groups (Palines et al., 2020).

The common mental health consequences that trafficking survivors experience include depression, anxiety, and posttraumatic stress disorder (PTSD) (Kiss et al., 2015). Additionally, the prevalence of psychological morbidity among female trafficking survivors was reported in a systematic review (Moyce & Schenker, 2018). A survey conducted in South Asia also demonstrated the prevalence of symptoms of PTSD among both male and female survivors of trafficking (Hopper & Gonzalez, 2018). Another study conducted with 1,387 trafficking returnees in Ethiopia found that 34.5% participants had symptoms of PTSD (Gezie et al., 2018). Trafficking survivors also experience stigma upon returning to their home country (Vijeyarasa, 2013). It has been reported that their psychological and emotional trauma is intensified when they experience stigma after returning to their home community (Baldwin et al., 2015).

The prevalence of suicidal ideation among trafficking survivors is also reported in the literature. A study conducted with more than 100 trafficked women reported that 41.5% of the participants attempted suicide (Lederer & Wetzel, 2014). Another study conducted in Ghana with 116 female victims of labor trafficking found that exposure to violence increases psychological distress (Edgemon et al., 2024). Additionally, a study conducted in the Greater Mekong subregion, which includes Cambodia, Thailand, Vietnam, Laos, Myanmar, and Yunnan Province of China, reported suicidal ideation among trafficking victims with PTSD symptoms (Kiss et al., 2015). In this same study, 58% of the children reported feelings of shame, and 54% reported concern over returning home as they were worried about how they would be treated there.

Similarly, a study conducted with 387 trafficking survivors aged 10 to 17 at the Greater Mekong subregion, which includes Thailand, Cambodia, and Vietnam, reported that 25.5% of the participants had PTSD symptoms. The same study revealed that 15.8% of the total 387 participants had suicidal ideation in the past month. Additionally, 5.4% of children who participated in the study had at least attempted suicide in the last month. This study also revealed the association between self-harm and feelings of shame. (Kiss et al., 2015). Women who were sex-trafficked or experienced sexual abuse as domestic laborers reported 24% of the women had sleep disturbance as the most common PTSD symptom, and they were assessed by the study after 90 days or more of their entering into posttrafficking services (Zimmerman et al., 2006). Also, female sexual assault survivors who had PTSD symptoms found an association between trauma-related sleep disorders and suicidality (Krakow et al., 2000; Okech et al., 2018). Self-harm behavior among child and adolescent trafficking survivors, such as suicide attempts and self-injury, was more than four times higher among participants with PTSD symptoms than those without PTSD (Kiss et al., 2015).

The consequences of domestic sex trafficking in the United States show that women face high rates of physical and sexual violence, as well as an increased risk of Human Immunodeficiency Virus (HIV)/ Acquired Immune Deficiency Syndrome (AIDS), Sexually Transmitted Infections (STIs), Hepatitis, and other infectious diseases (Raphael et al., 2010).

Similarly, commercially sexually exploited youth experience significant physical and sexual violence from pimps, customers, and others in the commercial sex industry (Fedina et al., 2019). These youth are also at heightened risk of HIV/AIDS, STIs, unintended pregnancies, and poor overall health (Fedina et al., 2019). Additionally, they often suffer from complex and untreated mental health issues, including depression and suicidal ideation (Fedina et al., 2019; Klain, 1999).

The long-term challenge that trafficking survivors experience after exiting human trafficking is financial difficulties, though this same risk factor, poverty, is responsible for making them human trafficking victims. The financial difficulties trafficking survivors face during their reintegration phase include unemployment, lack of savings, family debt, and inability to provide financially for their families. When they fail to support their families financially, it negatively affects their family relationship as well as their reintegration process (Tsai et al., 2017).

Challenges Associated with Prevention of Women and Child Trafficking

Preventing trafficking of women and children presents numerous challenges. One of the challenges is inadequate training of the local and state law enforcement on trafficking-related laws, victim identification, and interrogation procedures (Clawson et al., 2006). Additionally, the successful implementation of such training depends on improved coordination between law enforcement agencies, nongovernmental organizations working with this population (NGOs), and prosecutors, as each can share specialized knowledge from their respective sectors (Fordyce, 2012). However, these groups are usually unaware of each other's capabilities, which hinders collaborative efforts (Fordyce, 2012).

Moreover, brief training on trafficking indicators, such as limited English proficiency, nervousness when answering questions about citizenship status, and third-party control in conversations, could significantly improve the identification of trafficking victims (Clawson et al., 2006). Besides training law enforcement on victim identification, educating the public about human trafficking indicators is equally important, as it enables community members to recognize warning signs and report them to authorities (Fordyce, 2012). Further, there is a misconception in the United States that human trafficking is an issue confined to developing countries and that it does not occur within the United States (Fordyce, 2012). This misconception sometimes leads to a lack of media coverage of domestic human trafficking incidents (Clawson & Dutch, 2008). It has been emphasized that for combating trafficking, law enforcement agencies and service providers should collaborate with the media to ensure consistent and accurate reporting of trafficking cases rather than waiting for high-profile cases to emerge (Fordyce, 2012).

Another challenge in addressing human trafficking is the lack of resources, which include a limited number of personnel for investigations, victim identification training, service providers, and advocates to educate the public (Clawson & Dutch, 2008; Rand, 2010). To address this problem, community members can be a valuable resource in identifying victims, which may aid in reducing the burden on law enforcement (Fordyce, 2012). A unified community stance against child labor can play a crucial role in deterring traffickers (Fordyce, 2012). Additionally, public awareness campaigns should be expanded to the local level, as well as using multiple languages to engage communities (Logan et al., 2009). Further, since language barriers remain a significant issue for law enforcement in victim identification (Okech et al., 2012), emphasis should be given to recruiting individuals with these skills (Fordyce, 2012). Moreover, improved data collection and the creation of a national trafficking database, such as the Human Trafficking Reporting System (HTRS), could provide a more accurate picture of trafficking across the United States (Farrell et al., 2010).

A significant challenge in human trafficking investigations is the lack of proper techniques for interviewing victims and witnesses (Fordyce, 2012). According to a study, the current screening process of Customs and Border Patrol (CBP) for unaccompanied children is ineffective, as it is not conducted appropriately by child welfare specialists (United States Department of State [U.S. DOS], 2011). While progress has been made in enhancing penalties and investigations, more efforts are required on victim support, as victim testimony is crucial for successful prosecution (Fordyce, 2012). It has also been recommended that consular officers and border patrol agents be provided training on detecting visa fraud and weaknesses in visa programs, as this could greatly enhance trafficking prevention efforts (U.S. DOS, 2011).

Additionally, since 2005, the US government has actively worked to identify industries where exploitative labor practices are standard. Under the US Department of Labor, the Bureau of International Labor Affairs

(ILAB) publishes an annual list of goods and their countries of origin suspected of being produced through forced or child labor, violating international standards. In 2016, this list identified 139 goods from 75 countries linked to such exploitative practices (Aronowitz, 2019; US Department of Labor, 2016). However, the list does not account for labor abuses occurring within US farms and construction sites, nor does it address the role of the transportation and service industries, which are facilitating forced labor and sexual exploitation (Aronowitz, 2019). Addressing these gaps is crucial to developing comprehensive anti-trafficking strategies encompassing all sectors where exploitation persists.

Conclusion

In conclusion, the literature demonstrates that human trafficking affects individuals across gender, age, and nationality, with boys and men too often overlooked in both research and policy responses. Structural inequalities such as poverty, conflict, weak governance, and entrenched gender norms create conditions that make individuals vulnerable to exploitation. While girls and women face distinct risks due to systemic gender inequality, boys and men also experience exploitation, often hidden due to societal perceptions of masculinity. Trafficking prevention and intervention efforts must therefore move beyond binary understandings of victimhood and incorporate a nuanced, intersectional lens. Addressing the full scope of trafficking requires inclusive policies, structural reforms, and sustained attention to how gender, race, and socioeconomic status shape vulnerability. Only then can efforts truly ensure equitable protection and justice for all trafficking victims.

References

Abioro, T., & Akinyemi, O. (2020). Worsening women trafficking, multidimensional poverty and gender inequality: The vulnerabilities, playouts and governmental responses in West Africa. *Polish Political Science Yearbook, 4*(49), 87–104.

Albanese, J. (2007). *Commercial sexual exploitation of children: What do we know and what do we do about it?* NIJ Special Report, NCJ (No. 215733). U.S. Department of Justice, National Institute of Justice. https://www.ncjrs.gov/pdffiles1/nij/215733.pdf

Ariail, D. L., Smith, K. T., & Smith, L. M. (2024). Human trafficking and gender inequality: How businesses can lower risks and costs. *Journal of Risk and Financial Management, 17*(9), 418.

Aronowitz, A. A. (2019). Regulating business involvement in labor exploitation and human trafficking. *Journal of Labor and Society, 22*(1), 145–164.

Baldwin, S. B., Fehrenbacher, A. E., & Eisenman, D. P. (2015). Psychological coercion in human trafficking: An application of Biderman's framework. *Qualitative Health Research, 25*(9), 1171–1181.

Bales, K., Fletcher, L., & Stover, E. (2004). *Hidden slaves: Forced labor in the United States.* Human Rights Center, University of California, Berkeley. https://escholarship.org/uc/item/4jn4j0qg

Banks, D., & Kyckelhahn, T. (2011). *Characteristics of suspected human trafficking incidents, 2008–2010* (pp. 1–12). US Department of Justice, Office of Justice Programs, Bureau of Justice Statistics. https://justicestudies.com/pubs/hum-traffick.pdf

Barner, J. R., Okech, D., & Camp, M. A. (2014). Socio-economic inequality, human trafficking, and the global slave trade. *Societies, 4*(2), 148–160.

Barron, I. M., & Frost, C. (2018). Men, boys, and LGBTQ: Invisible victims of human trafficking. In *Handbook of sex trafficking: Feminist transnational perspectives* (pp. 73–84). Springer International Publishing. https://link.springer.com/chapter/10.1007/978-3-319-73621-1_8

Benería, L., Diana Deere, C., & Kabeer, N. (2012). Gender and international migration: Globalization, development, and governance. *Feminist Economics, 18*(2), 1–33.

Bronstein, S., Lyon, A., & Poolos, A. (2010). Held as slaves, now free. *CNN.* http://www.cnn.com/2010/CRIME/12/02/slave.labor.ring.busted/

Capaldi, M. (2014). *Unfinished business: Ending child prostitution, child pornography and child trafficking for sexual purposes.* Bangkok: ECPAT International. http://www.ecpat.org/wpcontent/uploads/2016/04/UNFINISHED%20BusinessReport_2015.pdf

Chong, N. G. (2017). Human trafficking and sex industry: Does ethnicity and race matter?. In *Human trafficking* (pp. 119–136). Routledge. https://doi.org/10.1080/07256868.2014.885413

Clawson, H. J., & Dutch, N. (2008). *Identifying victims of human trafficking: Inherent challenges and promising strategies from the field.* US Department of Health and Human Services (HHS), 3. https://www.aspe.hhs.gov/sites/default/files/migrated_legacy_files/42671/ib.pdf

Clawson, H., Dutch, N., & Cummings, M. (2006). *Law enforcement response to human trafficking and the implications for victims.* ICPSR Data Holdings. https://www.ojp.gov/pdffiles1/nij/grants/216547.pdf

Crawford, M. (2019). International sex trafficking. In *A feminist perspective on human trafficking of women and girls* (pp. 95–116). Routledge. https://doi.org/10.1080/02703149.2016.1206784

D'Cunha, J. (2002, November). Trafficking in persons: A gender and rights perspective. In *Expert group meeting on trafficking in women and girls* (pp. 18–22). https://static.un.org/womenwatch/daw/egm/trafficking2002/reports/EP-DCunha.PDF

Department of Homeland Security. (2022, January). *Department of Homeland Security strategy to combat human trafficking*, The importation of goods produced with forced labor, and child sexual exploitation. The Department of Homeland Security. https://www.dhs.gov/sites/default/files/publications/20_0115_plcy_human-trafficking-forced-labor-child-exploit-strategy.pdf

Edgemon, T. G., Clay-Warner, J., Kawashima, T., Anarfi, J. K., & Okech, D. (2024). Violence increases psychological distress among women trafficking survivors in Ghana. *Violence Against Women, 31*(6–7), 1469–1487.

Estes, R. J., & Weiner, N. A. (2001). *The commercial sexual exploitation of children in the US, Canada and Mexico.* University of Pennsylvania, School of Social Work, Center for the Study of Youth Policy. https://abolitionistmom.org/wp-content/uploads/2014/05/Complete_CSEC_0estes-weiner.pdf

Farrell, A., McDevitt, J., & Fahy, S. (2010). Where are all the victims? Understanding the determinants of official identification of human trafficking incidents. *Criminology & Public Policy, 9*(2), 201–233.

Fedina, L., Williamson, C., & Perdue, T. (2019). Risk factors for domestic child sex trafficking in the United States. *Journal of Interpersonal Violence, 34*(13), 2653–2673.

Fordyce, E. M. (2012). Identifying the unknown: Challenges and solutions to US human trafficking investigations. *PublicINReview, 1*(1), 23–32.

Fouladvand, S., & Ward, T. (2019). Human trafficking, vulnerability and the state. *The Journal of Criminal Law, 83*(1), 39–54.

Franchino-Olsen, H. (2021). Vulnerabilities relevant for commercial sexual exploitation of children/domestic minor sex trafficking: A systematic review of risk factors. *Trauma, Violence, & Abuse, 22*(1), 99–111.

Gezie, L. D., Yalew, A. W., Gete, Y. K., Azale, T., Brand, T., & Zeeb, H. (2018). Socio-economic, trafficking exposures and mental health symptoms of human trafficking returnees in Ethiopia: Using a generalized structural equation modelling. *International Journal of Mental Health Systems, 12*(1), 62.

Gozdziak, E., & Bump, M. N. (2008). Victims no longer: Research on child survivors of trafficking for sexual and labor exploitation in the United States (Final report). (NCJ No. 221891). *National Criminal Justice Reference Service.* https://www.ojp.gov/pdffiles1/nij/grants/221891.pdf

Greenbaum, V. J. (2014). Commercial sexual exploitation and sex trafficking of children in the United States. *Current Problems in Pediatric and Adolescent Health Care, 44*(9), 245–269.

Greenbaum, J. (2016). Identifying victims of human trafficking in the emergency department. *Clinical Pediatric Emergency Medicine, 17*(4), 241–248.

Hebert, L. A. (2016). Always victimizers, never victims: Engaging men and boys in human trafficking scholarship. *Journal of Human Trafficking, 2*(4), 281–296.

Hopper, E. K., & Gonzalez, L. D. (2018). A comparison of psychological symptoms in survivors of sex and labor trafficking. *Behavioral Medicine, 44*(3), 177–188.

Hounmenou, C. (2016). Exploring child prostitution in a major city in the West African region. *Child Abuse & Neglect, 59*, 26–35.

International Committee of the Red Cross. (2004). *Inter-agency guiding principles on unaccompanied and separated children*. International Committee of the Red Cross, Central Training Agency and Protection Division. http://www.unicef.org/protection/IAG_UASCs.pdf

International Labor Organization and Walk Free. (2022, September 15). *Global estimates of modern slavery: Forced labour and forced marriage*. https://www.ilo.org/sites/default/files/wcmsp5/groups/public/%40ed_norm/%40ipec/documents/publication/wcms_854795.pdf

Jaeckl, S., & Laughon, K. (2021). Risk factors and indicators for commercial sexual exploitation/domestic minor sex trafficking of adolescent girls in the United States in the context of school nursing: An integrative review of the literature. *The Journal of School Nursing, 37*(1), 6–16.

Jones, S. V. (2010). The invisible man: The conscious neglect of men and boys in the war on human trafficking. *Utah L. Rev., 1143*. https://repository.law.uic.edu/facpubs/30

Jones, T. R., & Kingshott, B. F. (2016). A feminist analysis of the American criminal justice system's response to human trafficking. *Criminal Justice Studies, 29*(3), 272–287.

Jordan, J., Patel, B., & Rapp, L. (2013). Domestic minor sex trafficking: A social work perspective on misidentification, victims, buyers, traffickers, treatment, and reform of current practice. *Journal of Human Behavior in the Social Environment, 23*(3), 356–369.

Kiss, L., Yun, K., Pocock, N., & Zimmerman, C. (2015). Exploitation, violence, and suicide risk among child and adolescent survivors of human trafficking in the Greater Mekong subregion. *JAMA Pediatrics, 169*(9), e152278.

Klain, E. J. (1999). *Prostitution of children and child-sex tourism: An analysis of domestic and internationals responses* (NCJ No. 189251). U.S. Department of Justice. https://www.ojp.gov/pdffiles1/Digitization/189251NCJRS.pdf

Klatt, T., Cavner, D., & Egan, V. (2014). Rationalising predictors of child sexual exploitation and sex-trading. *Child Abuse & Neglect, 38*(2), 252–260.

Kotrla, K. (2010). Domestic minor sex trafficking in the United States. *Social Work, 55*(2), 181–187.

Krakow, B., Artar, A., Warner, T. D., Melendrez, D., Johnston, L., Hollifield, M., Koss, M., et al. (2000). Sleep disorder, depression and suicidality in female sexual assault survivors. *Crisis: The Journal of Crisis Intervention and Suicide Prevention, 21*(4), 163.

Krushas, A. E., & Kulig, T. C. (2023). Exploring the physical, mental, and social health issues of sex trafficking victims by stage of exploitation. *Victims & Offenders, 18*(3), 447–472.

Kulig, T. C., & Cullen, F. T. (2021). A theory of sex trafficking victimization. In *Revitalizing victimization theory* (pp. 279–307). Routledge.

Lederer, L. J., & Wetzel, C. A. (2014). The health consequences of sex trafficking and their implications for identifying victims in healthcare facilities. *Annals Health L., 23*(1), 61.

Logan, T. K., Walker, R., & Hunt, G. (2009). Understanding human trafficking in the United States. *Trauma, Violence, & Abuse, 10*(1), 3–30.

Macias Konstantopoulos, W., Ahn, R., Alpert, E. J., Cafferty, E., McGahan, A., Williams, T. P., Burke, T. F., et al. (2013). An international comparative public health analysis of sex trafficking of women and girls in eight cities: Achieving a more effective health sector response. *Journal of Urban Health, 90*(6), 1194–1204.

MacKinnon, C. A. (2011). Trafficking, prostitution, and inequality. *Harvard Civil Rights-Civil Liberties Law, 46*(2), 271–309.

Martin, K., Vieraitis, L. M., & Britto, S. (2006). Gender equality and women's absolute status: A test of the feminist models of rape. *Violence Against Women, 12*(4), 321–339.

Meriläinen, N., & Vos, M. (2015). Public discourse on human trafficking in international issue arenas. *Societies, 5*(1), 14–42.

Miller-Perrin, C., & Wurtele, S. K. (2017). Sex trafficking and the commercial sexual exploitation of children. *Women & Therapy, 40*(1–2), 123–151.

Mo, C. H. (2018). Perceived relative deprivation and risk: An aspiration-based model of human trafficking vulnerability. *Political Behavior, 40*(2), 247–277.

Moyce, S. C., & Schenker, M. (2018). Migrant workers and their occupational health and safety. *Annual Review of Public Health, 39*(1), 351–365.

National Human Trafficking Hotline. (2022). *National human trafficking hotline data report: Report 1/1/2021 - 12/31/2021.* National Human Trafficking Hotline. Accessed January 25, 2023, from https://humantraffickinghotline.org/sites/default/files/2023-01/National%20Report%20For%202021.docx%20%283%29.pdf

Nnebedum, C., & Ogugua, C. P. (2022). The horrendous effects of child trafficking: A case study in Abakaliki urban area of Ebonyi state of Nigeria. *Open Journal of Social Science and Humanities, 3*(1), 18–32.

Noyori-Corbett, C., & Moxley, D. P. (2016). Inequality of women as a factor influencing migration from countries of origin to the United States and its implications for understanding human trafficking. *International Social Work, 59*(6), 890–903.

Okech, D., Morreau, W., & Benson, K. (2012). Human trafficking: Improving victim identification and service provision. *International Social Work, 55*(4), 488–503.

Okech, D., Hansen, N., Howard, W., Anarfi, J. K., & Burns, A. C. (2018). Social support, dysfunctional coping, and community reintegration as predictors of PTSD among human trafficking survivors. *Behavioral Medicine, 44*(3), 209–218.

Palines, P. A., Rabbitt, A. L., Pan, A. Y., Nugent, M. L., & Ehrman, W. G. (2020). Comparing mental health disorders among sex trafficked children and three groups of youth at high-risk for trafficking: A dual retrospective cohort and scoping review. *Child Abuse & Neglect, 100*, 104196.

Piper, N. (2005). *Gender and migration*. Global Commission on International Migration. https://www.incedes.org.gt/Master/pipersesentacuatro.pdf

Querol, A., & Lerner, A. (2024). The vulnerability of minors after a child trafficking situation. *Journal of Human Trafficking, 10*(1), 103–120.

Rahman, M. A. (2011). Human trafficking in the era of globalization: The case of trafficking in the global market economy. *Transcience Journal, 2*(1), 54–71.

Rand, A. (2010). It can't happen in my backyard: The commercial sexual exploitation of girls in the United States. *Child & Youth Services, 31*(3–4), 138–156.

Raphael, J., Reichert, J. A., & Powers, M. (2010). Pimp control and violence: Domestic sex trafficking of Chicago women and girls. *Women & Criminal Justice, 20*(1–2), 89–104.

Reid, J. A. (2016). Entrapment and enmeshment schemes used by sex traffickers. *Sexual Abuse: Journal of Research and Treatment, 28*(6), 491–511.

Reid, J. A., Baglivio, M. T., Piquero, A. R., Greenwald, M. A., & Epps, N. (2018). No youth left behind to human trafficking: Exploring profiles of risk. *American Journal of Orthopsychiatry, 89*(6), 704–715.

Roe-Sepowitz, D. (2019). A six-year analysis of sex traffickers of minors: Exploring characteristics and sex trafficking patterns. *Journal of Human Behavior in the Social Environment, 29*(5), 608–629.

Sabine, K. A. (2008). Armed conflict in Ivory Coast and its impact on women's human rights. *Women's World, 43*, 24–32.

Sanders, J. D. (2025). *How gender inequality drives the human trafficking industry*. Sociology and Criminology Undergraduate Honors Theses, University of Arkansas, Fayetteville. https://scholarworks.uark.edu/sociuht/24

Smolenski, C., & Ingerman, S. (2017). Trafficking of children within the United States. In *Human trafficking is a public health issue: A paradigm expansion in the United States* (pp. 93–104). Springer International Publishing. https://link.springer.com/chapter/10.1007/978-3-319-47824-1_6

Tien, M. T. (2012). Human trafficking: The missing male victim. *Public Interest Law Reporter, 18*(3), 207.

Todres, J. (2010). Taking prevention seriously: Developing a comprehensive response to child trafficking and sexual exploitation. *Vanderbilt Journal of Transnational Law, 43*(1), 1–56.

Tsai, L. C., Seballos-Llena, I. F., & Datta, R. (2017, May). Participatory assessment of a matched savings program for human trafficking survivors and their family members in The Philippines. *Forum Qualitative Sozialforschung Forum: Qualitative Social Research, 18*(2), 27.

United Nations International Children's Emergency Fund (UNICEF). (2006). *UNICEF Annual Report 2006*. United Nations International Children's Emergency Fund. https://www.unicef.org/media/93006/file/UNICEF-annual-report-2006.pdf?utm_source=chatgpt.com

United States Department of Labor. (2016). *List of goods produced by child labor and forced labor. Bureau of International Labor Affairs*. United States Department of Labor. https://www.dol.gov/sites/default/files/documents/ilab/reports/child-labor/findings/TVPRA_Report2016.pdf

United States Department of State (USDOS). (2004). *Traffic in person report*. United States Department of State. https://www.ojp.gov/ncjrs/virtual-library/abstracts/victims-trafficking-and-violence-protection-act-2000-trafficking-1

United States Department of State (USDOS). (2005). *The facts about human trafficking for forced labor*. United States Department of State. https://2001-2009.state.gov/documents/organization/51174.pdf

United States Department of State (USDOS). (2011). *Traffic in person report*. United States Department of State. https://2009-2017.state.gov/j/tip/rls/tiprpt/2011/

United States Department of State (USDOS). (2023, June). *Traffic in Person Report*. United States Department of State. https://www.state.gov/wp-content/uploads/2023/05/Trafficking-in-Persons-Report-2023_Introduction-Additional-Pagesv4_FINAL.pdf

Vijeyarasa, R. (2013). Stigma, stereotypes and Brazilian soap operas: Road-blocks to ending human trafficking in Vietnam, Ghana and Ukraine. *Gender, Place & Culture, 20*(8), 1015–1032.

Voronova, S., & Radjenovic, A. (2016). *The gender dimension of human trafficking*. European Parliamentary Research Service. https://www.europarl.europa.eu/RegData/etudes/BRIE/2016/577950/EPRS_BRI(2016)577950_EN.pdf

Vyas, S., & Heise, L. (2016). How do area-level socioeconomic status and gender norms affect partner violence against women? Evidence from Tanzania. *International Journal of Public Health, 61*(8), 971–980.

Wakgari, G. (2014). Causes and consequences of human trafficking in Ethiopia: The case of women in the Middle East. *International Journal of Gender and Women's Studies, 2*(2), 233–246.

Wallace, C., Greenbaum, J., & Albright, K. (2022). Global perspectives on the health and social impacts of child trafficking. *Pediatrics, 150*(4). https://doi.org/10.1542/peds.2021-055840

Warria, A. (2020). "The child goes back to the trafficking situation": Consequences of inappropriate assistance procedures during reintegration of child victims of trafficking. *Child Abuse Research in South Africa, 21*(1), 47–57.

Weatherburn, A. (2015). The effects of political and socio-economic factors on human trafficking. In *Bulgaria (Sofia):* Conference paper. https://www.researchgate.net/publication/284725360

Wilson, H. W., & Widom, C. S. (2010). The role of youth problem behaviors in the path from child abuse and neglect to prostitution: A prospective examination. *Journal of Research on Adolescence, 20*(1), 210–236.

Zhang, S. X. (2022). Progress and challenges in human trafficking research: Two decades after the Palermo protocol. *Journal of Human Trafficking, 8*(1), 4–12.

Zimmerman, C., Hossain, M., Yun, K., Roche, B., Morison, L., & Watts, C. (2006). *Stolen smiles: A summary report on the physical and psychological health consequences of women and adolescents trafficked in Europe*. London School of Hygiene & Tropical Medicine. https://www.icmec.org/wp-content/uploads/2015/10/Stolen-Smiles-Physical-and-Psych-Consequences-of-Traffic-Victims-in-Europe-Zimmerman.pdf

CHAPTER 2

School Violence and Immigrant Youth

Jennifer M. Bondy, Kay S. Varela, Janice Iwama, Sarah Lindstrom-Johnson, Anthony A. Peguero, and Angelica Lopez

Introduction

The United States has long had more immigrants than any other country. It is home to one-fifth of the world's international migrants. These immigrants come from just about every country in the world (US Census Bureau, 2022). For this chapter, immigrant youth are defined as those under age 18 who are either foreign-born or US-born to immigrant parents, which now accounts for one-fourth of the US (or 75 million) youth population; by 2050, immigrant youth are projected to make up one-third (or one-hundred million) of the US youth population (US Census Bureau,

J. M. Bondy (✉)
School of Social Transformation, Arizona State University, Tempe, AZ, USA
e-mail: jmbondy@asu.edu

K. S. Varela • A. A. Peguero
School of Criminology and Criminal Justice, Arizona State University, Tempe, AZ, USA
e-mail: Kay.Varela@asu.edu

J. S. Hong et al. (eds.), *Violence and Trauma Without Borders*,
https://doi.org/10.1007/978-3-032-29221-6_2

2022). Considering that safety could facilitate, while trauma and adverse experiences with crime and violence could derail, healthy youth development and educational progress, understanding how these connections occur for a vulnerable segment of the youth population (i.e., children of immigrants) is paramount as the United States becomes more diverse. Interest in the relationships between immigration, violence, trauma, and schooling is gaining social, public, and policy concern (Miller et al., 2020; Peguero & Bondy, 2021).

Research evidence indicates that immigrant youth have increased reports of anxiety and trauma due to the stress and pressure that they and their families experience in the migration process (Peguero & Bondy, 2021; Portes & Rumbaut, 2024). Moreover, the migration experience denotes a major life transition that often engenders fear, loss, isolation, confusion, and uncertainty about the present and future for immigrant youth and their family (Peguero & Bondy, 2021; Portes & Rumbaut, 2024). While there are a wide array of reasons for migration, such as war, famine, religious persecution, and disaster, the process of leaving one's home, country, and culture can each contribute to anxiety and trauma (Peguero & Bondy, 2021; Portes & Rumbaut, 2024). It is also clear that migration is a lengthy and difficult process that can sometimes involve danger for immigrant youth and their families once they arrive, reside, live, and attend schools. Language barriers, racism, discrimination, prejudice, xenophobia, and unfamiliar customs are all part of the diverse social and cultural experiences for immigrant youth (Hong et al., 2014, 2016; Peguero & Bondy, 2021; Portes & Rumbaut, 2024). Unfortunately, immigrant youth are being victimized and endure trauma within their schools, such as exposure to school violence and disorder, bullying and harassment, increased security and surveillance, disproportionate

J. Iwama
Department of Justice, Law and Criminology, American University, Washington, DC, USA
e-mail: iwama@american.edu

S. Lindstrom-Johnson • A. Lopez
T. Denny Sanford School of Social and Family Dynamics, Arizona State University, Tempe, AZ, USA
e-mail: sarahlj@asu.edu; alope277@asu.edu

discipline, prejudice and xenophobia, and threats of deportation (Hong et al., 2014, 2016; Peguero & Bondy, 2021; Verma et al., 2017).

In this chapter, we first present and demonstrate the significance of how adversity, stress, and trauma exist and matter for immigrant youth within schools, as well as the potential efforts to prevent violence and ameliorate trauma for this vulnerable population while also ensuring safe learning environments. We then discuss how utilizing a socioecological framework could inform researchers, educators, policymakers, and stakeholders toward understanding the connections between violence, victimization, and trauma for immigrant youth. Next, we highlight how laws, public and political discourses, and educational policies are potentially contributing to the harm and traumatic experiences that immigrant youth endure within schools. We then denote student factors associated with violence and victimization for immigrant youth, such as English-language proficiency, legal status, race/ethnicity, generational status, nationality, religion, and gender. Finally, we present implications for considering violence and trauma for immigrant youth. Thus, with the evident rapid growth of immigrant youth in US schools, any effort to address school violence and implement school safety policies must consider barriers and hurdles associated with immigrant youth's schooling and educational experiences.

The Significance of Trauma and Immigrant Youth

The relationship between trauma and migration is multifaceted, particularly in the context of youth. We define trauma as a reaction to the experience of adversity in which there is a diminished ability to cope, often in the face of overwhelming or life-threatening circumstances (Bartlett & Steber, 2019; SAMHSA, 2014). Frequently, immigrants are moving from environments where they are exposed to traumatic events in the form of war, political violence, natural disasters, or economic uncertainty, with the ability to migrate and change this context indicating a source of strength. This, along with other cultural strengths, is often the explanation for what has been called the "immigrant paradox," or the fact that first-generation immigrant youth usually have improved health and developmental outcomes than later generations of more acculturated youth (Marks et al., 2014). However, there is also acknowledgment that the process of migration is itself a source of trauma. A study of Hispanic immigrant youth identified that in-transit traumatic events, such as witnessing or experiencing sexual assault or physical violence, or seeing another person-injured, were experienced by 30% of the sample (De Arellano et al., 2018). Additionally, ethnic-racial discrimination can also be a source of trauma for youth (Umaña-Taylor, 2016), with models documenting exposure to traumatic experience (e.g., Adverse Childhood Experiences or ACEs) being expanded to both capture direct experience of discrimination as well as understanding structural consequences of discrimination as explanatory for differences in rates of trauma for minoritized populations (Mélenedez Guevara et al., 2024). Finally, youth of immigrants report high levels of fear, as they worry about their parents being deported (Gandara, 2020). Understanding the above as co-existing and influencing adolescent well-being likely explains a recent meta-analysis that found higher rates of internalizing problems (i.e., anxiety and depression) for first-generation immigrant youth but lower rates of externalizing problems (i.e., delinquency and substance use; Tilley et al., 2021). Additionally, studies have suggested that more than half of immigrant youth meet the cutoff for clinically significant posttraumatic stress disorder (PTSD) symptoms (Venta & Mercado, 2019). Thus, schools need to take a trauma-informed approach to supporting immigrant youths' success in schools.

Trauma has been known to be associated with the ability to succeed in schools. Specifically, trauma impacts students' ability to focus on schooling, form relationships, and address conflict and problem-solve (Kataoka et al., 2018). This is likely an understudied mechanism that contributes to immigrant students' challenges in school, including a lower likelihood of graduation than native-born peers (Sibley & Brabeck, 2017). Besides being an understudied mechanism, it also represents an underutilized approach to support immigrant youth. In addition to addressing the overt discrimination reported by immigrant youth (Brown, 2015), schools can and should be aware of the effect of migration-related trauma as well as the broader narrative around immigrants that is related to social isolation, increased family tension, and worries about deportation (Barajas-Gonzales et al., 2018). This can be as straightforward as being transparent around policies related to migration status, including the obligation to provide education to all students regardless of immigration status and the protections of student records from Immigration and Customs Enforcement (e.g., no Family Educational Rights and Privacy Act (FERPA) exception), to focusing on parent–school engagement being cognizant of barriers to education including those related to material-hardship and familiarity with the US educational system (Lindstrom Johnson et al., 2024). While these activities might not at first be conceptualized as part of a trauma-informed school model, if the goal is to ensure that children are safe, supported, and ready to learn, for immigrant families and students, these may be foundational to even engaging in the school environment. Other considerations of trauma-informed schools, including professional development of staff on the signs and symptoms of trauma responses, practices supporting the regulation of emotions and a shift away from the punishment of behavior, and supports for mental health services and referrals, are likely beneficial, but need to be tailored to be culturally sensitive (Burgund Isakov & Markovic, 2024). However, the role of the school in supporting immigrants is even broader, as it can serve as a source of resilience for students.

Research has suggested that increased sensitivity to the process of second-language acquisition may be especially pertinent to establishing positive and empathetic relationships between teachers and immigrant students (Bollin, 2007; Jones & Fuller, 2003). Furthermore, developing a better understanding of the strengths and diversity within Hispanic culture may enable teachers to place higher value and expectations on their immigrant students, promoting inclusion and academic success (Bollin, 2007; Bondy & Braunstein, 2019; Goodwin, 2017). Studies show that extracurricular involvement and volunteerism might be particularly important predictors of intrinsic motivation, school belonging, and grade point average for immigrant students (Camacho & Fuligni, 2015; Perez et al., 2009). Unfortunately, studies also suggest that immigrant students are less likely to be called upon in class and are more likely to attend under-resourced schools with greater amounts of violence (Sibley & Brabeck, 2017), which undermines school climate and the use of schools and schooling as protective factors for immigrant youth.

Utilizing a Social-Ecological Framework Toward School Violence and Immigrant Youth

This chapter utilizes Bronfenbrenner's (1979) social-ecological model as a descriptive framework to understand the multilevel complexities associated with a youth's experience with violence and victimization and how they are connected to broader social-ecological factors, such as societal, community, institutional, group, and individual. The power of the socio-ecological model lies not just in identifying multiple levels of influence but in analyzing their interactions. For immigrant youth, individual experiences of trauma often reflect policies and practices at the societal and institutional levels, making it essential to understand these influences not as isolated and individual, but as mutually reinforcing. The socioecological model will therefore be used as a guide to understand the multifaceted links between school violence and trauma for immigrant youth.

At the *societal level*, there are harmful processes that have historically marginalized immigrant youth and contributed to their experiences with violence in school. These societal-level factors highlight historical, structural, and systemic immigration disparities in the United States that are associated with school violence and safety. For instance, as we will describe in more detail later in this chapter, heated and controversial social, political, and educational debates about US immigration policies may detrimentally influence school relationships and interactions between immigrant families/parents, school friends and classmates, and teachers and administrators (Hong et al., 2014, 2016; Peguero & Bondy, 2021; Peguero & Hong, 2020). These broader societal discourses about immigration can seep into schools, negatively shaping how teachers, friends and classmates, and administrators perceive and interact with immigrant youth, thereby reinforcing a climate of fear and exclusion.

At the *community level*, because schools are embedded within communities, a disadvantaged and underresourced neighborhood environment can also contribute to school violence and trauma. For example, as we will detail later in this chapter, schools serving predominantly immigrant communities are often embedded within urban communities with higher levels of poverty, unemployment, crime, and violence (Peguero & Bondy, 2021; Portes Rumbaut, 2024). Schools' ability and socioeconomic resources to address violence, ameliorate trauma, and enact safety policies to stem the tide of community violence entering the school are limited (Peguero & Bondy, 2021). That is, the socioeconomic constraints of a school's community can limit access to resources and create an institutional environment where trauma is less likely to be adequately acknowledged and addressed.

At the *institutional level*, school climate can influence youths' academic, behavioral, and social outcomes (Lindstrom Johnson et al., 2017; Peguero & Bondy, 2021; Peguero & Hong, 2020). Immigrant youth who attend schools where disorder, crime, and violence are prevalent are often presented with limited opportunities for academic success and social mobility, which contribute to immigrant youth's vulnerability and exposure to that dangerous and traumatic environment. That environment can also manifest in immigrant youth misbehavior, delinquency, depression, and isolation (Peguero & Bondy, 2021; Peguero & Hong, 2020). Immigrant youth who designate their schools as unfair spaces are more likely to engage in deviant behavior and experience biased treatment, victimization, and diminished educational aspirations (Hong et al., 2014, 2016; Peguero & Bondy, 2021; Peguero & Hong, 2020). The institutional context of schools, such as punitive discipline policies, is shaped by broader societal policies and narratives about immigration and community-level disparities. Institutional contexts of schools, therefore, in turn, influence peer and student–teacher relationships, as well as immigrant students' coping strategies.

At the *group level*, immigrant youth who have limited English proficiency may find it difficult to establish friendships with native-born peers and find school group membership (Kao et al., 2013; Peguero & Bondy, 2021). Some suggest that same-ethnicity friendship, shared language, and congruent cultural beliefs could serve as an insulating factor from victimization, with same-ethnicity peers providing social and emotional support (Kao et al., 2013; Peguero & Bondy, 2021); moreover, others suggest that friendships and group involvement with native-born youth could also promote victimization and influence increased misbehavior (Hong et al., 2014, 2016; Peguero & Bondy, 2021). These group dynamics are shaped by a school's institutional context and broader societal attitudes toward immigration. Such dynamics impact peer relationships, shape how immigrant youth navigate daily school routines, and influence how youth experience violence and trauma. Later in this chapter, we also provide more details about the role of English-language speaking proficiency regarding immigrant youths' experiences with school violence and trauma.

At the *individual level*, the behaviors and student activity, movement, or patterns within the daily school routines may expose the children of immigrants to violence, victimization, and harassment (Abu El-Haj, 2015; Albdour et al., 2017; Peguero & Bondy, 2021). For example, Arab Muslim immigrant youth encounter religiously biased treatment and ignorance at school, factors which influence their school routines and activities (Abu El-Haj, 2015; Albdour et al., 2017; Peguero & Bondy, 2021). Basford (2010) cites an example, describing an incident involving an Arab Muslim immigrant youth who participated in a school book club exchange: They frequently heard students yell "there go the little terrorists" and observed several people in their math class, including the teacher, laugh loudly at Arab Muslim immigrant youth who engaged in this mainstream school activity. We will highlight more individual intersecting student factors associated with school violence for immigrant youth later in this chapter.

The Importance of the Social, Political, and Educational Climate of Immigration

The social, political, and educational rhetoric over immigration is multifaceted and often based on biased views as well as misinformation. For example, from 2016 to 2020, the myth of immigrants being criminals and diseased was spread (Ee & Gándara, 2020; Gibson, 2023; Oreskes, 2024). The presidential campaign and term, coupled with aggressive rhetoric, had detrimental impacts on immigrant youth by fueling surveillance, bullying, fear, and increasing racial/ethnic tensions in schools (Costello, 2016). School climates across the United States have been admonished with hostile remarks, such as "Go back to [insert foreign country name here, usually Mexico]" (Vara-Orta, 2018, p. 13), "[The President] is going to throw you back over the wall, you know?" (Costello, 2016, p. 6), and "Put the panic back in Hispanic" (Sharp, 2017). Many immigrant youth are fearful of their own or family members' deportation, which has prompted students to carry their birth certificates and social security cards for fear of being separated and deported from their families (Ee & Gándara, 2020; Sanchez et al., 2018). Even as the president campaigned to be reelected in 2024, campaign speeches and advertisements, as well as the presidential debate, highlighted the president's exclusionary discourses about immigrants, which continued to be virulent and toxic. The president has incorporated Nazi rhetoric to claim that "immigrants are poisoning the blood of our country" and are "killers" who rape and kill women (Gibson, 2023; Oreskes, 2024). The president's reelection lends even greater urgency to understanding and addressing the social, political, and educational rhetoric over immigration that traumatizes immigrant youth, especially within schools.

This social, political, and educational misinformation is focused on linking immigration to increased crime rates, derailing employment opportunities for native residents, and deteriorating educational progress and success of native students. To the contrary, there is much evidence indicating that immigration is associated with improved public safety, employment opportunities, and educational outcomes (Iwama et al., 2023; Peguero et al., 2023). Unfortunately, however, there is a ubiquitous depiction of immigrants as deviant, criminal, and lacking "intelligence" (Iwama et al., 2023; Chavez, 2013; Peguero et al., 2023). Immigrant youth are less likely to be involved in crime, substance use, and general deviance (Iwama et al., 2023; Peguero & Bondy, 2021). This is likely an understudied mechanism that contributes to immigrant students' challenges in school, including a lower likelihood of graduation than native-born peers (Sibley & Brabeck, 2017). Moreover, immigrant youth have increased beliefs that hard work, progress, and success within school will lead to adult educational and economic success (Kao et al., 2013; Peguero & Bondy, 2021; Portes & Rumbaut, 2024). Even though immigrant youth are outperforming their US native-born counterparts, immigrant youth report attending schools that vilify, criminalize, and traumatize immigrant youth.

It also appears that this problematic and traumatic social, political, and educational misinformation and discourse are being perpetuated by faculty, staff, administrators, and security personnel. Some teachers view immigrant youth as problems within their classrooms, burdened by what they perceive to be lacking capabilities, and argue that immigrant youth diminish the teacher's ability to teach all students effectively and efficiently. Teachers often hold negative and unwelcoming attitudes toward immigrant youth who are placed in their classes (Goodwin, 2017; Kao et al., 2013; Peguero & Bondy, 2021). Faculty and staff often rationalize holding negative or unwelcoming views based on chronic lack of time to address the unique needs of immigrant youth, perceived intensification of teacher workloads when immigrant youth are enrolled in their classes, and feelings of professional inadequacy to work with immigrant youth (Goodwin, 2017; Kao et al., 2013; Peguero & Bondy, 2021). Because the perception of immigrant youth restricts the advancement and educational progress for the entire class, it is not uncommon for teachers to be reluctant to accept and teach immigrant youth. Verma et al. (2017) reveal a school-to-deportation pipeline that indicates a process in which immigrant youth and their families find themselves in deportation hearings, including families seeking political asylum or amnesty from undocumented status. In some cases, school faculty, administrators, staff, and school resource officers have threatened and have reported immigrant youth suspected to be undocumented to immigration enforcement as a form of harassment and social control (Gonzales, 2016; Irwin et al., 2022; Verma et al., 2017). Of course, it can be argued that this social, political, and educational misinformation and hostile rhetoric against immigration is being "weaponized," resulting in traumatic school experiences for immigrant youth.

Intersecting Student Factors Associated with School Violence and Immigrant Youth

There are several student factors associated with susceptibility to violence, victimization, and trauma for immigrant youth. The following will describe how socioeconomic status, race/ethnicity, gender, country or region of origin, and English-language speaking proficiency impact and stratify the violence that immigrant youth endure at their schools. Several scholars (García Coll et al., 1996; García Coll & Marks, 2012; Peguero & Bondy, 2021; Peguero & Hong, 2020) highlight the significance of different forms of social inequality that intersect and further the importance of Bronfenbrenner's (1979) social-ecological model. Researchers must consider the significance of social inequality when investigating the connections between the social-ecological context and youth development. Extending Bronfenbrenner's (1979) social-ecological theoretical approach must consider: social position (e.g., socioeconomic status, race/ethnicity, and gender) as well as adaptive culture and current demands (e.g., assimilation or acculturation and language) when investigating the role that the social environment has for marginalized youth, such as immigrant youth (García Coll et al., 1996; García Coll & Marks, 2012; Peguero & Bondy, 2021; Peguero & Hong, 2020). Under this approach, the social environment, including within schools, is particularly important because norms about behavior and climate can influence life-course trajectories, adolescent development, overall well-being, and educational progress (Espelage & Swearer, 2010; Finkelhor, 2008). Factors fundamentally associated with the context of racial/ethnic stratification, inequality, and biased treatment are important factors to consider in this aforementioned relationship (Bradshaw et al., 2013; García Coll & Marks, 2012). Thus, the social-ecological environment matters for immigrant youth's experiences with school violence.

Across all social-ecological levels, being socioeconomically disadvantaged positions immigrant youth within vulnerable situations in their communities and schools, increasing their exposure to violence and likelihood of victimization. Immigrant families and their children are more likely to reside in disadvantaged and underresourced communities that report prolonged economic hardships, poverty, and disorder (Kao et al., 2013; Portes & Rumbaut, 2024). Additionally, at the community and institutional level, researchers have stressed that educational and community inequalities impose serious barriers and challenges to implementing anti-violence programs within schools (Peguero & Bondy, 2021; Peguero & Hong, 2020). At the group level, stress due to poverty and low socioeconomic circumstances is negatively correlated to school safety outcomes among immigrant youth, including being victimized, engagement in fighting, and being criminalized (Hong et al., 2016; Peguero & Bondy, 2021; Verma et al., 2017).

At the societal level, race/ethnicity also plays an important role in the distinct forms of violence, biased treatment, and trauma that immigrant youth report at their schools. Generally speaking, Black immigrant youth in the United States migrate from two major regions, the Caribbean Islands and the African continent. Despite the diversity among Black immigrant youth, they are often grouped into one racial/ethnic category, which dismisses, invalidates, and erases their different cultural, national, linguistic, and religious heritages at their school (Basford, 2010; Peguero & Bondy, 2021; Ray, 2022). Moreover, Black immigrant youth confront racial/ethnic segregation and biased treatment within their schools and communities. At the institutional level, evidence suggests that Black immigrant youth are isolated, marginalized, and disenfranchised from other racial/ethnic minority groups and are at increased risk of being victimized and harassed (Basford, 2010; Peguero & Bondy, 2021; Ray, 2022). Similarly, Latinx immigrant youth are overrepresented among those at risk for poor behavioral, physical, and mental well-being (Hong et al., 2014; Peguero & Bondy, 2021; Verma et al., 2017). Furthermore, at the societal level, the stereotype of the "model immigrant" is often assigned to Asian immigrant youth; however, that label is detrimental and arguably traumatizing. At the community level, although Asian immigrant youth are stereotypically portrayed as academically astute and economic overachievers, Asian immigrant families often live in poverty, are underserved by human services, are underpaid, and are often subjected to biased treatment and harassment (Hong et al., 2014; Peguero & Bondy, 2021). Due to teacher expectations and the "model minority syndrome," teachers often assume that the children of Asian immigrants do not need help or assistance because of "natural" or "biological" ability (Kao et al., 2013; Peguero & Bondy, 2021). In turn, at the institutional level, Asian immigrant youth report being "pushed" into particular academic subjects, such as math and science, to be accepted by school administrators, faculty, and staff. Otherwise, the children of Asian immigrants are harassed, "put down," and treated inequitably (Ee & Gándara, 2020; Hong et al., 2016; Kao et al., 2013; Peguero & Bondy, 2021). This was exacerbated during the COVID-19 pandemic, with detrimental effects on Asian-Americans' mental health.

Additionally, Arab immigrant youth are stereotyped to be well educated, relative to the American population as a whole, reflecting the high value placed on education. Because of this, the school experiences of the children of Arab immigrants are frequently characterized by marginalization (Abu El-Haj, 2015; Albdour et al., 2017). At the societal level, "Islamophobia" has become a form of xenophobia that has detrimentally impacted Arab immigrant youth despite their religious background (Abu El-Haj, 2015; Selod, 2018). Anti-Arab and Anti-Muslim sentiment has exponentially grown in scale and visibility since 2001, with the US government's "War on Terror" unfortunately becoming evident within US schools. At the group level, the bullying, victimization, harassment, verbal and physical threats, and hate that Arab immigrant youth experience continue to be a persistent social and educational problem within US schools (Abu El-Haj, 2015; Albdour et al., 2017; Peguero & Bondy, 2021).

Another student factor that diverges immigrant youth's experiences with violence and trauma within US schools is linked to gender. Oftentimes, immigrant youth must bridge gender expectations of two different cultures—their homeland culture and US culture—during the socialization and "Americanization" processes (Peguero & Bondy, 2021; Ray, 2022). At the group level, gender plays a key role in the educational struggles and biased treatment that immigrant girls and boys experience in their adjustment to the United States (Bondy, 2014, 2015, 2016; Kao et al., 2013; Ray, 2022). Many female immigrant youth report being ostracized by their American peers for dressing or wearing their hair differently (Peguero & Bondy, 2021; Ray, 2022). Additionally, at the group level, female immigrant youth are often sexualized or "exoticized" and, in turn, often endure increased sexual harassment, unwanted touching, gesturing, and inappropriate jokes (Bondy, 2014, 2015, 2016; Ray, 2022). Without proper support from teachers, administrators, and guidance counselors, social isolation can lead to low self-esteem, shame, and high depression rates the longer that female immigrant youth are in the United States (Kao et al., 2013; Peguero & Bondy, 2021; Ray, 2022). At the institutional level, immigrant boys are more likely to be surveilled and punished by teachers, administrators, and school security guards; less likely to be academically engaged; and more likely to report experiencing biased and unjust treatment in school than immigrant girls (Peguero & Bondy, 2021). Immigrant boys' detachment from school, rather than being attributed to laziness or lack of intellectual capabilities, may be a response to the school's hostile environment (Peguero & Bondy, 2021). Their disengagement might thus be better understood as their attempt to deal with largely negative encounters in US schools (Peguero & Bondy, 2021).

Although all people who speak English speak it with an accent, immigrant youth who speak English with an accent tend to experience negative, detrimental, and ridiculing feedback from their teachers and peers (Creese & Kambere, 2003; Goodwin, 2017; Peguero & Bondy, 2021). Immigrant youth report being patronized by and receiving lower grades from their teachers because of their English-speaking accents and skills (Kao et al., 2013; Peguero & Bondy, 2021). At the institutional level, teachers and administrators sometimes lack knowledge about how second language acquisition and second language literacy development can unintentionally result in lower grades and unique educational barriers and challenges for ELL students (Kao et al., 2013; Peguero & Bondy, 2021). At the group level, immigrant youth are verbally and physically bullied by their US-born peers who claim not to understand their spoken English (Hong et al., 2014; Peguero & Bondy, 2021). Perceptions of immigrant youths' English-speaking competencies restrict access to inclusion by their teachers and peers by creating obstacles to "fitting in" with and talking to US-born students (Kao et al., 2013; Peguero & Bondy, 2021). As Creese and Kambere (2003) note, language and accents are not about communication; rather, they are about "power and exclusion, marginalization and 'Othering', racism and discrimination" (p. 571). On the other hand, English-speaking accents and skills can distinguish between youths who are and who are not perceived as academically, socially, and culturally competent in US schools, which can be traumatizing.

Implications for Considering School Violence and Immigrant Youth

Here, we have documented and described the multifaceted exposure to violence and traumatic events that immigrant youth of color experience within US schools. We have sought to demonstrate that these experiences present unique challenges but also detail concrete opportunities for researchers, educators, policymakers, and other stakeholders to create safe and inclusive learning environments for all immigrant students. Addressing immigrant youths' trauma and safety cannot occur at just one level. School climate policies must address how broader political discourse, community contexts, and peer dynamics contribute to immigrant youths' lived experiences. The socioecological framework helps to ensure a multifaceted approach that is necessary for developing sustainable and just school safety policies.

First, given the rapid and sustained growth of immigrant children within US schools, school-wide efforts to ensure safety and equity should be purposeful and trauma-informed, particularly taking into consideration the impact of traumatic events and violence on immigrant youths' school safety experiences. Within schools, administrators should focus on and advocate for trauma-informed school safety policies that focus on creating and maintaining a safe and inclusive learning environment, taking special care to prioritize the well-being of immigrant students. To be effective, trauma-informed policies should be multifaceted, including not just administrators but also school safety personnel, teachers, and other staff, all of whom play an important role in addressing and reducing violence within schools. Furthermore, policies should move beyond individualized approaches and look toward broader, school-wide approaches. For example, considering the unique challenges that immigrant students face within schools, school safety personnel, teachers, and other staff should be actively trained in how to create and sustain culturally responsive and trauma-informed learning environments and learning routines that are responsive to students' needs. This includes sensitivity not only to immigration status but also to language barriers, differences in gender and ethnicity, and sexuality, among others. This will not only help immigrant students thrive personally and academically but also reduce biased attitudes, bullying, and harassment from other students (Craig et al., 2000; Dukes & Ming, 2008; Hong et al., 2014, 2016; Ronnau, 2014).

Second, with the increasing importance of school mental health professionals for school safety, mental health practices and protocols within schools should also take the unique challenges immigrant youth face into account when providing services. For example, mental health services within schools should include trauma-informed practices such as skill building for difficult situations for both students and teachers, culturally informed counseling services and resources to reduce bias, and a greater focus on creating safe spaces for students (Hong et al., 2014; Hong et al., 2016).

Finally, the importance of families and community for immigrants and immigrant youth indicates that parents must be considered when creating effective school safety policies intended to reduce trauma and harm for immigrant youth. For example, increased transparency between teachers, school safety personnel, and parents could not only greatly improve youth's experiences within schools but could also help improve youths' perceptions of schools overall. Given that the challenges faced by immigrant parents of school-aged children are well known (e.g., language and cultural barriers), school should strive to build resources to counteract limitations to parent involvement, such as language translators and interpreters, cultural brokers or partnerships with local immigrant organizations to increase transparency, or increased flexibility to facilitate parent involvement in school events and meetings (Clark & Ladd, 2000; Hong et al., 2014).

Strategies and practices such as those outlined here could potentially mitigate school-level and individual-level factors that contribute to increased trauma, lack of safety, and increased violence among or toward immigrant youth within US schools. By taking a holistic approach to school safety and violence reduction, school administrators, teachers, and school safety personnel can positively impact the educational journeys of immigrant youth.

Conclusion

With the rising number of immigrant youth in the United States, it is important to consider the significant impact that trauma has on these youth, given their experience before, during, and after the immigration process, to develop a better understanding of how it impacts their school experience. Utilizing a social-ecological model, we disentangle the multilevel complexities associated with immigrant youth's experience that stem from violence, victimization, and trauma. Immigrant youth are situated in a vulnerable place from the beginning, given their English-language proficiency, legal status, race/ethnicity, generational status, nationality, religion, and gender. Yet, these factors alone do not expose immigrant youth to violence and increase their chances of victimization. Other factors that exist in US communities, institutions, and societies also contribute to the harm and trauma that immigrant youth endure within schools. While considering how these factors negatively impact immigrant youth, this chapter offers researchers, educators, policymakers, and other stakeholders recommendations on how to improve immigrant youth's schooling and educational experiences. By adopting and implementing strategies and practices aimed directly at these barriers and hurdles, we can improve the experiences of immigrant youth by creating a safe and inclusive learning environment for all students.

References

Abu El-Haj, T. R. (2015). *Unsettled belonging: Educating Palestinian American youth after 9/11*. University of Chicago Press.

Albdour, M., Lewin, L., Kavanaugh, K., Hong, J. S., & Wilson, F. (2017). Arab American adolescents' perceived stress and bullying experiences: A qualitative study. *Western Journal of Nursing Research, 39*(12), 1567–1588.

Barajas-Gonzalez, R. G., Ayón, C., & Torres, F. (2018). Applying a community violence framework to understand the impact of immigration enforcement threat on Latino children. *Social Policy Report, 31*(3), 1–24.

Bartlett, J. D., & Steber, K. (2019). How to implement trauma informed care to build resilience to childhood trauma. *Trauma, 9*(10).

Basford, L. (2010). From mainstream to east African charter: Cultural and religious experiences of Somali youth in U.S. schools. *Journal of School Choice, 4*, 485–509.

Bollin, G. G. (2007). Preparing teachers for Hispanic immigrant children: A service learning approach. *Journal of Latinos and Education, 6*(2), 177–189.

Bondy, J. M. (2014). "Why do I have to pledge the US flag? It's not my country!": Latina youths rearticulating citizenship and national belonging. *Multicultural Perspectives, 16*(4), 193–202.

Bondy, J. M. (2015). Hybrid citizenship: Latina youth and the politics of belonging. *The High School Journal, 98*(4), 353–373.

Bondy, J. M. (2016). Latina youth, education, and citizenship: A feminist transnational analysis. *Theory & Research in Social Education, 44*(2), 212–243.

Bondy, J. M., & Braunstein, L. B. (2019). Racial politics, Latin@ youth, and teacher education. *Journal of Latinos and Education, 18*(2), 93–106.

Bradshaw, C. P., Waasdorp, T. E., Goldweber, A., & Johnson, S. L. (2013). Bullies, gangs, drugs, and school: Understanding the overlap and the role of ethnicity and urbanicity. *Journal of Youth and Adolescence, 42*, 220–234.

Brown, C. S. (2015). *The educational, psychological, and social impact of discrimination on the immigrant child*. Migration Policy Institute.

Burgund Isakov, A., & Markovic, V. (2024). Systematic review of trauma-informed approaches and trauma-informed care for forced migrant families: Concepts and contexts. *Trauma, Violence, & Abuse, 25*(5), 3999–4015.

Camacho, D. E., & Fuligni, A. J. (2015). Extracurricular participation among adolescents from immigrant families. *Journal of Youth and Adolescence, 44*, 1251–1262.

Chavez, L. (2013). *The Latino threat: Constructing immigrants, citizens and the nation*. Stanford University Press.

Clark, K. E., & Ladd, G. W. (2000). Connectedness and autonomy support in parent–child relationships: Links to children's socioemotional orientation and peer relationships. *Developmental Psychology, 36*(4), 485.

Costello, M. B. (2016). *After election day the Trump effect: The impact of the 2016 election on our nation's schools*. Southern Poverty Law Center.

Craig, S., Hull, K., Haggart, A. G., & Perez-Selles, M. (2000). Promoting cultural competence through teacher assistance teams. *Teaching Exceptional Children, 32*(3), 6–12.

Creese, G., & Kambere, E. N. (2003). What colour is your English? *Canadian Review of Sociology and Anthropology, 40*(5), 565–573.

De Arellano, M. A., Andrews, A. R., III, Reid-Quiñones, K., Vasquez, D., Doherty, L. S., Danielson, C. K., & Rheingold, A. (2018). Immigration trauma among Hispanic youth: Missed by trauma assessments and predictive of depression and PTSD symptoms. *Journal of Latina/o Psychology, 6*(3), 159.

Dukes, C., & Ming, K. (2008). Fostering cultural competence through school-based routines. In *The elusive what and the problematic how* (pp. 195–214). Brill.

Ee, J., & Gándara, P. (2020). The impact of immigration enforcement on the nation's schools. *American Educational Research Journal, 57*(2), 840–871.

Espelage, D. L., & Swearer, S. M. (2010). A social-ecological model for bullying prevention and intervention: understanding the impact of adults in the social ecology of youngsters. In: S. R. Jimerson, S. M. Swearer, & D. L. Espelage (Eds.), Handbook of Bullying in Schools: An International Perspective, (pp. 61–72). New York: Routledge.

Finkelhor, D. (2008). Childhood victimization. New York, NY: Oxford University Press.

Gándara, P. (2020). The students we share: Falling through the cracks on both sides of the US-Mexico border. In *The end of compassion* (pp. 38–59). Routledge.

García Coll, C., & Marks, A. K. (2012). *The immigrant paradox in children and adolescents: Is becoming American a developmental risk?* American Psychological Association Press.

García Coll, C., Lamberty, G., Jenkins, R., McAdoo, H. P., Crnic, K., Wasik, B. H., & García, H. V. (1996). An integrative model for the study of developmental competencies in minority children. *Child Development, 67*, 1891–1914.

Gibson, G. (2023, December 17). Trump says immigrants are 'poisoning the blood of our country.' Biden campaign likens comments to Hitler. *NBC News*. https://www.nbcnews.com/politics/2024-election/trump-says-immigrants-are-poisoning-blood-country-biden-campaign-liken-rcna130141

Gonzales, R. G. (2016). *Lives in limbo: Undocumented and coming of age in America*. University of California Press.

Goodwin, A. L. (2017). Who is in the classroom now? Teaching preparation and the education of immigrant children. *Educational Studies, 53*(5), 433–449.

Guevara, A. M. M., Cottam, S., Wall, C., & Johnson, S. L. (2024). Expanding ACES in child and family service systems: Incorporating context and resilience. *Child Protection and Practice, 3*, 100065.

Hong, J. S., Peguero, A. A., Choi, S., Lanesskog, D., Espelage, D. L., & Lee, N. Y. (2014). Social ecology of bullying and peer victimization of Latino and Asian youth in the United States: A review of the literature. *Journal of School Violence, 13*(3), 315–338.

Hong, J. S., Merrin, G. J., Crosby, S., Jozefowicz, D. M. H., Lee, J. M., & Allen-Meares, P. (2016). Individual and contextual factors associated with immigrant youth feeling unsafe in school: A social-ecological analysis. *Journal of Immigrant and Minority Health, 18*(5), 996–1006.

Irwin, K., Varela, K. S., & Peguero, A. (2022). Punishment and racial segregation of schools: Against racial threat and toward a racial control perspective. *Critical Criminology, 30*(4), 1075–1090.

Iwama, J., Peguero, A. A., Marchbanks, M. P. T., III, Eason, J. M., Blake, J., & Zhang, J. (2023). Immigration and school threat? Exploring the significance of the border. *Journal of Research in Crime and Delinquency, 60*(6), 703–739.

Jones, T. G., & Fuller, M. L. (2003). *Teaching Hispanic children*. Pearson.

Kao, G., Vaquera, E., & Goyette, K. (2013). *Education and immigration*. Wiley.

Kataoka, S. H., Vona, P., Acuna, A., Jaycox, L., Escudero, P., Rojas, C., Stein, B. D., et al. (2018). Applying a trauma informed school systems approach: Examples from school community-academic partnerships. *Ethnicity & Disease, 28*(Suppl 2), 417.

Lindstrom Johnson, S., Waasdorp, T. E., Cash, A. H., Debnam, K. J., Milam, A. J., & Bradshaw, C. P. (2017). Assessing the association between observed school disorganization and school violence: Implications for school climate interventions. *Psychology of Violence, 7*(2), 181.

Lindstrom Johnson, S., Kulkarni, N., Rodríguez De Jesús, S. A., Cottam, S., Fillhouer, M., & Guevara, A. M. (2024). School-family partnerships to support attendance: Advancing an equity-centered theoretical framework. *Journal of School Health, 94*(8), 777–785.

Marks, A. K., Ejesi, K., & García Coll, C. (2014). Understanding the US immigrant paradox in childhood and adolescence. *Child Development Perspectives, 8*(2), 59–64.

Miller, H. V., Ripepi, M., Ernstes, A. M., & Peguero, A. A. (2020). Immigration policy and justice in the era of COVID-19. *American Journal of Criminal Justice, 45*, 793–809.

Oreskes, B. (2024, June 27). Trump says millions of immigrants are criminals. Biden says he's lying. *Los Angeles Times*. https://www.latimes.com/california/story/2024-06-27/2024-election-trump-biden-presidential-debate-immigration

Peguero, A. A., & Bondy, J. M. (2021). *Immigration and school safety*. Routledge.

Peguero, A. A., & Hong, J. S. (2020). *School bullying: Youth vulnerability, marginalization, and victimization*. Springer Nature.

Peguero, A. A., Irizarry, Y., Iwama, J., King, S., Dunning-Lozano, J. L., Hong, J. S., & Bondy, J. M. (2023). Is there an immigration and school-level crime link? *Crime & Delinquency, 69*(8), 1339–1368.

Perez, W., Espinoza, R., Ramos, K., Coronado, H. M., & Cortes, R. (2009). Academic resilience among undocumented Latino students. *Hispanic Journal of Behavioral Sciences, 31*(2), 149–181.

Portes, A., & Rumbaut, R. G. (2024). *Immigrant America: A portrait*. University of California Press.

Ray, R. (2022). School as a hostile institution: How black and immigrant girls of color experience the classroom. *Gender & Society, 36*(1), 88–111.

Ronnau, J. P. (2014). Teaching cultural competence: Practical ideas for social work educators. In *School social workers in the multicultural environment* (pp. 29–42). Routledge.

Sanchez, S., Freeman, R., & Martin, P. (2018). *Stressed, overworked, and not sure whom to trust: How public school educators are navigating recent immigration enforcement*. The Civil Rights Project. Retrieved from https://www.civilrightsproject.ucla.edu/research/k-12-education/immigration-immigrant-students/stressed-overworked-and-not-sure-whom-to-trust-the-impacts-of-recent-immigration-enforcement-on-our-public-school-educators/teachers-Immig-Enforcement-DRAFT-7.pdf

Selod, S. (2018). *Forever suspect: Racialized surveillance of Muslim Americans in the war on terror*. Rutgers University Press.

Sharp, J. (2017, September 16). *'Put the panic back in Hispanic': Photo at Robertsdale pep rally sparks criticism*. Retrieved from https://www.al.com/news/mobile/index.ssf/2017/09/baldwin_school_officials.html

Sibley, E., & Brabeck, K. (2017). Latino immigrant students' school experiences in the United States: The importance of family-school-community collaborations. *School Community Journal, 27*(1), 137–157.

Substance Abuse and Mental Health Services Administration. (2014). *SAMHSA's guidance for a trauma-informed approach*.

Tilley, J. L., Huey, S. J., Jr., Farver, J. M., Lai, M. H., & Wang, C. X. (2021). The immigrant paradox in the problem behaviors of youth in the United States: A meta-analysis. *Child Development, 92*(2), 502–516.

Umaña-Taylor, A. J. (2016). A post-racial society in which ethnic-racial discrimination still exists and has significant consequences for youths' adjustment. *Current Directions in Psychological Science, 25*(2), 111–118.

United States Census Bureau. (2022). *Current population survey.* U.S. Census Bureau, Population Division.

Vara-Orta, F. (2018, August 6). *Hate in schools: An in-depth look.* Retrieved from https://www.edweek.org/ew/projects/hate-in-schools.html

Venta, A. C., & Mercado, A. (2019). Trauma screening in recently immigrated youth: Data from two Spanish-speaking samples. *Journal of Child and Family Studies, 28*, 84–90.

Verma, S., Maloney, P., & Austin, D. W. (2017). The school to deportation pipeline: The perspectives of immigrant students and their teachers on profiling and surveillance within the school system. *The Annals of the American Academy of Political and Social Science, 673*(1), 209–229.

CHAPTER 3

The Outsider Within: Violence, Black Bodies, and the Road to Citizenry

Dante' D. Bryant and Dexter R. Voisin

Introduction

Give me your tired, your poor,
Your huddled masses yearning to breathe free,
The wretched refuse of your teeming shore.
Send these, the homeless, tempest-tossed to me,
I lift my lamp beside the golden door!
—Emma Lazarus (1883)

In 1903, Emma Lazarus's poem "The New Colossus" was etched onto a bronze plaque and placed at the Statue of Liberty's feet (National Park

D. D. Bryant (✉)
School of Social Work, University of North Carolina,
Charlotte, NC, USA

Department of Africana Studies, University of North Carolina,
Charlotte, NC, USA
e-mail: dante.bryant@uncc.edu

D. R. Voisin
Jack, Joseph and Morton Mandel School of Applied Social Sciences, Case
Western Reserve University, Cleveland, OH, USA
e-mail: drv22@case.edu

J. S. Hong et al. (eds.), *Violence and Trauma Without Borders*,
https://doi.org/10.1007/978-3-032-29221-6_3

Service, 2019). This act aimed to capture and concretize the United States as a country welcoming to all. As such, America professed to stand as a nation of possibilities for anyone who touched its "teeming shore." To be clear, this is the American ideal, a story of hope, which was authored byformer immigrants seeking the dream of a better tomorrow (National Park Service, 2019).

Still, the American story is complex and nuanced, and despite its dependence on the transformation of the immigrant into the citizenry, all those who have dawned on its shores have not been equally greeted with a welcoming embrace. For example, many northern and western European immigrants have a long history of being immediately adopted and offered a path to citizenship that was cleared and paved. In contrast, others, such as Asians and many southern and eastern Europeans, were, and at times continue to be, scorned and placed on roads covered with thickets and barbs (Cohn, 2015). Yet there are still others, such as formerly enslaved Africans and their descendants, who, despite their tenure, have been conceptually confined to communities whose existence has been relegated to the shadows of the stars and stripes. As such, every group of "huddled masses yearning to breathe free" has, and continues to, walk their own paths; each offering a unique set of experiences and scars notating the price they paid to live out the "American dream." To this point, it is fruitless to rank comparative oppressions, for example, the Oppression Olympics, or to actively engage in the collation of sufferings by the group.

Still, it is important to acknowledge that there are those, and their successive generations, who have not only tasted but found their place within the promise of America, while others remain outsiders within. For instance, in contrast to many who assimilated after voluntarily broaching American shores, Africans, who were brought as slaves, have been, and in many ways continue to be, subject to a form of integration that is marked by a unique form of ontological violence, trauma, and resistance (Bryant & Swafford, 2024; Bryant & Vision, 2024; Voisin, 2019; Warren, 2018).

To this point, this chapter will focus on the social-cultural challenges of citizenry faced by African Americans. In doing so, we hope to establish a dialogue that allows us to better engage and understand the ongoing experiences of African Americans as commensurate with the social traumas noted by many of those who have and continue to approach the promise of American citizenship.

In addition, this chapter will explore the ongoing significance of racial hierarchies, social contracts, and America's investment in keeping African Americans at the bottom of the social order. In closing, we will discuss the potential costs borne by all Americans for maintaining the subjugated status of African Americans and some general arguments for advancing a more just and inclusive society where all can thrive.

Trauma, Violence, and Social Outcomes

It is first important to define what we mean by the term violence. Violence is often defined as a singular act—a push, a slap, a violent blow, or a gunshot resulting in harm, injury, or even death. While this is indeed one aspect of violence, a broader aspect of violence that is hidden in plain sight influences the daily lives, opportunities, and reach of many subjugated populations in America (Voisin, 2019). This form of violence, termed structural violence, refers to "the social arrangements that put individuals and populations in harm's way. … The arrangements are *structural* because they are embedded in the political and economic organization of our social world; they are *violent* because they cause injury to people" (Farmer et al., 2006).

Structural violence often disproportionately burdens African Americans as a result of centuries of legislative and cultural discrimination that often manifests itself through the social determinants of health. The social determinants of health are the conditions in which people are born, live, work, and grow and shape their health outcomes, including factors such as education, employment, food, and healthcare access (World Health Organization, n.d.). Cultural and interpersonal racism operates through the social determinants of health to negatively impact not only health outcomes but also wealth, societal opportunities, and social and economic advancement.

Redlining, for example, refers to the discriminatory practices of restricting loans, business opportunities, and homeownership from African Americans, which resulted in a disproportionate number of Blacks living in low-resourced communities (Lynch et al., 2021). Researchers have posited that the "redlining practices of the 1930s potentially contribute to increased rates of firearm violence through changes to neighborhood environments, namely through preclusion from homeownership, poverty, poor educational attainment, and concentration (i.e., segregation) of Black communities" (Poulson et al., 2021). The effects of redlining persisted for decades, and sociologists and demographers have documented that the neighborhoods with the highest rates of health and social disparities such as gun violence, homicide rates, lung cancer, Human

Immunodeficienicy Virus (HIV) infections, and infant and maternal mortality are the communities that have been subject to redlining (Krieger et al., 2020; Lynch et al., 2021; Nardone et al., 2020; Poulson et al., 2021; Swope et al., 2022), which further deepened these social inequalities. For example, despite *Brown v. Board of Education* (1954) desegregating schools, de facto school education persists in America due to the lingering effects of redlining. This means that most Black and Brown children are educated in majority-minority schools with fewer resources (Voisin, 2019). Research provides evidence that neighborhood environment impacts health: Housing and environmental data show that Black Americans are more likely to live in neighborhoods with poor air quality, exposure to toxins and lead, fewer green spaces, and more food deserts. Studies show that in America, one's zip code is a stronger predictor of their health than their genetic makeup (Chambers et al., 2019; Drewnowski et al., 2007; Graham, 2016).

American Citizenry, Whiteness, and the White Adjacent

> But what on earth is whiteness that one should so desire it? ... I am given to understand that whiteness is the ownership of the earth forever and ever, Amen! - Du Bois (1920/1987)

Geneticists have long debunked the biological myth of Whiteness and provided evidence that the genetic makeup of groups that are typically classified as "White" shares more differences and no set of consistent genetic or biological characteristics. Ethnic groups typically classified as White share more similar genetic characteristics with groups that are typically considered non-White (Kampourakis, 2023; Rutherford, 2021). In 2020, the American Medical Association adopted new policies to acknowledge race as a social construct (American Medical Association, 2020).

The concept of "Whiteness" in the United States has been socially constructed. It is a fluid classification that has evolved over time and mirrored changing demographic, cultural, political, and economic shifts within America. Consequently, the social contract of who is allowed to be seen or treated as White has evolved. Whiteness, primarily reserved for White Anglo-Saxon Protestants (WASPs), began to loosen in the late nineteenth and early twentieth centuries with the arrival of millions of immigrants from Southern and Eastern Europe, including Polish, Italian, Jewish, and

Irish groups. These ethnic groups were initially marginalized as "non-White" and relegated to living in racialized ghettos. These immigrant groups faced considerable discrimination and were often excluded from the privileges associated with being White. Nevertheless, over generations, many of these groups gradually assimilated into the broader category of Whiteness because of several contextual factors, a few of which are discussed below.

Economic Opportunity and Whiteness

Historical and ongoing racial trauma has continued to hamper the economic opportunities and upward mobility of African Americans. The legacy of slavery has had profound and enduring negative economic impacts on African American communities. Chattel slavery subjected African Americans to brutal treatment, denied them basic human rights, and deprived them of opportunities for education and economic advancement. Even after the abolition of slavery in 1865, the subsequent Jim Crow laws enforced racial segregation and institutionalized discrimination, followed by the retooling of the New Jim Crow (i.e., the War on Drugs and the rise of the prison industrial complex that disproportionately targeted Black people; Alexander, 2010, 2011), creating significant barriers to social, political, and economic opportunities for African Americans. These laws entrenched systemic racism and reinforced the notion of African Americans as second-class citizens and their "othering" in America (Alexander, 2011).

Undeniability and economic opportunities are associated with the assimilation and acceptance of some immigrants, who came to America voluntarily, being accepted into the category of "White Americans." The post–World War II period was characterized by economic prosperity and the expansion of the middle class. Federal policies, such as the GI Bill, excessively benefited immigrant families who could take advantage of educational and housing opportunities. This access contributed to a redefinition of what it meant to be White in America; achieving a stable economic standing became a pathway to acceptance within the White American identity. Owning homes, beginning small businesses, and solidifying stable jobs, some immigrants solidified their place within society, aligning more closely with the ideals of Whiteness—upward mobility, homeownership, and economic stability.

While many immigrant groups assimilated into White American culture through economic mobility and cultural integration, African Americans have often faced significant economic barriers that inhibit similar pathways. Lower wages, high rates of unemployment, less healthcare access, limited access to quality education, higher tracking into child welfare systems, over-policing, and high incarceration rates have perpetuated cycles of poverty within African American communities (Voisin, 2019). These economic challenges hinder the ability to achieve the same level of economic assimilation into the dominant culture, as seen with some immigrant groups. James Baldwin (1963) describes these individuals who live "in the shadow of the stars and stripes," and former president Bill Clinton (1997) speaks of the communities "not yet touched by our prosperity."

Cultural Integration and Whiteness

Over successive generations, many immigrants and their descendants adopted the language, customs, and social practices of dominant American culture. This cultural integration often involved a conscious effort by immigrants to distance themselves from their ethnic origins (e.g., language, customs, culture) in trade for a gradual shift in identity toward being viewed and accepted as being White. Intermarriage between different European ethnic groups with native-born White Americans further accelerated this transition to Whiteness, muddling the lines of racial distinction and identification. For some researchers, the evidence of becoming White American is the change in socioeconomic status for these groups (Yang & Koshy, 2016).

In contrast, race and identity are central components for African Americans, shaped by a long history of slavery, oppression, resilience, and community cohesion. Many African Americans embrace their cultural heritage (e.g., food, culture, linguistic traditions, and presentation of their natural hair), which can create a sense of unity and strength within the community. However, the pride in cultural identity can sometimes lead to societal perceptions of "otherness," further complicating the assimilation process into a predominantly White culture that has historically marginalized them.

Negative stereotypes about African Americans have been pervasive in American culture, leading to structural violence and reinforced by prejudice and discrimination that further entrench second-class status. The historical portrayal of African Americans in media and societal narratives has contributed to enduring biases, suggesting that they are less capable, deserving, or valuable than their White counterparts. These stereotypes can curtail educational gains, which hampers acceptance and inclusion, making it more difficult for African Americans to assimilate into mainstream society (Nelson, 2008; Prince et al., 2018; Wilson, 2012).

Becoming White Adjacent

Legislation and the political process have also played a pivotal role in defining and reshaping the concept of opportunity, success, and ultimately, Whiteness in America. For instance, in 1691, the Virginian General Assembly outlawed intermarriage between free Black people and White people (Wolfe, 2020). This law remained in effect until the US Supreme Court in *Loving v. Virginia* (1967) decreed all state anti-miscegenation laws unconstitutional. Another example of anti-Black racism and the marginalization of Blacks and Black identities is the Immigration and Nationality Act (1965), which marked a significant turning point in immigration policy, promoting family reunification and enabling diverse groups from Asia and Latin America to enter the United States, but more restrictions on persons entering from African countries (McKanders, 2019).

Although many of these newer immigrant groups faced challenges in achieving societal acceptance, over time, many have been able to experience many of the social and economic markers of success, which have allowed them to achieve societal integration and be viewed as White adjacent. To be clear, it is not that African Americans have not achieved many of these social markers of American success. However, relative to other ethnic populations who came to America as immigrants, they disproportionately lag on many of these social markers and bear a higher disease burden and societal inequalities, as noted earlier.

In contrast, some legislation and its biased application have further constrained the social and economic mobility of large numbers of African Americans, creating a large underclass. The differential application of welfare benefits to African American mothers, which discouraged Black family formation, and the War on Drugs, which targeted low-income Black substance users, are a few examples of biased legislative policy applications (Alexander, 2011; Voisin, 2019). African Americans have often faced significant barriers to political participation and representation, from voter suppression tactics to systemic exclusion from political power. This lack of political voice affects their ability to advocate for their rights and influence policies that could improve their social standing (Voisin, 2019). In contrast, many immigrant groups have found avenues for political engagement that help them assimilate and establish their place within society.

This transition is often influenced by public perceptions of immigrant identity and economic success and mobility. As certain groups gained visibility, prominence, and success in American society, their acceptance as "White adjacent" was reinforced through cultural representations, media portrayals, and political and social narratives, as examined later in this chapter. The need for acceptance created pressures to conform to the norms and values associated with Whiteness, leading many to navigate their ethnic identities in a way that aligned with broader societal expectations and led to the adoption and propagation of America's racial contract.

Such inequities have hampered the ability of African Americans to assimilate in the same way as many immigrant groups have, by leveraging economic opportunities, gained acceptance into the broader society as "White adjacent." Given that socioeconomic status is so inextricably linked to race in America (Crimmins et al., 2004), African Americans who reach economic heights that have been traditionally reserved for WASPs are often seen as achieving racelessness or defying the barriers of race (Hall, 2008). Examples of such persons include Michael Jordan (Georgia Tech, n.d.; Smith, 2023) and Oprah Winfrey (Hall, 2008), but only when they are recognized and identified as their iconic profiles; the effect does not extend to the average African American person on the streets, for whom the violence of racism persists.

Stigma Theory

Goffman's theory provides one of several frameworks for understanding the racial and structural violence enacted on African Americans. According to Goffman (1963), stigma is an intensely discrediting attribute that can lead a person to be considered almost nonhuman. Goffman (1963, p. 4) identifies three types of stigmas: "abominations of the body," "blemishes of individual character," and stigmas associated with group affiliations. All three designations have been applied to African Americans, and ongoing forms of anti-Black racism represent present violence and threat. Indeed, the stark disproportionate social outcomes reported by this population are sober reminders that anti-Black racism persists within America.

The three-fifths clause of the United States Constitution (1787), often misinterpreted as stating that Blacks were considered three-fifths human, meant that "for purposes of representation in Congress, enslaved blacks in a state would be counted as three-fifths of the number of white inhabitants" (Simba, 2014). Regardless of the interpretation, it signaled legislatively that Black bodies were less valuable than those considered White. In addition, the "one drop of Black blood" further reinforced the "othering" and stigma of Blackness, and findings have shown that persons who are half Black consider themselves as Black or are not permitted by society to be seen or treated as anything other than being Black (Khanna, 2010). Indeed, immigrant groups have often culturally, socially, and politically distanced themselves from Blacks and have enacted anti-Black racism, furthering their distance from Blackness and approximation to Whiteness (Khanna, 2010; Wilderson, 2020).

Blackness remains stigmatized in American society, and as a result, African Americans, despite the legal designation as citizens, experience significant social disparities and bear a higher disease burden, higher rates of poverty and infant mortality, overrepresentation in the child welfare system, and other systemic inequalities (Voisin, 2019). Consequently, cultural and medical racism, which views Black bodies as deficit-based, threatening, or deserving of less sympathy or respect, further perpetuates individual, societal, and structural racism.

Often, these disparities lead Black people in the United States to experience toxic stress, the "frequent, chronic stress that has harmful and potentially lasting effects on physical and mental health" (Shafir, 2023; see also Odgers & Jaffee, 2013; Shonkoff et al., 2009). The human body is not designed to function in a state of heightened hypervigilance; scientists believe that excessive stress can cause significant harm to the body and the brain, causing lifelong health problems. Toxic stress has been linked to compromises to the immune systems, poorer sleep and memory recall, higher blood pressure and heart disease, obesity, changes to the onset of puberty, and high rates of depression and anxiety, among the many aftereffects (Benjet et al., 2013; Garner, 2013).

Some might say that the Black body, physically, is bleeding to death by a thousand papercuts and the everyday lacerations to the soul. At the same time, the Black body suffers under the cultural weight of racism—a conceptual burden imposed by the construction of American identity.

Violence, Black Bodies, and the Road to American Citizenry

Black bodies define the humanity and the human condition they are forbidden to participate in. —Warren 2018

Black bodies have and continue to occupy a unique space in the development and maintenance of American citizenry and identity (Alexander, 2010; Baldwin, 2010; Coates, 2015; Du Bois, 1920/1987; Fanon, 1967; Glaude, 2016; Wilderson, 2020). More specifically, individuals such as Sylvia Wynter (McKittrick, 2015) and Hortense Spillers (2003) have suggested that the very idea of the *American* has been, and continues to be, heavily dependent on the Western (re)production of the Black body as the canvas on which Whiteness and American citizenry are painted (Baldwin, 2010; General Assembly, 1705).

To this point, Baldwin (2010) argues that as created, Black bodies are not bodies at all; instead, they are what Ellison (1947) once referred to as "figments of their [White America's] imaginations" (p. 3). As imagined, "Black," when ascribed to bodies, does not evidence a race of people but functions as a marker of a person's reduction to a social standing outside society, thus demarcating society itself (Mills, 1997; Wilderson, 2020).

Put differently, the idea of the Black body was not produced to index the color of a people but rather to indicate a specific state of social standing, or noncitizenry (General Assembly, 1705; Mills, 1997; Warren, 2018; Wilderson, 2020). Scholars such as Mills (1997) and Warren (2018) assert that from its inception, the Black body has been repeatedly used to clarify the outer limits of, and standards for, group participation in a society in which those same bodies are denied full attendance (Baldwin, 2010; Wilderson, 2020).

For example, one of the first legally documented usages of race as a proxy for social standing and citizenry occurred in the Virginia Slave Codes of 1705, in which the General Assembly drew clear distinctions between those identified as Black and those identified as White (Hening, 1832; Morgan, 1975/2003; Wood, 1998). One of the more salient distinctions was the sociological designation of Black people as slaves and White people as free. Patterson (1982) argues that the fundamental nature of the slave is wholly contingent on the needs, conditions, and desires of the slaveholder. As such, the slave is denied any unique identifiers independent of subjugation. Therefore, to the extent the Black body was (re) classified as a slave, it was rendered valueless apart from its ability to serve, define, and accentuate the value of those socially identified as free, slave-holding citizens.

Additionally, the formlessness attributed to the slave (Patterson, 1982) extends beyond its sociological condition, ultimately touching and reshaping its biological constitution. For example, according to the Virginia Act XII of 1662, any child who was born of a slave was subject to the same conditions as the mother's biological lineage (Hening, 1832). Conversely, those designated as slaves were not known by the status of their labor but rather by the predetermined and eternal condition of their being, particularly in relation to those who were not. Thus, according to Patterson (1982), the conditions and functions of the slave are contingent on, and change according to, the personal and social needs, value statuses, and standings of the American citizen. As the perceived needs of the citizenry change, so too do the activities and character of the enslaved. In this way, the social value, standing, and conditions of the two exist in codependence, maintaining their inherent relationship despite fluctuations in time.

Persistent Representation of the Black Body as a Slave

Examples of stability over time include, but are not limited to, campaigns to reimagine Americanness and Whiteness after the Revolutionary and Civil Wars. For example, postrevolutionary American theater flourished, enabling recently liberated American audiences to engage in imaginative exercises exploring the possibilities of their newfound nationalism. These new stories sought to establish and situate the elevated value, dignity, and status of those who had come to reside in the new colonial America. However, the landscape of the colonies forced such identities to emerge within the context of slavery and the mass killing and colonization of Indigenous populations. The result was the othering of non-Europeans, and the rise in popularity of characters such as the Yankee, the Ingine/Savage, and the Sambo (Meserve, 1994).

Unfortunately, such performative efforts to define the character and value of post-British America often relied on the erasure or overdetermination of Black and Indigenous bodies (Dorson, 1940; Meserve, 1994). For instance, stories of American progress and values such as virtue, nationalism, patriotism, courage, and conquest were often reduced to and depended on images of Indigenous and Black populations as savages, antagonists, and racial tropes (Meserve, 1994). In these distorted images,

Black bodies were most commonly personified as happy, childlike servants in minstrel shows and blackface, both of which saw their greatest popularity during the nineteenth and twentieth centuries (Dorson, 1940; Rea, 2024; Meserve, 1994; Wilson, 2016). Once disseminated, these stories and images captured and concretized the existing cultural iconography, which helped to shape and normalize the postrevolutionary (White) American identity and the subaltern status of Black bodies as slaves—that is, subject to the needs of the freed and slaveholding (Dunn, 2019; Marks, 2017).

Similarly, when confronted with the legal emancipation of slaves in 1865 and the quickly evolving social tapestry, southern White Americans sought to reconstitute their place in society by reimagining the role of Black bodies. The personification of this was captured in D. W. Griffith's 1915 film *The Birth of a Nation*. Touted as the first feature-length American major motion picture, this three-hour film drew on the fears, anxieties, and imaginings of White, post–Civil War America. *The Birth of a Nation* defined and differentiated Black and White bodies by tethering Black bodies to violence, criminality, hypersexuality, deviance, and the desire to defame White purity (Glaude, 2016). White Americans in the South relied on this portrayal of Black bodies to reconcile their expressed Christian identity/ethics with their development and propagation of racially biased practices, laws, policies, and procedures.

In addition, the (re)constitution of Black bodies established a set of narratives that served to justify and reinforce the differential freedoms, protections, and consequences granted to these disparate social groups—essentially rendering the Black body a slave to the American narrative. In his 2018 work *Ontological Terror*, Warren argues that an "onto-metaphysical holocaust" (p. 27; see also Patterson, 1982) occurs when one group successfully reconstitutes another's being in ways that deny the full breadth of that group's humanity and civic participation. Under such conditions, those who are (re)defined cease to exist in any meaningful way independent of the narratives propagated by those who have sociopolitical power to define what is.

According to social dominance theory, these narratives, or "legitimizing myths," are the persistent, but often unacknowledged, culturally integrated mythologies that shape and are shaped by underlying beliefs and values (Sidanius & Pratto, 1999; Sidanius et al., 1992). As representations of these values and beliefs, legitimizing myths provide individuals, communities, and nations with the moral and intellectual justifications that define, normalize, and shape their participation, experience, and sense of belonging within mainstream society (Appiah, 2005; Sidanius & Pratto, 1999; Sidanius et al., 1992). Yet these myths—these identities—impose limits, and come at a cost to all.

The Cost of Racial Trauma and Unequal Citizenry

To illustrate these costs, we offer some commentary on the broader direct and indirect impact of racism, especially anti-Black racism and inequality, on the overall American citizenry. These costs amount to an exorbitant economic, health, social, moral, and spiritual tax, though such costs are too seldom articulated in the extant academic literature. As Martin Luther King Jr. articulated in "Letter from a Birmingham Jail" (1963), "We are ... tied in a single garment of destiny. Whatever affects one directly, affects all indirectly."

Economists have long tried to quantify the cost of racism. "For instance, the wealth gap between American Whites and Blacks is projected to cost the US economy between $1 trillion and $1.5 trillion in lost consumption and investment between 2019 and 2028. This translates to a projected [gross domestic product] penalty of 4 to 6 percent in 2028" (Losavio, 2020, citing data from Noel et al., 2019). In addition, economists calculate that the lost productivity due to chronic disease and preventable death alone costs the United States $3.7 trillion annually (Waters & Graf, 2018).

Studies in population health have shown that societies that report greater social and racial inequalities also document higher mortality rates and lower levels of life satisfaction (Smedley & Syme, 2000; Wilkinson & Pickett, 2006; Williams & Collins, 1995). Higher population disease burdens are also correlated to higher healthcare costs, which are borne by the insured, the uninsured, and the government and city budgets (Waters & Graf, 2018). Americans can expect to live about 5 years less than their Canadian counterparts (Wilkie & Ho, 2024). While the roots of such differences are complex, access to health care and resources that are rooted in race in America are part of these complex reasons (Yearby et al., 2022). When pandemics such as COVID-19 occur, it is a reminder that personal wealth does not always protect us when these deep societal inequalities exist.

While there is no doubt a tangible price every country must pay for the unwarranted marginalization of any one of its citizens, there is, although often unacknowledged, an additional tariff incurred via the morality of being itself. The spiritual and moral cost of watching the suffering of our fellow Americans cannot be understated. The proposition is captured by Baldwin's (2010) idea that there are always two men in prison: the prisoner and the one keeping him there—the guard. For Baldwin (2010), the idea of prison has little to do with the carceral system proper. To the contrary, Baldwin (2010) argues that the true American prison is the persistence of a racially informed caste system that relies on the intentional distortion and devaluation of black bodies.

For example, in a society where race serves as a proxy for one's humanity, social value, and level of citizenry, there must be a race that is void of such (Patterson, 1982; Warren, 2018; Wilderson, 2020). According to Glaude (2016), Warren (2018), Wilderson (2020), and others, not only have Black bodies been ascribed this role, but as the outsider within, they have and continue to function as a cultural zero point, denoting the outer limits of full citizenry (Baldwin, 2010; Patterson, 1982).

If that is correct, then within American discourse, Black bodies mark, for all other immigrants and populations, that which must be surpassed if they are to assume their allocated place within the social hierarchy. In addition, the value and social standing that is garnered via comparison retains its validity only insofar as Black bodies remain socially fixed at the bottom of the proverbial well (Bell, 1992). Thus, not only is the status of White Americans predicated on the persistent distortion and devaluation of Black bodies, but so too is the status of all other cultural, racial, and ethnic groups that breach the nation's "teeming shore" (Lazarus, 1883; Wilderson, 2020).

Unfortunately, one's ability to distort the intrinsic value and humanity of another requires, above all, the willingness to distort one's own. This persistent investment in preserving a lie capable of altering one's perception manifests dishonest and distorted identification of, and relationships to, others, oneself, and the world we inhabit. Put differently, the guard's investment in the lie discourages them from broaching the truth. And if the investment continues long enough, it mars their capacity to differentiate between the two, imprisoning them in a lie that actively facilitates their moral demise while simultaneously assuring them that they are standing in truth.

It is clear, then, that America cannot truly stand as a beacon of welcome—a "golden door" for the "huddled masses"—until we shine light upon, and deeply reckon with, the violence against Black bodies that is at the foundation of our nation's history and self-perception.

References

Alexander, M. (2010). *The new Jim Crow: Mass incarceration in the age of colorblindness*. The New Press.

Alexander, M. (2011). The new Jim Crow. *Ohio State Journal of Criminal Law, 9*(1), 7–26.

American Medical Association. (2020, November 16). *New AMA policies recognize race as a social, not biological, construct* [Press release]. https://www.ama-assn.org/press-center/press-releases/new-ama-policies-recognize-race-social-not-biological-construct

Appiah, K. A. (2005). *The ethics of identity*. Princeton University Press.

Baldwin, J. (1963). A talk to teachers. In R. Simonson & S. Walker (Eds.), *Multiculturalism literacy* (pp. 3–12). Graywolf Press.

Baldwin, J. (2010). *The cross of redemption: Uncollected writings*. Vintage Books.

Bell, D. (1992). *Faces at the bottom of the well: The permanence of racism*. Basic Books.

Benjet, C., Borges, G., Medina-Mora, M. E., & Méndez, E. (2013). Chronic childhood adversity and stages of substance use involvement in adolescents. *Drug and Alcohol Dependence, 131*(1–2), 85–91.

Brown v. Board of Education, 347 U.S. 483 (1954).

Bryant, D., & Swafford, T. (2024). Race, space, and culture: Exploring the educational experiences of African American doctoral social work students. *Journal of Social Work Education*.

Bryant, D., & Vision, D. (2024). Black male bodies in White female spaces: Power, dominance, and myth in social work education. *Journal of Social Work Education*.

Chambers, B. D., Baer, R. J., McLemore, M. R., & Jelliffe-Pawlowski, L. L. (2019). Using index of concentration at the extremes as indicators of structural racism to evaluate the association with preterm birth and infant mortality—California, 2011–2012. *Journal of Urban Health, 96*, 159–170.

Coates, T. (2015). *Between the world and me*. Random House.

Cohn, D. (2015, September 30). How U.S. immigration laws and rules have changed through history. *Pew Research Center*. https://www.pewresearch.org/short-reads/2015/09/30/how-u-s-immigration-laws-and-rules-have-changed-through-history/

Crimmins, E. M., Hayward, M. D., & Seeman, T. E. (2004). Race/ethnicity, socioeconomic status, and health. In National Research Council, Panel on Race, Ethnicity, and Health in Later Life, Committee on Population, Division of Behavioral and Social Sciences and Education, N.B. Anderson, R.A. Bulatao, & B. Cohen (Eds.), *Critical perspectives on racial and ethnic differences in health in late life* (pp. 310–352). The National Academies Press.

Dorson, R. M. (1940). The Yankee on the stage—a folk hero of American drama. *The New England Quarterly, 13*(3), 467–493.

Drewnowski, A., Rehm, C. D., & Solet, D. (2007). Disparities in obesity rates: Analysis by ZIP code area. *Social Science & Medicine, 65*(12), 2458–2463.

Du Bois, W. E. B. (1920/1987). *W.E.B. Du Bois: Writings* (pp. 923–938). Library of America. https://loa-shared.s3.amazonaws.com/static/pdf/Du_Bois_White_Folk.pdf

Dunn, K. (2019). Hidden damage: When uninformed casting and actor training disregard the effects of character embodiment on students of color. *Theatre Symposium, 27*(1), 68–79.

Ellison, R. (1947). *Invisible man.* Random House.

Fanon, F. (1967). *Black skin, White mask.* Grove Press.

Farmer, P. E., Nizeye, B., Stulac, S., & Keshavjee, S. (2006). Structural violence and clinical medicine. *PLoS Medicine, 3*(10), e449.

Garner, A. S. (2013). Home visiting and the biology of toxic stress: Opportunities to address early childhood adversity. *Pediatrics, 132*(Suppl. 2), S65–S73.

General Assembly. (1705). An act concerning servants and slaves. *Encyclopedia Virginia.* https://encyclopediavirginia.org/primary-documents/an-act-concerning-servants-and-slaves-1705/

Georgia Tech. (n.d.). *Michael Jordan famously didn't talk about race — that doesn't mean it didn't shape his career.* https://iac.gatech.edu/featured-news/2023/11/michael-jordan

Glaude, E. S., Jr. (2016). *Democracy in black: How race still enslaves the American soul.* Broadway Books.

Goffman, E. (1963). *Stigma: Notes on the management of spoiled identity.* Simon & Schuster.

Graham, G. N. (2016). Why your ZIP code matters more than your genetic code: Promoting healthy outcomes from mother to child. *Breastfeeding Medicine, 11*(8), 396–397.

Hall, K. (2008, May 27). Transcending race and racism [Video interview]. In *Explorations in Black Leadership.* UVA Arts & Sciences. https://blackleadership.virginia.edu/videos/hall-katori/khh11

Hening, W. W. (1832). *The statutes at large: Being a collection of all the laws of Virginia, from the first session of the legislature, in the year 1619. Published pursuant to an act of the General Assembly of Virginia, passed on the fifth day of February one thousand eight hundred and eight.* HathiTrust. https://babel.hathitrust.org/cgi/pt?id=hvd.hxh5uc&seq=22

Kampourakis, K. (2023). *Ancestry reimagined: Dismantling the myth of genetic ethnicities.* Oxford University Press.

Khanna, N. (2010). "If you're half black, you're just black": Reflected appraisals and the persistence of the one-drop rule. *The Sociological Quarterly, 51*(1), 96–121.

King, M. L. (1963, April 16). *Letter from a Birmingham jail.* https://www.africa.upenn.edu/Articles_Gen/Letter_Birmingham.html

Krieger, N., Van Wye, G., Huynh, M., Waterman, P. D., Maduro, G., Li, W., Gwynn, R. C., Barbot, O., & Bassett, M. T. (2020). Structural racism, historical redlining, and risk of preterm birth in New York City, 2013–2017. *American Journal of Public Health, 110*(7), 1046–1053.

Lazarus, E. (1883). *The new Colossus.* https://www.poetryfoundation.org/poems/46550/the-new-colossus

Losavio, J. (2020, September). What racism costs us all. F&D: Finance & Development Magazine. *International Monetary Fund.* https://www.imf.org/en/Publications/fandd/issues/2020/09/the-economic-cost-of-racism-losavio

Loving v. Virginia, 388 U.S. 1 (1967).

Lynch, E. E., Malcoe, L. H., Laurent, S. E., Richardson, J., Mitchell, B. C., & Meier, H. C. S. (2021). The legacy of structural racism: Associations between historic redlining, current mortgage lending, and health. *SSM–Population Health, 14*, 100793.

Marks, P. (2017, June 29). Black actresses still have to play maids on Broadway. How do they feel about it? *The Washington Post.* https://www.washingtonpost.com/entertainment/theater_danc/black-actresses-still-have-to-play-maids-on-broadway-how-do-they-feel-about-it/2017/06/29/60311162-5a8f-11e7-8e2f-ef443171f6bd_story.html

McKanders, K. (2019). Immigration and blackness: What's race got to do with it? *Human Rights, 44*(1), 20–23.

McKittrick, K. (Ed.). (2015). *Sylvia Wynter: On being human as praxis.* Duke University Press.

Meserve, W. J. (1994). *An outline history of American drama.* Feedback/Prospero.

Mills, C. W. (1997). *The racial contract.* Cornell University Press.

Morgan, E. S. (1975/2003). *American slavery, American freedom.* W. W. Norton.

Nardone, A., Chiang, J., & Corburn, J. (2020). Historic redlining and urban health today in U.S. cities. *Environmental Justice, 13*(4), 109–119.

National Park Service. (2019, August 14). *The New Colossus.* https://www.nps.gov/stli/learn/historyculture/colossus.htm

Nelson, A. (2008). African American stereotypes in prime-time television: An overview, 1948–2007. In T. Boyd (Ed.), *African Americans and popular culture* (Vol. 1, pp. 185–216). Greenwood Publishing Group.

Noel, N., Pinder, D., Stewart, S., & Wright, J. (2019, August 13). *The economic impact of closing the racial wealth gap.* McKinsey Institute for Black Economic Mobility. https://www.mckinsey.com/industries/public-and-social-sector/our-insights/the-economic-impact-of-closing-the-racial-wealth-gap

Odgers, C. L., & Jaffee, S. R. (2013). Routine versus catastrophic influences on the developing child. *Annual Review of Public Health, 34*, 29–48.

Patterson, O. (1982). *Slavery and social death: A comparative study*. Harvard University Press.

Poulson, M., Neufeld, M. Y., Dechert, T., Allee, L., & Kenzik, K. M. (2021). Historic redlining, structural racism, and firearm violence: A structural equation modeling approach. *The Lancet Regional Health–Americas, 3*, Article 100052.

Prince, D. M., Rocha, A., & Nurius, P. S. (2018). Multiple disadvantage and discrimination: Implications for adolescent health and education. *Social Work Research, 42*(3), 169–179.

Rea, K. G. (2024, September 23). Western theater. *Encyclopedia Britannica*. https://www.britannica.com/art/Western-theatre

Rutherford, A. (2021). *How to argue with a racist: What our genes do (and don't) say about human difference*. The Experiment, LLC.

Shafir, H. (2023, September 14). Toxic stress: Definition, causes, & treatment. *Choosing Therapy*. https://www.choosingtherapy.com/toxic-stress/

Shonkoff, J. P., Boyce, W. T., & McEwen, B. S. (2009). Neuroscience, molecular biology, and the childhood roots of health disparities: Building a new framework for health promotion and disease prevention. *JAMA, 301*(21), 2252–2259.

Sidanius, J., & Pratto, F. (1999). *Social dominance: An intergroup theory of social hierarchy and oppression*. Cambridge University Press.

Sidanius, J., Devereux, E., & Pratto, F. (1992). A comparison of symbolic racism theory and social dominance theory as explanations for racial policy attitudes. *The Journal of Social Psychology, 132*(3), 377–395.

Simba, M. (2014, October 3). The three-fifths clause of the United States Constitution (1787). *BlackPast.org*. https://www.blackpast.org/african-american-history/events-african-american-history/three-fifths-clause-united-states-constitution-1787/

Smedley, B. D., & Syme, S. L. (2000). *Promoting health: Intervention strategies from social and behavioral research*. National Academies Press (US).

Smith, J. (2023). *Jumpman: The making and meaning of Michael Jordan*. Basic Books.

Spillers, H. J. (2003). *Black, white, and in color: Essays on American literature and culture*. University of Chicago Press.

Swope, C. B., Hernández, D., & Cushing, L. J. (2022). The relationship of historical redlining with present-day neighborhood environmental and health outcomes: A scoping review and conceptual model. *Journal of Urban Health, 99*(6), 959–983.

Voisin, D. (2019). *America the beautiful and violent: Black youth and neighborhood trauma in Chicago*. Columbia University Press.

Warren, C. L. (2018). *Ontological terror: Blackness, nihilism and emancipation*. Duke University Press.

Waters, H., & Graf, M. (2018, August). The costs of chronic disease in the U.S. *Milken Institute*. https://milkeninstitute.org/sites/default/files/reports-pdf/ChronicDiseases-HighRes-FINAL.pdf

Wilderson, F. B. (2020). *Afropessimism*. W. W. Norton.

Wilkinson, R. G., & Pickett, K. E. (2006). Income inequality and population health: A review and explanation of the evidence. *Social Science & Medicine, 62*(7), 1768–1784.

Wilkie, R. Z., & Ho, J. Y. (2024). Life expectancy and geographic variation in mortality: An observational comparison study of six high-income Anglophone countries. *BMJ Open, 14*(7), e079365.

Williams, D. R., & Collins, C. (1995). US socioeconomic and racial differences in health: patterns and explanations. *Annual Review of Sociology, 21*(1), 349–386.

Wilson, A. (2016, July/August). The ground on which I stand [text of speech delivered on June 26, 1996]. *Theatre Communications Group*. https://www.americantheatre.org/2016/06/20/the-ground-on-which-i-stand/

Wilson, W. J. (2012). *The truly disadvantaged: The inner city, the underclass, and public policy* (2nd ed.). University of Chicago Press.

Wolfe, B. (2020, December 7). *Free Blacks in Colonial Virginia*. Encyclopedia Virginia. https://encyclopediavirginia.org/entries/free-blacks-in-colonial-virginia

Wood, G. S. (1998). *The creation of the American Republic, 1776–1787*. Omohundro Institute and University of North Carolina Press.

World Health Organization. (n.d.). *Social determinants of health*. https://www.who.int/health-topics/social-determinants-of-health

Yang, P., & Koshy, K. (2016). The "becoming white thesis" revisited. *The Journal of Public and Professional Sociology, 8*(1), 1.

Yearby, R., Clark, B., & Figueroa, J. F. (2022). Structural racism in historical and modern US health care policy. *Health Affairs, 41*(2), 187–194.

CHAPTER 4

Violence, Displacement, and Transformation: The Ukrainian Experience

Viktor Burlaka, Irena L. C. Connon, Kateryna Buchko, Lena Dominelli, Holly Feen-Calligan, Anna Burlaka, Valeriia Peshkova, and Arash Javanbakht

Introduction

On February 24, 2022, Russia invaded Ukraine, escalating the war that has been going on between Russia and Ukraine since 2014, when Russia annexed Crimea and supported separatist movements in the eastern Donbas region (Brands, 2024). The invasion followed a long and complex history of Russian political, cultural, and military domination over Ukraine, marked by periods of colonization, suppression of national identity, and forced assimilation (Burlaka et al., 2018). In the years following the start of the war, both

V. Burlaka (✉)
Department of Social Work, University of North Carolina, Greensboro, NC, USA

American University Kyiv, Kyiv, Ukraine
e-mail: v_burlaka@uncg.edu

I. L. C. Connon • L. Dominelli
Faculty of Social Sciences, University of Stirling, Stirling, Scotland, UK
e-mail: irena.connon@stir.ac.uk; lena.dominelli@stir.ac.uk

J. S. Hong et al. (eds.), *Violence and Trauma Without Borders*,
https://doi.org/10.1007/978-3-032-29221-6_4

countries engaged in efforts to establish ceasefires and negotiate agreements. However, violence continued in eastern Ukraine. The conflict then expanded geographically, with Russia launching widespread artillery and rocket attacks across the country. Major cities such as Kyiv, Kharkiv, and Mariupol were subjected to intense bombardments, resulting in extensive destruction and civilian casualties (Center for Preventative Action, 2025). The conflict now continues into its third year, with frontlines shifting and both sides suffering heavy losses. Civilian infrastructure has also been targeted, exacerbating the trauma and hardships experienced. Approximately 3.7 million people remain internally displaced within Ukraine due to the ongoing Russian invasion (International Organization of Migration, 2025). Most internally displaced persons (IDPs) originate from the heavily affected eastern and southern regions, including Donetsk, Kharkiv, Kherson, and Zaporizhzhia oblasts.

As of April 17, 2025, approximately 6.36 million Ukrainian refugees have been recorded across Europe (UNHRC, 2025). Multiple European countries have granted temporary protection status to Ukrainian migrants. Among these, over 4.25 million individuals are hosted by Germany (1.18 million), Poland (997,000), and Czechia (365,000) (Eurostat, 2025), while 28,137 now reside in Scotland (Scottish Parliament, 2025). Approximately 560,200 Ukrainian refugees have been received in countries outside the European continent (UNHRC, 2025). This includes

K. Buchko
Faculty of Social Sciences, University of Stirling, Stirling, Scotland, UK

Department of Pedagogy, Ukraine and Social Work, Ukrainian Catholic University, Lviv, Ukraine
e-mail: katebuchko@ucu.edu.ua

H. Feen-Calligan
College of Education, Wayne State University, Detroit, MI, USA
e-mail: Hfeen@wayne.edu

A. Burlaka
Grimsley High School, Greensboro, NC, USA

V. Peshkova
Private Practice in Odesa, Odesa, Ukraine

A. Javanbakht
Department of Psychiatry and Behavioral Neurosciences, Wayne State University School of Medicine, Detroit, MI, USA
e-mail: ajavanba@med.wayne.edu

individuals who have sought refuge in nations such as Canada and the United States (UNHRC, 2025).

Social relationships with other members of the diaspora, with receiving communities, and with people back home feature in facilitating the successful transitions of forcibly displaced people to life in new countries (Anthias, 2018). However, little is known about how displaced Ukrainians renegotiate worldviews and consolidate identities during the migration process and in new surroundings.

This chapter employs a narrative case study methodology, drawing on a combination of clinical practice, program implementation, informal interviews, and personal and familial experiences. This approach aligns with qualitative traditions in trauma, migration, and identity studies, particularly those that emphasize rich, context-sensitive understandings of lived experience (Riessman, 2008; Stake, 1995). Our goal is not statistical generalization but analytic illumination: to show how Ukrainian displacement is navigated through shifting emotional and social anchors and to explore the transformation of identity over time and space. The cases were purposefully selected to exemplify theoretical dimensions observed in practice and community-based settings in Ukraine, Europe, and the United States.

Reasons for Leaving Home

The decision to flee one's home during war is deeply personal and shaped by a complex mix of anchors and shifting obligations. Research with healthcare workers in Syria found that the most common reason for displacement was concern for personal and family safety (Kallström et al., 2021), a pattern echoed in the experiences of many Ukrainians. Another reason some participants in that study chose to migrate was that they no longer wanted to live in a state of perpetual fear, or they had witnessed a colleague being killed or captured.

According to Aslany et al. (2021), other reasons individuals aspire to migrate include demographic factors such as youth; gender; socioeconomic motivations such as unemployment, low income, and lack of homeownership; individual-level drivers, including education level, subjective well-being, and risk tolerance; and contextual factors such as poor governance, corruption, inadequate public services, violence, and insecurity, alongside perceptions of better opportunities abroad. Isański et al. (2022) also noted that Ukrainian refugees cited the search for a safer location as a primary motivation for fleeing. One component of living under the constant threat of missile attacks and occupation is that these emotional, psychological, and physical stressors compel people to leave their homes in pursuit of security and peace.

In contrast, Bendix et al. conducted interviews with people who lived through the War of 1967 in the Middle East and found that many of them chose to stay to avoid the humiliation of becoming displaced people outside the country (2022). Furthermore, the findings of a study involving people living in Tajikistan's Pamir Mountains, where numerous environmental and socioeconomic threats are present, revealed that many remained in this environment due to their attachment to the places where they lived, connection with a sense of tradition, and family (Blondin, 2021).

The decision to flee, then, exists on a spectrum—shaped by danger, attachment, social roles, emotional resilience, and personal preferences. But how is this evident in the context of Ukraine?

For many Ukrainians, the decision to leave was not a single momentary decision, but one that evolved over a series of cascading disruptions, emotional reckonings, and unintended consequences of war. One such story is Maria's (*a pseudonym*), a Ukrainian woman whose experience illustrates the complexity and emotional depth behind migration decisions.

Maria shared with us that her decision to move to the United States wasn't something she had planned. "My situation is very atypical," she said. "All of us Ukrainians who came under U4U [the US Government Program Uniting for Ukraine, allowing Ukrainian citizens to come to the US for up to two years under humanitarian parole] have non-typical stories, but mine is rather specific." Her son had already started the process of applying to universities in the United States before the war began. "That process is very complex and takes years," she explained. Even as the war escalated, Maria stayed. "I had no intention of coming to the US myself—despite the bombs, I kept working. I had a good job, and I had to pay for my son's education. I wasn't even thinking of leaving."

She described how things began to unravel. "Everything started falling apart—like puzzle pieces no longer fitting together." Already worn down by the emotional toll of the pandemic, the war pushed her further. "I was already on antidepressants. Everything was hard." Losing her job was the final blow. "They gave my position to the schoolmate of the company's owner… I'm a person who fights to the end—until my last breath. But they just said there was no chance."

When her son left for college in the United States, she started thinking about following. "The son I had raised and lived with all my life. And I was going to be left completely alone." She briefly looked into going to

Canada or England but realized, "I don't just want to leave. I want to be with my son." Then came her first panic attack, on a train ride home. "You just can't tolerate it—sitting, lying, walking, breathing—it's unbearable." Eventually, she told her mother, "I'm going to the US" Her mother was shocked, but by the next morning, she said she'd come to terms with it. Maria found a sponsor in Indiana, closer to her son. But when she arrived, he said, "I'm not ready." They didn't see each other until December. "I lost almost all my inner strength," she recalled. "I had this feeling like everything had shut down."

Another Ukrainian family—a father, Ivan; a mother, Natalia; and two daughters, Ella and Svitlana (*pseudonyms*)—had no intention of leaving Ukraine. However, when the father's mother, Lidia, was offered an opportunity to go to Germany, where family friends had agreed to support her, the two daughters decided to accompany their grandmother. The parents agreed, saying, "We can't risk losing our children. Drones are flying over our heads, and a missile just exploded less than a kilometer from our home."

After some time apart, the parents began to miss their daughters and eventually decided to join them in Germany. Adjusting to the German system was difficult, especially navigating the bureaucracy and language. Meanwhile, the family who hosted the grandmother and daughters had grown emotionally attached to the girls, and the daughters, in turn, became closely bonded with their German hosts.

Wanting to be together again, the entire family later moved to the United States and stayed for four months with Ivan's brother. But Ivan, who has a disability, was unable to work in the United States, and the family began to miss their home, friends, and the rhythm of their former life. They eventually decided to return to Europe—the parents moved back to Ukraine, while the daughters returned to live with their German host family.

Over time, the older daughter became independent and moved into her apartment, while the younger daughter came to see the German family as her own. Months later, Ivan reflected, "Why should I live here in Ukraine when my children and my mother are in Germany? I have a disability and cannot fight. My life feels meaningless."

The parents decided to move back to Germany to live closer to their children. Today, one daughter lives independently while the other remains with her German host family. The father confided, "I feel betrayed because my younger daughter chose the stability and lifestyle of the German home over staying with her immigrant father and mother."

Anchored Migration Theory (Grzymała-Kazłowska & Brzozowska, 2017) suggests decisions to migrate are not merely responses to danger but are shaped by the weakening, loss, or reorientation of one's anchors—social, familial, cultural, and emotional. Maria's case illustrates this clearly. Her professional identity, caregiving role, and ties to home initially kept her grounded despite wartime danger. Her eventual decision to migrate was catalyzed not by a single event, but through cascading disruptions to those anchors: job loss, mental health decline, and emotional separation from her son.

Likewise, Ivan and Natalia's evolving family configuration reveals how migration decisions reflect dynamic reanchoring. They prioritized safety and family unity, even at the cost of physical distance. Over time, these relational anchors pulled them from Ukraine to Germany, to the United States, back to Ukraine, and again to Germany. These cases, while few, converge with others we have encountered in clinical and community practice, illustrating the nuanced and gradual process of reanchoring that defines forced migration.

Challenges of Displacement

Displacement involves the disruption of anchors and identity structures. The Transformational Identity Theory of Migration (Cormoş, 2022) emphasizes how identity must be renegotiated in the wake of loss. Maria's narrative is emblematic: her professional, social, and cultural anchors were weakened, and she experienced dislocation both physically and existentially. Her experience of culture shock, isolation, and marginalization in the United States is not just about geography but about being untethered from her prior sense of self.

By framing these challenges through identity theory, we move beyond merely describing hardship to demonstrating how identity must be reconstructed amidst systemic, emotional, and cultural upheaval. Her story exemplifies not just trauma but transformation in progress. As Bogic et al. (2015) explained, stress caused by migration, as well as trauma from the violence that led to it, can result in post-traumatic stress disorder (PTSD), depression, and anxiety. This highlights the psychological weight that makes such a transformation especially profound.

Children of survivors may internalize their parents' unresolved trauma, developing a melancholic attachment to an idealized prewar past and experiencing identity confusion due to the absence of a coherent narrative about their family's war experiences (Yordanova, 2024). While postmigration environments have the potential to support the well-being of war refugees, sociocultural barriers in host countries frequently obstruct or delay psychosocial recovery (Metersky et al., 2024).

Refugees often face significant challenges in accessing basic services, such as healthcare; Karadag et al. (2021) found that fewer than 10% of refugees in Turkey accessed mental health services, largely due to language barriers and limited awareness of available care. Examining gender-based violence, Amodu et al. (2020) reported that internally displaced African women experienced significantly greater negative impacts on their mental health compared to men living in the same communities.

Similarly, Maria, a Ukrainian who migrated to the United States under the U4U program, faced a cascade of psychological, economic, and relational stressors that uniquely burdened her as a woman navigating displacement. A highly educated HR professional from Kyiv, she arrived in rural Indiana and was immediately struck by culture shock. "I came from Kyiv, a city of millions, to a house surrounded by cornfields," she said. "I felt like I was in prison." Despite her preparation and strong English skills, communication proved difficult due to regional dialects and her sponsor's hearing loss, adding to her sense of isolation.

Living as a guest in someone else's home brought additional stress. She described being surrounded by noise and interruptions, unable to find a private space to focus on learning English or applying for jobs. "Even the laundry machines were on my wall," she noted, describing the constant tension between gratitude and discomfort. Professionally, she encountered multiple barriers. Although she had years of experience in human resources, she failed the US HR certification exam three times: "I'm a strong HR professional, but I couldn't pass. I realized the system isn't built for people like me." Even when she began working at a nonprofit refugee agency, she experienced controlling behavior from her supervisor, who denied her access to the office and undermined her autonomy.

Emotionally, Maria faced the cumulative weight of trauma, displacement, and loneliness. She endured panic attacks, family separation, and a sense of disconnection from herself and others. "My third eye was closed," she said, describing her spiritual and psychological shutdown.

Coping Mechanisms and Adjustment Processes

Given the significant psychological burden migration imposes, refugees often rely on a range of coping strategies to manage stress, loss, and uncertainty. In a study of Ukrainian war refugees, nearly half of the participants cited social support from close relationships as their primary coping mechanism (Oviedo et al., 2022). Others turned to religious practices, with explicit prayer serving as a source of emotional grounding and hope. Similarly, among refugees from the former Soviet Union resettled in New York, those who reported the freedom to practice their religion experienced greater psychological well-being (Wu et al., 2021), underscoring the importance of cultural and spiritual safety in the host society.

Others may demonstrate a more individualized approach to coping, such as Maria, a Ukrainian refugee interviewed in our study. Isolated from her family and religious community, she turned inward and leaned on self-structure and personal growth. "Education is my treatment," she shared, describing how the pursuit of professional certifications helped restore her sense of purpose and agency. Physical activity, including walking, biking, and yoga, also became integral to her mental resilience. Notably, she engaged in deliberate self-dialogue: "I love talking to myself… I support myself," she said. Over time, her coping evolved into meaning-making through service. By working at a refugee agency, Maria found a sense of mission: "Now I have a purpose—to help others and not give up."

Research supports the value of adaptive coping. In a systematic review of psychosocial interventions for displaced populations, Nguyen et al. (2023) found that modest programs had a positive effect on mental health outcomes. Building on this evidence, the *Conflict Trauma Technical Assistance for School Districts and School Impact Providers in Michigan* project aimed to strengthen the capacity of educators to support children who have experienced war and forced displacement, including newly arrived Ukrainian students. These children often faced significant emotional and behavioral challenges as they adjusted to unfamiliar environments while processing trauma.

To address this, we delivered targeted training for school staff, practical resources such as infographics and handouts, and individualized consultations. These tools help educators recognize signs of trauma, foster emotional regulation in the classroom, and implement developmentally appropriate interventions such as expressive arts and sensory-based strategies. By engaging school personnel through listening sessions and capacity-building workshops, the initiative bridges critical support gaps and fosters inclusive, trauma-sensitive learning environments. Ultimately, it equips educators with the trauma-informed, culturally responsive tools needed to ease acculturation and promote resilience among refugee youth, allowing healing and learning to coexist in the classroom.

One component of this initiative included art therapy sessions delivered in a Michigan elementary school, providing a supportive space for Ukrainian refugee children to express their experiences. Conducted over two academic years, these sessions brought together students in grades K-11. Sessions began with mind–body activities—guided movement and stretching—to help the youth regulate emotionally and feel grounded. Each student received a name tag they could personalize to represent something about themselves, and then engaged in creative tasks such as painting or crafting. During these sessions, students were guided by a certified art therapist who presented art prompts chosen to facilitate their expression, help reduce stress, and build strengths and resilience. Students were free to create at their own pace while interacting with the facilitators, who documented emotional themes emerging through both verbal and visual expression.

The fifth author of this chapter, herself a bilingual first-generation immigrant, was a member of the facilitation team. Through informal conversations and close observation, she noted many of the children's drawings included images of their former homes, pets, family members, and school life in Ukraine. When prompted, the children shared fond memories of their past, demonstrating an ongoing emotional attachment to the lives they had left behind. These sessions revealed rich, vivid recollections of what "home" meant to them, often centered around nature, family traditions, and a sense of belonging. Although less common, some children also depicted aspects of their current lives in Michigan, signaling the beginnings of integration and adaptation. Across the groups, recurring themes in their artwork included family connections in both countries, natural landscapes, Ukrainian houses, and cultural memories, revealing that art therapy served not only as a tool for emotional expression but also as a bridge between past and present identities.

Together, these examples illustrate how displaced individuals and communities develop new anchors and cope through meaning-making. Anchored Migration Theory helps interpret these behaviors not as isolated responses but as deliberate efforts to reestablish coherence and stability in unfamiliar environments. Moreover, the Michigan school initiative demonstrates how anchors can be formed not only interpersonally but also institutionally and symbolically—through consistent support, cultural affirmation, and emotionally safe spaces. In this way, trauma-informed and culturally responsive programming becomes central not just to healing, but to identity continuity and reconstruction.

Transformations in Identity and Worldview

Changes brought by migration affect multiple areas of life, including familial and community roles. Migration often alters one's sense of identity and belonging, forcing individuals to rebuild their lives while adapting to unfamiliar social and economic systems. A study of internally displaced women in Georgia found that leaving agriculturally rich communities to escape conflict pushed many to seek new sources of income, often challenging traditional norms that positioned men as the primary breadwinners (Fiddian-Qasmiyeh, 2020). Similarly, Syrian refugees interviewed by Bunn et al. (2023) described a profound sense of loss, not only of place but of community and culture. Separation from social networks disrupted their sense of self and made adjustment in host countries more difficult. Many spoke of living between two realities—the home they now inhabit and the one they were forced to leave, often feeling a stronger emotional tie to the past (Bunn et al., 2023).

This sense of living in a "dual reality" is also evident among Ukrainian refugees, who navigate unfamiliar surroundings while remaining exposed to the realities of war at home via social media. However, others experience a broader sense of identity transformation. Using transformational identity theory, we analyze how displaced Ukrainians not only mourn the loss of prior identities but also cocreate new ones through service, community, and ritual. For example, Maria, a former Ukrainian HR director, described her life in Ukraine as professionally fulfilling and financially stable, but after arriving in the United States, she found herself struggling to regain her footing, failing multiple certification exams, and experiencing deep discouragement. Maria's identity shifted from HR professional to case manager; from isolated migrant to helper; from disoriented to grounded through meaning and mission. This kind of transformation illustrates how new identities are forged through adaptation and agency, even amidst significant upheaval. Yet, despite this professional displacement, Maria found renewed purpose by working with Ukrainian refugees as a case manager. "This wasn't the plan," she said, "but now I have a mission—to help others and not give up." Her story reflects the broader identity transformation experienced by many displaced individuals—redefining success, rediscovering purpose, and forming new identities grounded not in status but in service and resilience.

This theme of identity reconstruction is not unique to one individual or restricted to the individual level. Consolidation of collective identities is also critical to endorsing a unified sense of nationhood among forcibly displaced people living overseas (Anthias, 2018). Activities that consolidate shared identities assist this goal and enhance social interconnectedness through the building of support networks among members of the diaspora and between them and members of receiving communities (Anthias, 2018). The celebration of national festivals, such as Christmas, which are recognized and celebrated by most people at home and in receiving countries, represents important activities for facilitating a sense of unity among sociocultural and ethnically diverse individuals. This is because widely celebrated events have the potential to reach beyond ethnic, cultural, geographic, and social divides.

In Scotland, where 28,137 displaced Ukrainians have resettled (Scottish Parliament, 2025), one initiative was developed to address this very need. In December 2022, a public event titled *Christmas with Ukraine* was hosted in Stirling by five members of the Ukrainian diaspora from the Stirling-Ukraine Solidarity group. Attendees included recently displaced Ukrainians, long-standing Ukrainian residents of Scotland, members of voluntary organizations, local community members, researchers, and students. The event included presentations on Ukrainian Christmas customs—foods, music, and the evolution of celebration through pre- and post-Soviet times. Traditional dishes were shared, and informal conversations flourished between members of the diaspora and the local Scottish public.

This event aimed to build solidarity not only among displaced Ukrainians from different regions but also between Ukrainians and Scots. Although variations exist in how Christmas is celebrated within Ukraine, the organizers intentionally presented a unified narrative. As one participant noted, this was because: "We are all Ukrainian, and we need to show how great our country is… traditions are part of our culture; they can be different, but we have a similar history, and when you have something that you all celebrate in different parts of the country, you have that layer of sameness." The act of focusing on similarities allowed the organizers to transcend regional and linguistic divisions, replacing them with a shared identity.

The absence of discussion about the war during the event was notable, even though its impact was deeply felt by everyone present. The "Christmas with Ukraine" event can thus be reframed not as a programmatic aside but rather as a symbolic anchor that fosters identity consolidation. This is because it represents collective reanchoring through public cultural affirmation, bridging past and present identities, and offering belonging to both Ukrainians and Scots. The emphasis on resilience rather than victimhood also illustrates how displaced people strategically shape their identities to embody empowerment, continuity, and pride. The choice not to center the event on war trauma was deliberate, as one organizer reflected, "When the war started, it's like you feel someone's pain and grief and how it is terrible and unites from within… we presented on the level of the state because [members of the diaspora] are united regardless of diversity. It's this unity in Ukraine as a nation that's something unique and something you want to belong to. That's what we wanted to encourage… and I think that's what we did."

This vision of national unity and strength was also interwoven with the desire to educate receiving communities about Ukraine beyond its image of destruction: "Everybody knows what happened to Ukraine and how [war] destroyed everything, and so the world now know[s] Ukraine as destroyed… but we wanted to show Ukraine is not only about that. Before, it was a wonderful country, with lots of interesting stories to tell. We wanted to make people feel what we felt before the war. Show [that] we have something to fight for." This emphasis on cultural resilience rather than victimhood shifted the narrative toward empowerment and shared pride.

Support from family members in Ukraine further motivated participation, as described by one of the organizers: "My friends and family were supportive of me doing the event. They thought it very important because they also say we need to show people what there is about Ukraine for obtaining help [from] them." Importantly, however, the event also fostered understanding with the Scottish public. By highlighting distinct aspects of Ukrainian identity, organizers hoped to correct misconceptions, such as the idea that Ukraine and Russia are culturally interchangeable. One organizer explained how the workshop emphasized how Ukraine has its "own culture and language, which is something beautiful and something that we have to fight for." These efforts aimed to cultivate empathy through knowledge and not just emotional appeal.

These efforts proved successful, with one attendee reflecting, "We see we are different, but at that moment when celebrating Christmas, we are all the same. You can't see the divide." That quote captures the emotional essence of the gathering. The event offered a moment of cultural continuity amid rupture, unity amid fragmentation. It also served as a microcosm of broader diasporic resilience, demonstrating how even modest, community-driven actions can reinforce identity, forge bonds across difference, and frame displacement not solely as loss but also as transformation.

Conclusion

The narratives presented in this chapter offer important insights into the lived realities of migration and reveal that migration is not a singular or isolated event but a relational, emotional, and identity-shifting process. Two theoretical frameworks—*Anchored Migration Theory* (Grzymała-Kazłowska & Brzozowska, 2017) and *Transformational Identity Theory of Migration* (Cormoş, 2022)—when combined, provide a relational lens that helps conceptualize these motivations for migration and the resulting transformations.

Anchored Migration Theory suggests people's decisions to stay or leave are shaped not only by external push and pull factors such as violence, war, or opportunity but also by their social and emotional anchors—family ties, professional roles, cultural belonging, and personal meaning (Grzymała-Kazłowska & Brzozowska, 2017). Migration occurs when anchors shift, weaken, or reorient. Importantly, it is not the absence of anchors that leads to movement, but the redefinition of what—and whom—one is anchored to (Grzymała-Kazłowska & Brzozowska, 2017). Maria, for example, initially refused to leave Ukraine despite the danger, holding tightly to her professional identity and caregiving role. However, when her son left, her job disappeared, and her mental health declined, her anchors realigned. Her decision to migrate was less about fleeing than about following new relational and existential connections. Similarly, Ivan and his wife allowed their daughters to go to Germany with their grandmother, not because they wanted to separate but because preserving life and family required new configurations of trust, distance, and reunion.

Their later move to the United States and then back to Europe reveals the ongoing work of adjusting one's anchors to new realities.

Transformational Identity Theory of Migration builds on this by examining how migration forces the redefinition of the self (Cormoş, 2022). Migration unsettles the roles people once occupied and invites new forms of identity grounded in adaptation, resilience, and reattachment (Cormoş, 2022). Maria found a renewed sense of purpose not in reclaiming her old professional status but in serving other displaced Ukrainians. Her new identity—as a helper, a survivor, a member of a transnational community—was not a loss of self but a reconfiguration. For Ivan's younger daughter, the connection she formed with her German host family shifted her understanding of family and belonging. These transformations do not erase the past but integrate it into a new narrative of self that transcends place, time, and culture.

When combined, these theories offer a helpful relational lens for understanding migration and identity change. They recognize that people are not simply pushed or pulled across borders but moved by the reorientation of what matters most to them—relationships, values, memories, and futures—and highlight how identity is negotiated across time and space, in dialogue with both personal history and new contexts.

Our analysis enriches existing theory in two ways:

1. Anchored Migration Theory is deepened by showing how it is not only the presence of anchors but their emotional intensity, temporal change, and symbolic significance that shape migration trajectories.
2. Transformational Identity Theory is advanced by illustrating how public rituals and institutional supports (such as trauma-informed schools) act as key mechanisms for identity reconstruction.

This perspective is further supported by collective initiatives such as *Christmas with Ukraine* in Scotland and trauma-informed programming in Michigan schools, which illustrate how cultural rituals, shared stories, and emotionally safe spaces help migrants establish new anchors and reconstruct coherent, meaningful identities in unfamiliar environments. Such interventions are not peripheral but central to recovery and belonging.

Migration, especially war-related, is not a binary event or a geographical relocation from point A to point B, but a multilayered and nonlinear unfolding process of disconnection and reconnection, identity loss and renewal. By grounding these abstract dynamics in the lived experience of Ukrainians, this chapter offers a relational, nuanced framework to understand forced migration as not just displacement but transformation.

Migration is not only about movement but about meaning and how people stay connected to their past, navigate the present, and imagine new futures. By framing migration through the lenses of anchoring and identity transformation, we move toward a deeper, more humane understanding of what it means to leave—and what it means to arrive.

References

Amodu, O. C., Richter, M. S., & Salami, B. O. (2020). A scoping review of the health of conflict-induced internally displaced women in Africa. *International Journal of Environmental Research and Public Health.* https://doi.org/10.3390/ijerph17041280

Anthias, F. (2018). Identity and belonging: Conceptualizations and reframings through a translocational lens. In H. Ghorashi, K. Davis, & P. Smets (Eds.), *Contested Belonging: Spaces, Practices, Biographies.* Emerald Publishing Limited. https://doi.org/10.1108/9781787432062

Aslany, M., Carling, J., Mjelva, M. B., & Sommerfelt, T. (2021). *Systematic review of determinants of migration aspirations.* https://www.quantmig.eu/res/files/QuantMig%20D22%202021-01-29.pdf

Bendix, R. F., Haidar, A., & Salamon, H. (2022). *June 1967 in* Personal Stories of Palestinians and Israelis.

Blondin, S. (2021). Staying despite disaster risks: Place attachment, voluntary immobility and adaptation in Tajikistan's Pamir Mountains. *Geoforum, 126.* https://doi.org/10.1016/j.geoforum.2021.08.009

Bogic, M., Njoku, A., & Priebe, S. (2015). Long-term mental health of war-refugees: A systematic literature review. *BMC International Health and Human Rights, 15.* https://doi.org/10.1186/s12914-015-0064-9

Brands, H. (Ed.). (2024). *War in Ukraine: Conflict, strategy, and the return of a fractured world.* Johns Hopkins University Press.

Bunn, M., Samuels, G., & Higson-Smith, C. (2023). Ambiguous loss of home: Syrian refugees and the process of losing and remaking home. *Wellbeing, Space and Society.* https://doi.org/10.1016/j.wss.2023.100136

Burlaka, V., Serdiuk, O., Nickelsen, T., Tkach, B., & Khvorova, H. (2018). Family life education in Ukraine. In M. Robila & A. C. Taylor (Eds.), *Global perspectives on family life education.* Springer International Publishing AG.

Center for Preventative Action. (2025, May 27). *War in Ukraine | Global Conflict Tracker.* https://www.cfr.org/global-conflict-tracker/conflict/conflict-ukraine

Cormoş, V. C. (2022). The processes of adaptation, assimilation and integration in the country of migration: A psychosocial perspective on place identity changes. *Sustainability, 14*(16), 10296. https://doi.org/10.3390/su141610296

Eurostat. (2025, May 6). *Temporary protection for persons fleeing Ukraine—Monthly statistics.* https://ec.europa.eu/eurostat/statistics-explained/index.php?title=Temporary_protection_for_persons_fleeing_Ukraine_-_monthly_statistics

Fiddian-Qasmiyeh, E. (2020). Aspects of loss and coping among internally displaced populations: Towards a psychosocial approach. In *Refuge in a moving world: Tracing refugee and migrant journeys across disciplines.* University College London. https://muse.jhu.edu/pub/354/oa_edited_volume/chapter/2777919

Grzymała-Kazłowska, A., & Brzozowska, A. (2017). From drifting to anchoring. Capturing the experience of Ukrainian migrants in Poland. *Central and Eastern European Migration Review, 6*(2), 103–122. https://doi.org/10.17467/ceemr.2017.04

International Organization of Migration. (2025). *Ukraine Internal Displacement Report* (p. 16).

Isański, J., Nowak, M., & Michalski, M. A. (2022). *Social reception and inclusion of refugees from Ukraine.* University of Adam Mickiewicz. https://philpapers.org/archive/ISASRA.pdf

Kallström, A., Al-Abdulla, O., Parkki, J., Häkkinen, M., Juusola, H., & Kauhanen, J. (2021). I had to leave. I had to leave my clinic, my city, leave everything behind in Syria. Qualitative research of Syrian healthcare workers migrating from the war-torn country. *BMJ Open.* https://doi.org/10.1136/bmjopen-2021-049941

Karadag, O., Kilic, C., Kaya, E., &Uner, S. (2021). Challenges and lessons learned in mental health research among refugees: A community-based study in Turkey. *BMC Public Health.* https://doi.org/10.1186/s12889-021-11571-5

Metersky, K., Jordan, A., Al-Hamad, A., & El-Masri, M. (2024). Psycho-social stressors experienced by young war refugees in developed countries: A scoping review. *The Canadian Journal of Nursing Research.* https://doi.org/10.1177/08445621241263459

Nguyen, A. J., Lasater, M. E., Lee, C., Mallawaarachchi, I. V., Joshua, K., Bassett, L., & Gelsdorf, K. (2023). Psychosocial support interventions in the context of forced displacement: A systematic review and meta-analysis. *Journal of Migration and Health.* https://doi.org/10.1016/j.jmh.2023.100168

Oviedo, L., Seryczyńska, B., Torralba, J., Roszak, P., Del Angel, J., Vyshynska, O., Muzychuk, I., &Churpita, S. (2022). Coping and resilience strategies among Ukraine war refugees. *International Journal of Environmental Research and Public Health.* https://doi.org/10.3390/ijerph192013094

Riessman, C. K. (2008). *Narrative methods for the human sciences.* Sage.
Scottish Parliament. (2025). Ukraine. Constitution, Europe, external affairs and culture committee 7th meeting (Thursday 27 February 2025). *Scottish Parliament. CEEAC/S6/25/7/1: Annex A.* https://www.google.com/search?q=Scottish+Parliament+(2025)%2C+Ukraine.+Constitution%2C+Europe%2C+External+Affairs+and+Culture+Committee+7th+Meeting+(Thursday+27+February+2025).+Scottish+Parliament.+CEEAC%2FS6%2F25%2F7%2F1%3A+Annex+A&oq=Scottish+Parliament+(2025)%2C+Ukraine.+Constitution%2C+Europe%2C+External+Affairs+and+Culture+Committee+7th+Meeting+(Thursday+27+February+2025).+Scottish+Parliament.+CEEAC%2FS6%2F25%2F7%2F1%3A+Annex+A&gs_lcrp=EgZjaHJvbWUyBggAEEUYOTIGCAEQRRg80gEHMzQ3ajBqNKgCALACAQ&sourceid=chrome&ie=UTF-8
Stake, R. E. (1995). *The art of case study research.* Sage.
UNHRC. (2025, April 17). *Ukraine Refugee Situation.* United Nations High Commissioner for Refugees. https://data.unhcr.org/en/situations/ukraine/location/680
Wu, S., Ellingson, S., Hagstrom, P., & Kucinskas, J. (2021). Religion and refugee well-being: The importance of inclusive community. *Journal for the Scientific Study of Religion.* https://doi.org/10.1111/jssr.12702
Yordanova, K. (2024). Socio-psychological aspects of war and their transgenerational dimension. *Journal of Sociology: Bulletin of Yerevan University, 15*(39), 1. https://doi.org/10.46991/BYSU:F/2024.15.1.005

CHAPTER 5

Elder Abuse Among Korean Immigrants in the United States

Miya Chang

Introduction

Elder abuse is a growing social issue, and it is still gaining recognition as a growing concern. However, few studies have been conducted so far on the scope and nature of elder abuse among Asian Americans in general or Korean immigrants in particular. One significant challenge in elder abuse is lack of knowledge about abuse within racial and ethnic minority groups in the United States. In addition to perceptions of what could constitute elder abuse, cultural factors may also affect risks for the abused and approaches to problem-solving among Korean immigrants in the United States.

This chapter begins with the demographic characteristics of Korean elderly immigrants, which is followed by prevalence of elder abuse,

This chapter was supported by the National Research Foundation of Korea Grant founded by the South Korean government (NRF-2022S1A5C2A04093439).

M. Chang (✉)
Center for Multicultural Studies, Daegu Catholic University,
Daegu, South Korea
e-mail: philsaram@cu.ac.kr

J. S. Hong et al. (eds.), *Violence and Trauma Without Borders*,
https://doi.org/10.1007/978-3-032-29221-6_5

definition and types of elder abuse, characteristics of Korean immigrant victims and perpetrators, perceptions of elder abuse, consequences of elder abuse, help-seeking behaviors of Korean immigrant victims, and implications for practice.

Demographic Characteristics of Korean Elderly Immigrants

The US population is expected to increase from 338 million people in 2022 to 373 million people in 2053. Population growth is increasingly directed by a large number of immigrants, which will account for all population growth beginning in 2042. Specifically, the year 2030 will mark a demographic turning point for the United States. By 2030, all baby boomers will be older than 65 years of age. This will expand the size of the older population in the United States so that one in every five Americans is projected to be of retirement age. The older American population was 62 million in 2022, and it represented 18% of the population. By 2054, 84 million older adults will make up an estimated 23% of the population. Older immigrants are one of the fastest-growing segments of the US population. The continued influx of older immigrants from different Asian countries contributes to the increasing diversity found among older Asian immigrants. In addition to the variety of immigration backgrounds, older Asian immigrants reflect a number of distinct cultures, languages, values, and histories of their countries of origin. All of these factors influence their well-being.

Over the past 30 years, the number of Asian Americans in the United States has increased significantly. In 2022, around 24 million US resident adults self-identified as Asian. Now, Asian Americans make up 7% of the general population and are the fastest-growing major racial or ethnic group in the country. Asian Americans trace their roots to more than 20 countries, but the large majority (77%) have origins in just six countries: China, India, the Philippines, Vietnam, South Korea, and Japan. Chinese Americans were the largest Asian group, followed by Indian (4.8 million), Filipino (4.4 million), Vietnamese (2.3 million), Korean (2.0 million), and Japanese Americans (1.6 million).

Due in part to Korean immigration, Koreans now make up 8% of all Asian Americans. The population of Korean immigrants grew from 1.4 million in 2010 to around 1.8 million in 2022. Over that time, Korean immigrants have become the fifth-largest foreign-born ethnic group in the United States (Budiman & Ruiz, 2021). And while Korean immigrants live all over the United States, 38% of the total Korean population resides in two states: California and New York. Areas with large Korean immigrant populations generally have established Korean communities with enriched ethnic resources.[1]

The current population of older Koreans is mostly foreign-born because of their relatively recent immigration history (Pew Research Center, 2021). Because most of these Korean immigrants have come to the United States since the Immigration and Nationality Act of 1965, the current generation of older Korean Americans is predominantly foreign-born immigrants and is challenged by linguistic and cultural barriers (Esterline & Batalova, 2022; Pew Research Center, 2021). The majority of older Korean Americans are first-generation immigrants and tend to conserve traditional cultural values from their country of origin, including filial piety and familism. Compared to younger Korean immigrants, older Korean immigrants face greater difficulties in acculturation due to limited language proficiency and restricted access to public services, as well as their high level of familiarity with and adherence to their original culture.

As a result of the rapid growth of the older Korean immigrant population in the United States, a very limited number of studies have been done about the nature and scope of elder abuse. To better understand the phenomenon of elder abuse, it is important to first understand the prevalence of elder abuse.

Prevalence of Elder Abuse

Despite a rapid increase in the number of older Asian immigrants in the United States, very little information is available regarding the prevalence of elder abuse in these ethnic communities. Most studies estimate that approximately 10% of people aged 65 or older have been abused by someone on whom they depend for care or protection in the United States (Acierno et al., 2010; Lachs & Pillemer, 2015; Pillemer et al., 2015). According to the National Center of Elder Abuse, the prevalence of elder

[1] According to the US Census Bureau (2019), 21% of all Korean immigrants are over 65 years old, which is greater than the percentage of US population that is composed of immigrants. Under 18 years old: 5%, 18 to 64 years old: 74%, and 65 years and over: 21%.

abuse is approximately 10%, including psychological abuse, physical abuse, financial abuse, sexual abuse, and neglect.[2]

Furthermore, the long-term care settings (i.e., nursing homes and assisted living facilities) population is rapidly growing, and research suggests that elder abuse may be common in such settings. Older adults who live in institutional settings that offer long-term care services are at much higher risk for abuse than older adults who live at home. Older adults in long-term care settings are particularly vulnerable because most suffer from multiple chronic diseases or conditions that lead to limitations in physical and cognitive functioning and are therefore dependent on others (Daly, 2017). Especially, elder abuse research in institutions, compared with research on other forms of interpersonal violence, is still very limited. Previous studies have shown that elder abuse occurs in every country with long-term care settings, and evidence indicates that abuse is probably common (Yon et al., 2019). Specifically, older adults with severe cognitive and physical impairments (e.g., dementia) are at increased risk of elder abuse (Dong et al., 2014; Lee et al., 2011). For example, Dong et al. (2014) found that older adults with greater levels of cognitive impairment were more often victims of abuse, and there was a significant correlation between caregiver stress and occurrences of violence.

Prevalence of elder abuse varies widely across all subgroup studies, largely due to methodological differences. Many studies suggest that older adults were more likely to have experienced multiple types of abuse than one type of abuse simultaneously. A study by Chang (2016) found that 58.3% of Korean immigrants reported experiencing some form of elder abuse. According to this study, emotional abuse was the most common form experienced, followed in terms of frequency by neglect, financial abuse, physical abuse, and sexual abuse. In a recent study, Chang (2019) reported that 26% of older Korean immigrants in the United States had experienced elder abuse in the past year. This study also reported that emotional abuse, such as "name calling" and "silent treatment," was the most frequent type of abuse, followed by neglect, physical abuse, financial abuse, and sexual abuse. There was no incident of rape among older Korean immigrants in the United States. An earlier study found that older Korean Americans had a high tolerance for neglect, with the majority of

[2]According to the United Nations (UN) report, prevalence rates in certain developed countries vary between 1% and 10%. Many studies estimate that *about 10% of all people over the age of 65 experience some form of abuse* (National Institutes of Health (NIH).

that population not identifying neglect situations as abusive. On the other hand, respondents were sensitive to situations of emotional abuse (Lee et al., 2011). In a recent study, Park et al. (2024) reported that emotional abuse (37.9%) was the most frequent type of elder abuse, followed by financial abuse (16.1%) and physical abuse (3%), during the past year among older Korean Americans. In addition, a study of Asian American older adults, including Koreans, Chinese, and others, revealed that about 27% of respondents experienced at least one form of elder abuse in the past year (Choi et al., 2024). According to interviews of social workers and professionals in San Francisco, Lee et al. (2014) reported that emotional abuse was the most frequent type of abuse. This result was consistent with recent research, which found that emotional abuse was the most common form of abuse among older Korean Americans (Chang, 2019).

Annual reports of elder abuse compiled by Adult Protective Services (APS) are the basis for statistics on how prevalent such abuse is. However, APS does not utilize consistent definitions of what constitutes abuse, and APS institutions exhibit considerable variance from state to state, so these statistics are insufficient for understanding the true scope of elder abuse. Not surprisingly, older Asian immigrants have suggested that elder abuse was more challenging to report when the perpetrator was a family member (Lee et al., 2014). The majority of older Korean immigrants avoid reporting abuse because of fear of retaliation, tolerance, protection of abusive family members, preservation of family harmony and privacy, and self-blame. In general, older Korean immigrants might avoid seeking help or be reluctant to report abuse, even in cases where they perceive that abuse is happening. This reluctance to report is even more likely when the abuse is perpetrated by family members, making the prevalence of abuse by family members difficult to determine (Myhre et al., 2020; Skirbekk & James, 2014). In addition, studies have found that elder abuse, particularly among Asian older adults, may be considerably underestimated and underreported (Chang, 2016; Falk et al., 2012). A study by the National Center on Elder Abuse (2006) found that Asian communities were far more likely to underreport abuse than white communities. Most incidences of elder abuse go unreported or are underestimated due to factors such as fear, denial, lack of perception of abuse, feelings of helplessness, the perceived powerlessness of police, and a lack of knowledge about reporting systems (Chang, 2016).

Definition and Types of Elder Abuse

Although a universally agreed-upon definition of elder abuse does not yet exist, it may be defined here as harmful or hurtful behavior that is intentionally inflicted upon older adults (National Center on Elder Abuse, 2011).[3] As these behaviors may range in severity, terms such as elder abuse, elder mistreatment, and elder maltreatment are used interchangeably (Roberto, 2016).

Elder abuse is usually classified into five types: emotional abuse, physical abuse, financial abuse, sexual abuse, and neglect. Emotional (or psychological) abuse is defined as the infliction of distress, anguish, or pain through verbal or nonverbal acts. It includes verbal insults, threats, humiliation, intimidation, isolation from one's family, friends, or regular activities, infantilizing, and giving silent treatment. Physical abuse is defined as the use of physical force that may result in physical injury, such as hitting, beating, pushing, grabbing, punching, slapping, kicking, and inappropriate use of drugs and physical restraints. Financial abuse (or material exploitation) is defined as the illegal or improper use of an older adult's funds, having the older adult's checks cashed without permission, forging the older adult's signature, stealing his or her money or valuable possessions, coercing or deceiving an older adult into signing any legal documents, and improper efforts to take on guardianship of an older adult. Sexual abuse is defined as any kind of nonconsensual sexual contact with older adults, such as unwanted touching, rape, coerced nudity, and exposure to sexually explicit photography. Finally, neglect is defined as the refusal or failure to fulfill any part of an obligation or duties of care to an older adult, such as failure to pay for necessary home care services, lack of necessary care, and refusal or failure to have necessities provided (National Center on Elder Abuse, 2011).

Emotional Abuse

Interestingly, older Korean immigrants were found to be highly sensitive to emotional abuse, including silent treatment, humiliation, yelling, or ignoring (Chang, 2016). Older Korean immigrants, compared to white

[3] Elder abuse was defined by NCEA as "An intentional act or failure to act by a caregiver or another person in a relationship involving an expectation of trust that causes or creates a risk of harm to an older adult."

Americans, were significantly less likely to tolerate verbal abuse. However, the majority of older adults agree that emotional abuse is as hurtful as physical abuse.

Attitudes toward *older adults* are typically informed by *values* of *respect* and filial piety in Asian societies. Specifically, disrespect and "silent treatment" were commonly perceived by Korean elders as extreme forms of psychological abuse (Lee et al., 2014). Such behaviors had greater impact due to cultural expectations regarding the treatment of elders. Traditionally, Asian communities placed great value on the respect of all older adults, who were given great authority and power in all spheres of family dynamics and big decision-making.

Among Asian communities, disrespect is often perceived as a primary form of elder abuse. In such communities, respect is highly valued, particularly in intergenerational relationships. According to one study, nearly 59% of older Korean immigrants cited not receiving the proper level of respect from their family members as the most serious abuse they had encountered (Chang, 2019). This was followed by verbal abuse as the second most serious form. Similarly, disrespect was reported as the most serious form of elder abuse in Chinese communities (Tam & Neysmith, 2006), where neglect is often included as the most commonly experienced form of disrespect. The fact that Asian communities consider disrespect toward and neglect of one's elders to be elder abuse points to the impact of culture on how elder abuse is defined, how it is reported, and what help-seeking behaviors one is likely to find among older Asian populations.

Physical Abuse

Physical abuse was the most obvious form of elder abuse identified. Many subtypes of physical abuse found in the general population were reported, including biting, hitting, slapping, pushing, grabbing, kicking, punching, or threatening with a knife. Older Korean immigrants reported several forms of physical abuse, such as pushing, shoving, and shaking (Chang, 2016). Another study reported forms of physical abuse such as disciplining elders by pinching their skin in order to put a stop to certain behaviors, forcing victims to eat nonfood items, and depriving victims of necessary items in order to inflict physical harm (Lee et al., 2014). In fact, physical abuse against older adults was uncommon in the Korean community, compared to other forms of abuse. The cultural value of filial piety and respect makes physical abuse even more harmful among older Korean immigrants. Other factors include traditional patriarchal norms of male dominance, which provide a basis for the cultural toleration of wife battering found in Korean culture.

Financial Abuse

Older adults highlighted significant problems pertaining to financial exploitation. Older Korean immigrants reported that several forms were similar to the financial abuse reported in the general population, including the transference of property from older parent to adult children (e.g., unauthorized transfer of legal title of property); using an older parent's money or economic resources (e.g., supplementary security income, social security benefits, or pensions); and restricting an older parent's financial freedom (Lee et al., 2014).

With regard to financial abuse, most older Korean immigrant who were financially abused reported voluntarily sharing their economic resources and property. In addition, some older immigrants may not perceive that they have been financially abused or may not consider certain behaviors as exploitive. In particular, there seems to be a high tolerance of financial abuse related to Asian cultural values (Lee & Eaton, 2009). Most Korean immigrants who were financially abused reported that they were voluntarily sharing their economic resources and property with family members (Lee et al., 2014). Within this cultural context, older Korean immigrants did not identify or perceive the behavior as exploitive because of the values of collectivism and family ties as opposed to values centering on individual rights.

Furthermore, a majority of older Korean immigrants reported that adult children have an obligation to help their older parents with care issues and, if necessary, to provide financial assistance to their parents. On the other hand, older Korean immigrants agreed that it is acceptable for adult children not to reimburse their older parents, even if the parent asks for the money. High tolerance of financial abuse by adult children comes from the long-standing Korean cultural practice of transferring one's wealth and property to adult children. This cultural norm still prevails in the Korean immigrant community, and children's entitlement to their parents' wealth often happens voluntarily. For this reason, financial abuse is not identified or perceived as the most frequently occurring form of elder abuse among older Korean immigrants.

Another source of financial abuse lies in dependency. Due to language barriers, cultural differences, and general unfamiliarity with government bureaucracy, many older immigrants rely on their children for important financial transactions such as managing bank accounts and receiving government SSI or Social Security benefits. Such dependency makes older immigrant adults vulnerable to exploitation. This vulnerability should be considered together with the fact that Korean victims tended not to report financial exploitation when it was done by a family member.

Sexual Abuse

Previous studies reported that sexual abuse against older immigrants was uncommon in Korean communities (Chang, 2016, 2019). Older Korean immigrants may underreport any incidents of rape committed by adult offspring or relatives. Sexual abuse mostly affected women, and the perpetrators were usually known and in a relationship of trust. Older Asian victims of sexual abuse were at a particular risk of experiencing sexual abuse. It is difficult for victims to disclose this abuse in Asian communities because of stigma, shame, and victim-blaming. Moreover, Asian cultural factors regarding male superiority and control of women's behaviors are important factors to account for in the examination of sexual abuse. Such strong patriarchal values could serve to exacerbate victimization and discourage help-seeking.

Neglect

Unlike the general population, the majority of older Korean immigrants perceived neglect by family members, which frequently occurred in the Korean community, as particularly abusive. Other culturally specific types of abuse or neglect commonly reported by Korean immigrants include the following: the unwillingness of married sons to provide care, the avoidance of caregiving responsibilities by adult children, the placement of impaired parents in a nursing home, the infrequency of visits or otherwise sparse contact with adult children, and the interference of family members with necessary medical treatment or key decisions resulting in inadequate care or physical harm (Lee et al., 2014). Many older Korean immigrants have the cultural expectation, driven by norms of filial piety, that they will live with their adult children, typically with their oldest son. Adult children who live far away from their parents are expected to fulfill their responsibilities of care through phone calls or regular visits. The practice of institutionalizing older parents was perceived as abusive across all racial and ethnic communities.

In conclusion, different cultural definitions exist as to what constitutes elder abuse and how elder abuse occurs and is perceived, reported, and investigated. Older Asian immigrants, compared to white Americans, may have different perceptions as to the situations that constitute abuse (Dong et al., 2011). That is, given the traditional Confucian teaching associated with respect for parents and older adults (Dong et al., 2014). Older Asian immigrants are more likely to identify culturally specific forms of elder abuse that are different from those seen in a Western cultural perspective.

Characteristics of the Korean Immigrant Victims and Perpetrators

Victims

Elder abuse is a serious problem among older Korean immigrants in the United States. However, little is known about the incidence of elder abuse and risk factors predicting violence experienced in family relationships. Victim risk factors are investigated based on a relatively small set of studies reporting victim data among older Korean immigrants in the United States.

With regard to gender, there are gender differences in the risk factors of elder abuse, although few studies have investigated gender differences in elder abuse. There have been mixed results on the gender issue, with some identifying different rates across genders. A greater risk for elder abuse among older females was found in studies of Asian countries. However, a study of older Korean immigrants in the United States reported that older men experienced a higher prevalence of most types of abuse than older women (Chang, 2016).

Regarding educational attainment, several research findings suggest the impact of educational attainment on elder abuse. Several studies have found that lower educational attainment among older immigrants is a high-risk factor for elder abuse (Chang, 2016). For example, older Korean immigrants in the United States with high educational attainment were less likely to be abused than those with lower levels of education (Chang, 2016).

Regarding health status, several studies have shown that poor health status and functional limitations make older Asians vulnerable to elder abuse (Chang, 2016; Chokkanathan, 2015; Chokkanathan & Lee, 2006; Sasaki et al., 2007). For example, Chang (2016) reported that older Korean immigrants with poor health status were over six times more likely to have experienced elder abuse than those who had good health status. Similarly, Dong et al. (2014) found that those with cognitive and physical impairments were more likely to experience elder abuse. In addition, older adults who live in long-term care facilities (e.g., nursing homes or assisted living) are particularly vulnerable to elder abuse (Castle et al., 2015; Gimm et al., 2018; Lachs & Pillemer, 2015). Overall, physical limitations and functional dependency are significantly associated with elder abuse.

Regarding economic status, studies on the impact of economic status on elder abuse reported mixed findings. However, many studies of older Asian populations, including Chinese, Indian, and Korean immigrants, found that those with lower income status and economic dependence on family members were more vulnerable to abuse than those who did not have such economic status (Chang, 2019; Dong & Simon, 2013; Sebastian & Sekher, 2011). For example, Chang (2019) found that older Koreans with lower incomes had an increased risk of abuse. Therefore, income is one of the major predictors of elder abuse.

Perpetrators

Perpetrators of elder abuse often include family members or intimate partners. Many studies find that family members are more likely to perpetrate elder abuse (Chang, 2016; Reisig & Holtfreter, 2013). Chang (2016) reported that perpetrators were most likely to be adult children of the victims, followed by spouses, relatives, friends, and others. The majority of the perpetrators were the victim's adult children and their spouses/partners.

The prevalence of abuse was significantly related to the sociodemographic (e.g., age, gender, education, unemployment, living arrangements, and financial dependence) and health of perpetrators and victim–perpetrator relationships (Park et al., 2024). There is no difference in age across types of elder abuse. As for gender differences among perpetrators of elder abuse, most studies found that the majority of perpetrators were men (Jackson, 2016; Kosberg, 2014). According to meta-analyses of elder abuse, older women, especially those living in Asian countries, are more likely to be abused (Yon et al., 2017). Therefore, most perpetrators were male, living with the victim, and not caring for the victim.

The prevalence of a victim–perpetrator relationship differs by the type of abuse. Neglect was most often perpetrated by adult children, followed by partners, acquaintances, and other relatives. Studies generally find that adult children are the most frequent perpetrators of neglect (Acierno et al., 2010). Physical abuse was most often perpetrated by partners (57%), followed by acquaintances, adult children, other relatives, and strangers (Acierno et al., 2010). Generally, spouses/intimate partners are the most frequent perpetrators of physical abuse. According to previous studies, the most frequent perpetrators of emotional abuse are spouses/intimate partners. Therefore, spouses/intimate partners are more likely to perpetrate emotional/verbal abuse and physical abuse, while adult children are more likely to perpetrate neglect.

Perceptions of Elder Abuse

Older adults with immigrant backgrounds perceive or define elder abuse within the specific scope of their original culture. What people perceive as elder abuse is significantly influenced by cultural factors. A review of elder abuse literature reveals that ethnicity or culture determines the way elder abuse is defined, perceived, and reported. In particular, the level of acculturation among older immigrants has a critical function in the recognition of elder abuse. In this regard, the degree of acculturation is substantial evidence that older adults with a higher level of acculturation to mainstream culture may perceive elder abuse differently compared to older adults who are less acculturated to mainstream culture. For example, Chang (2019) points out that Korean culture, characterized by strong family orientation and interdependency, is a critical predictor of elder abuse identification.

The most important finding of previous studies is that subjective perceptions of abuse and actual experiences of abuse are inconsistent among older Korean immigrants. Such inconsistencies may arise from different cultural definitions and values concerning the proper treatment of elders and what constitutes abuse (Chang, 2016; Selwood et al., 2007). For example, Chang (2016) reported that 39.5% of respondents admitted to experiencing some form of elder abuse. However, this measure of subjective perceptions was inconsistent with the number of respondents who answered "Yes" to specific questions about different forms of elder abuse.

The researcher therefore constructed another answer category designed to identify specific forms of elder abuse and found that 58.3% of respondents reported having experienced one or more forms of what researchers themselves would classify as abuse. Most likely, the older Korean immigrants responding to the questions in this survey had very limited knowledge and cultural perception of what could constitute elder abuse. That is, they either did not know what elder abuse is, they had a different understanding of what it is, or they may have been reluctant to recognize elder abuse in general as a problem. The inconsistencies found in this report point to an underlying problem with how the Korean older immigrant population perceives and understands elder abuse.

Older Korean immigrants have reported various culturally specific types of abuse. These include adult children who did not want to live with older parents, lack of contact and visits with adult children, adult children not fulfilling their duties of filial piety, lack of respect, adult children not offering money regularly to their older parents, and adult children placing frail older adults in a nursing home. Specifically, traditional Korean culture, including familism, filial piety, family harmony, and collectivism, affects perceptions of elder abuse. Another study of older Korean immigrants disclosed that elder abuse is a culturally reluctant taboo, and the norms (beliefs) of traditional culture and acculturation are significant contextual factors that strongly influence perceptions of elder abuse (Lee & Eaton, 2009).

Consequences of Elder Abuse

Elder abuse is associated with negative health outcomes such as physical injuries, psychological distress, depression, anxiety, social isolation, fear, and mortality among older adults (Chang, 2019; Pengpid & Peltzer, 2021). Older adults who experience abuse show an increased mortality rate compared to others (Dong et al., 2014). In addition, it has been reported that elderly abuse victims were more likely to experience disability and suicidal ideation in comparison to others who never experienced elder abuse (Schofield et al., 2013). For example, Dong et al. (2014) examined the relationship between elder abuse and mortality. The results showed that those who experience abuse have a 300% higher risk of mortality when compared to those who have not experienced elder abuse. Previous research has consistently reported that elder abuse is a significant factor in reduced quality of life among older adults (Atim et al., 2023;

Honarvar et al., 2019). Therefore, elder abuse can harm the victim in a number of ways.

Help-Seeking Behaviors of Korean Immigrant Victims

Perception is a strong predictor of the victim's intention to seek help. In fact, older adults' definition and tolerance of elder abuse impacts their perception of whether and from where they would seek help for abuse. A help-seeking intention is associated with perceiving a situation as abusive. At the same time, cultural factors such as cultural norms and expectations should be considered when seeking resources related to elder abuse. Previous studies found that a reluctance to expose family difficulties made Korean immigrants much less likely than whites to seek help with any problems (Chang, 2016). Generally speaking, culture will influence not only how elderly people perceive abuse but how they will seek help when it occurs.

Studies on help-seeking in Asian communities found that older Korean immigrants tended to prefer informal to formal assistance. In other words, they were more likely to go to family, relatives, or friends for help than to seek out social service professionals, social workers, or psychologists (Chang, 2016; Lee & Eaton, 2009). Chang (2016) in particular reported that all of the 47% of respondents who had sought help had sought informal rather than formal assistance. Furthermore, most of the reasons given for not seeking help (63%) arose from such cultural factors as the reluctance to expose family problems, tolerance for abuse, and feelings of shame. Since the family is expected to give care and help each other in Asian cultures, older Korean immigrants are often unlikely to be aware of what formal resources may be available to them as compared with the general population of older adults. As existing research shows, cultural contexts determine what is perceived as abuse and how relief from abuse will be sought.

In addition, older Korean immigrants face additional barriers, such as limited English proficiency, lack of knowledge about elder abuse, fear of involvement with government institutions, and fear of being sent to institutional care settings. Sociocultural barriers faced by immigrants were particularly salient across the Korean immigrant population, particularly among recent older Korean immigrants. Generally, older Korean immigrants, as compared to white older adults, had significantly lower levels of awareness and utilization of professional resources for help available to victims of elder abuse. This situation implies that seeking help directly from professionals such as the APS agency or the Elder Abuse Hotline may be impossible for older Korean immigrants, and informal helping agencies would be their primary source of help.

According to Asian cultural values, caring for older adults is a responsibility that maintains cultural norms and continuity, and strengthens family solidarity (Scharlach et al., 2006). From this cultural perspective, caring for one's family members is a responsibility rather than a matter of choice. When family members do not fulfill their duties to provide care, the entire family may be shamed and looked down on for failing to provide properly for their elders (Spitzer et al., 2003). Since the existence of formal sources of help is relatively new to such cultures, it is to be expected that help-seeking behaviors will differ, particularly among elders raised in such cultures when formal sources of help may scarcely have existed.

Significant differences were found across Asian subgroups in their perceptions toward elder abuse and intention to seek help from APS as a formal institution in the event of elder abuse. However, many older Asian immigrants did not recognize APS and other formal sources of help. Older adults from Asian cultural contexts are less willing to seek out professional help than those from other American contexts. Feeling shame and being stigmatized often impedes the help-seeking behavior of older adults suffering from abuse. Such barriers make it more difficult for people to come to terms with elder abuse and seek services. Culture, when it comes to professional help-seeking, influences when problems are perceived, how decisions are made regarding help-seeking, and how coping strategies are evaluated (Cauce et al., 2002). A strong prohibition against openly admitting to elder abuse is associated with cultural norms against the public disclosure of family problems and seeking outside assistance and services.

As a result, considerations of cultural differences when it comes to the perception of elder abuse are very important. What constitutes abuse in one culture may not be considered abuse in another culture, which makes abuse difficult to identify (Bagshaw et al., 2013; Fang et al., 2023). Therefore, people from different cultural backgrounds may respond differently to varying approaches to intervention. The design of culturally appropriate service programs with respect to elder abuse victims and perpetrators not only requires information on how older adults perceive interventions but also how they are likely to report abuse or seek help.

Implications for Practice

Although limited in sample size, measures, sampling methods, and representation of the population, several studies have contributed to this important area of knowledge. Many older Korean immigrants have suffered elder abuse, mostly perpetrated by their own family members. Above all, older Korean immigrants face inconsistency between older immigrants' (subjective) awareness of the term elder abuse and actual experiences of elder abuse. For this reason, the actual prevalence of elder abuse may be underestimated. Therefore, social workers who work with older Koreans should be aware that there is a substantial difference among older Korean immigrants in their understanding of the term elder abuse. Older Koreans in the United States may not open up about problems within their families to outsiders for a variety of strong cultural factors that mitigate against such disclosures.

There is a significant relationship between education and the experience of elder abuse. Older Korean immigrants with a lower level of education, compared to a higher level of education, are more vulnerable and at a higher risk for elder abuse by family members. Therefore, this finding suggests that collaborative outreach programs aimed at older Korean immigrants living in ethnic enclaves should be developed. Such programs should be aimed at increasing awareness of what constitutes elder abuse and also provide appropriate education and training to prevent abuse from occurring and to guide victims in how to seek help when it does occur.

Poor health status is highly correlated with elder abuse. When older adults who have poor health and functional impairments are dependent on their family caregivers, they are more likely to experience abuse. Furthermore, when older adults needing long-term care are dependent on family caregivers, they are more likely to experience abuse by their family members and relatives. Many older Korean immigrants turn to informal health practitioners such as herb doctors and acupuncturists when living in their ethnic enclaves. Such practitioners may also be utilized to spread awareness about elder abuse and the existence of formal resources available to victims. Religious leaders may be used for such awareness-raising programs as well. Furthermore, social work practitioners should have outreach programs in place to provide necessary services and improve the quality of information available to possible victims of elder abuse.

Conclusion

Few studies have been conducted so far regarding the range and scope of Asian American elder abuse. Asian immigrants are a growing minority that deserves further attention and research. Most existing research examines elder abuse in the general population, and very few studies focus specifically on Asian Americans. Previous research has revealed that there are different definitional variations of elder abuse among diverse racial and ethnic groups. However, defining the issue is problematic as there is no current universally agreed-upon understanding of elder abuse.

Due to the limited study of Asian Americans, our knowledge of the extent and type of elder abuse among older Korean immigrants in the United States is very scarce. It is important to investigate those factors that contribute to elder abuse. Despite strong cultural values regarding the respect and care due to older adults, many older Korean immigrants have reported experiencing one or more forms of elder abuse. It is even possible that older Korean immigrants are more likely than others to experience abuse due to a lack of economic opportunities, stressful life events, and a decrease in the family's role in caregiving (Choi et al., 2009).

The most important finding on this subject involves the inconsistencies in the subjective perceptions of abuse and the actual experiences of abuse found among older Korean immigrants. Such inconsistencies may reflect culturally specific understandings of what constitutes abuse and proper treatment of elders (Selwood et al., 2007). Most likely, older Korean immigrants have a limited perception of what might constitute abuse, making them both more vulnerable to instances of abuse and less likely to seek help when it occurs. It is possible that this immigrant population is completely unfamiliar with how the Western cultural perspective conceives of elder abuse, and therefore does not know what elder abuse is as seen from that perspective. In addition to lack of knowledge, culture also plays a significant role in how older Korean immigrants perceive abuse and how they respond to it. Thus, professionals should provide guidelines about what constitutes elder abuse.

There is a relationship between elder abuse and sociodemographic factors among older Korean immigrants in the United States. In particular, having a poor health status was the most important predictor of elder abuse among older Korean immigrants in the United States. Poor health status tends to increase dependency on caregivers, consequently increasing their burden for longer periods of time and contributing to the greater likelihood of incidences of elder abuse (Chang, 2016). Educational attainment was also an important predictor of elder abuse in older Korean immigrants in the United States (Chang, 2016). The level of education was significantly associated with the experience of elder abuse among older Korean immigrants in the United States. It is highly likely that those who are well educated may have resources and knowledge to protect themselves from abuse, whereas those who are less educated may lack either the resources or the knowledge, leaving them more vulnerable. It is possible that a higher education level enhances older Korean immigrants' knowledge about their own well-being, their safety, and their rights. Therefore, comprehensive programs should include education and training to increase awareness of elder abuse, and by doing so, should help decrease the prevalence of elder abuse among older Korean immigrants.

Regarding types of elder abuse, the most common form of abuse found among older Korean immigrants was emotional abuse. With regard to emotional abuse, the most frequent types of abuse were silent treatment and disrespect (Chang, 2016). While considerable numbers of older Korean immigrants are less likely to identify emotional abuse as elder abuse (Chang, 2016), certain forms of emotional abuse, such as lack of respect, are perceived as serious by them. Disrespect is the most common form of elder abuse in traditional Asian cultures (Dong et al., 2014). Physical and sexual abuse incidents were found to be significantly less typical compared to other types of elder abuse. However, there was no incident of rape in the Korean community (Chang, 2016, 2019). It is noteworthy that while many Korean immigrants experienced financial abuse, they were less likely than others to identify such experiences as abuse (Lee & Eaton, 2009). Thus, this population is less likely to seek help or make claims regarding financial abuse. Cultural factors may play a role here, as parents typically transfer their wealth and property to their children in traditional Korean households. In turn, adult children are expected to fulfill their duties of filial piety by taking care of their parents. Such expectations leave older Korean immigrants particularly vulnerable to financial abuse. Generally speaking, financial abuse by family members is a common form of elder abuse (Gibson & Greene, 2013), and most perpetrators of this form of abuse are family members and relatives (Acierno et al., 2010; National Center on Elder Abuse, 2006).

Regarding help-seeking behaviors, older Korean immigrants typically rely on informal resources such as family members and relatives for help. Such immigrants may even be reluctant to seek any help at all if it lies outside their family. It is also possible that they may feel that people outside the family should not intervene, even in abuse situations. This review reflects the traditional Korean value of preserving social harmony and social unity.

There is also the perception that disclosing family problems to outsiders will bring shame to the family. This makes victims less likely to open up about their family problems even in abusive situations (Yan, 2014). Many older Korean immigrants avoid seeking professional help in abuse situations because they see such behavior as lowering their own dignity and bringing shame to their family (Lee & Shin, 2010). In addition, older Korean immigrants have been shown to be much less aware of what formal resources for help may be available to them. Cultural differences, as well as lack of knowledge, may play a role in the underutilization of social services in this community. It is critical to develop culturally appropriate services and programs to provide support. Both formal and informal services may be necessary. Also, future research should examine what differences exist in the experience and definition of elder abuse among different Asian ethnic groups.

References

Acierno, R., Hernandez, M. A., Amstadter, A. B., Resnick, H. S., Steve, K., Muzzy, W., & Kilpatrick, D. G. (2010). Prevalence and correlates of emotional, physical, sexual, and financial abuse and potential neglect in the United States: The National Elder Mistreatment Study. *American Journal of Public Health, 100*(2), 292–297.

Atim, L. M., Kaggwa, M. M., Mamum, M. A., Kule, M., Ashaba, S., & Maling, S. (2023). Factors associated with elder abuse and neglect in rural Uganda: A cross-sectional study of community older adults attending an outpatient clinic. *PLoS One, 18*(2), e0280826.

Bagshaw, D., Wendt, S., Zannettino, L., & Adams, V. (2013). Financial abuse of older people by family members: Views and experiences of older Australians and their family members. *Australian Social Work, 66*(1), 86–103.

Budiman, A., & Ruiz, N. G. (2021). *Key facts about Asian Americans, a diverse and growing population.* Pew Research Center. https://www.pewresearch.org/short-reads/2021/04/29/key-facts-about-asian-americans/

Castle, N., Ferguson-Rome, J. C., & Teresi, J. A. (2015). Elder abuse in residential long term care: An update. To the 2003 National Research Council report. *Journal of Applied Gerontology, 34*, 407–443.

Cauce, A. M., Domenech-Rodríguez, M., Paradise, M., Cochran, B. N., Shea, J. M., Srebnik, D., & Baydar, N. (2002). Cultural and contextual influences in mental health help seeking: A focus on ethnic minority youth. *Journal of Consulting and Clinical Psychology, 70*(1), 44.

Chang, M. (2016). Experience of elder abuse among older Korean immigrants. *Journal of Elder Abuse & Neglect, 28*(2), 76–94.

Chang, M. (2019). Comparative study on subjective experience of elder abuse between older Korean immigrants in the United States and older Koreans in Korea. *The International Journal of Aging and Human Development, 88*(2), 187–210.

Choi, N. G., Kim, J., & Asseff, J. (2009). Self-neglect and neglect of vulnerable older adults: Reexamination of etiology. *Journal of Gerontological Social Work, 52*(2), 171–187.

Choi, G. Y., Koh, E., Lee, E. J., & Rhee, S. (2024). Elder mistreatment experiences, perceptions, and help-seeking behaviors of Asian American older adults. *Journal of Elder Abuse & Neglect, 36*(1), 41–66.

Chokkanathan, S. (2015). Elder mistreatment and health status of rural older adults. *Journal of Interpersonal Violence, 30*(18), 3267–3282.

Chokkanathan, S., & Lee, A. E. (2006). Elder mistreatment in urban India: A community based study. *Journal of Elder Abuse and Neglect, 17*(2), 45–61.

Daly, J. M. (2017). Elder abuse in long term care and assisted living settings. In X. Dong (Ed.), *Elder abuse: Research, practice and policy* (pp. 67–91). Springer International Publishing.

Dong, X., & Simon, M. A. (2013). Elder abuse as a risk factor for hospitalization in older persons. *JAMA Internal Medicine, 173*(10), 911–917.

Dong, X., Simon, M. A., Fulmer, T., Mendes de Leon, C. F., Hebert, L. E., Beck, T., Evans, D. A., et al. (2011). A prospective population-based study of differences in elder self-neglect and mortality between black and white older adults. *Journals of Gerontology Series A: Biomedical Sciences and Medical Sciences, 66*(6), 695–704.

Dong, X., Simon, M., & Evans, D. (2014). A population-based study of physical function and risk for elder abuse reported to social service agency: Findings from the Chicago health and aging project. *Journal of Applied Gerontology, 33*(7), 808–830.

Esterline, C., & Batalova, J. (2022). *Korean immigrants in the United States*. Migration Policy Institute. https://www.migrationpolicy.org/article/korean-immigrants-united-states

Falk, N. L., Baigis, J., & Kopac, C. (2012). Elder mistreatment and the elder justice act. *Online Journal of Issues in Nursing, 17*(3).

Fang, B., Li, D., Yan, E., Zhou, Y., Yu, Z., & Hu, J. (2023). Associated factors of discrepancy between older adults and their family caregivers in reporting elder abuse. *Journal of Clinical Nursing, 32*(5–6), 688–700.

Gibson, S. C., & Greene, E. (2013). Assessing knowledge of elder financial abuse: A first step in enhancing prosecutions. *Journal of Elder Abuse & Neglect, 25*(2), 162–182.

Gimm, G., Chowdhury, S., & Castle, N. (2018). Resident aggression and abuse in assisted living. *Journal of Applied Gerontology, 37*(8), 947–964.

Honarvar, B., Gheibi, Z., Asadollahi, A., Bahadori, F., Khaksar, E., Faradonbeh, M. R., & Farjami, M. (2019). The impact of abuse on the quality of life of the elderly: A population-based survey in Iran. *Journal of Preventive Medicine and Public Health, 53*(2), 89.

Jackson, S. L. (2016). All elder abuse perpetrators are not alike: The heterogeneity of elder abuse perpetrators and implications for intervention. *International Journal of Offender Therapy and Comparative Criminology, 60*(3), 265–285.

Kosberg, J. I. (2014). Rosalie Wolf Memorial Lecture: Reconsidering assumptions regarding men as elder abuse perpetrators and as elder abuse victims. *Journal of Elder Abuse & Neglect, 26*(3), 207–222.

Lachs, M. S., & Pillemer, K. A. (2015). Elder abuse. *New England Journal of Medicine, 373*(20), 1947–1956.

Lee, H. Y., & Eaton, C. K. (2009). Financial abuse in elderly Korean immigrants: Mixed analysis of the role of culture on perception and help-seeking intention. *Journal of Gerontological Social Work, 52*(5), 463–488.

Lee, H. Y., & Shin, N. (2010). Cultural view on and response to mistreatment of elderly Korean American immigrants: A social development intervention. *Social Development Issues, 32*(1), 89–110.

Lee, H. Y., Yoon, H. S., Shin, N., Moon, J. Y., Kwon, J. H., Park, E. S., Park, K. H., et al. (2011). Perception of elder mistreatment and its link to help-seeking intention: A comparison of elderly Korean and Korean American immigrants. *Clinical Gerontologist, 34*(4), 287–304.

Lee, Y. S., Kaplan, C. P., & Perez-Stable, E. J. (2014). Elder mistreatment among Chinese and Korean immigrants: The roles of sociocultural contexts on perceptions and help-seeking behaviors. *Journal of Aggression, Maltreatment & Trauma, 23*(1), 20–44.

Myhre, J., Saga, S., Malmedal, W., Ostaszkiewicz, J., & Nakrem, S. (2020). Elder abuse and neglect: An overlooked patient safety issue: A focus group study of nursing home leaders' perceptions of elder abuse and neglect. *BMC Health Services Research, 20*(1), 1–14.

National Center on Elder Abuse. (2006). *The 2004 study of survey of state adult protective services: Abuse of adults 60 years of age and older*. Author.

National Center on Elder Abuse. (2011). *Frequently asked questions*. http://www.ncea.aoa.gov/faq/index.aspx

Park, J., Wilber, K., Wu, S., Aranda, M. P., Oh, H., & Jang, Y. (2024). Risk factors for elder mistreatment among older Korean Americans. *The International Journal of Aging and Human Development*, 00914150241253235.

Pengpid, S., & Peltzer, K. (2021). Elder abuse and health outcomes among community-dwelling older adults in India: Results of a national survey in 2017–2018. *Journal of Elder Abuse & Neglect, 33*(4), 327–341.

Pew Research Center. (2021). *Koreans in the U.S. Fact sheet.* https://www.pewresearch.org/social-trends/fact-sheet/asian-americans-Koreans-in-the-u-s/

Pillemer, K., Connolly, M. T., Breckman, R., Spreng, N., & Lachs, M. S. (2015). Elder mistreatment: Priorities for consideration by the white house conference on aging. *The Gerontologist, 55*(2), 320–327.

Reisig, M. D., & Holtfreter, K. (2013). Shopping fraud victimization among the elderly. *Journal of Financial Crime, 20*(3), 324–337.

Roberto, K. A. (2016). The complexities of elder abuse. *American Psychologist, 71*(4), 302.

Sasaki, M., Arai, Y., Kumamoto, K., Abe, K., Arai, A., & Mizuno, Y. (2007). Factors related to potentially harmful behaviors towards disabled older people by family caregivers in Japan. *International Journal of Geriatric Psychiatry, 22*(3), 250–257.

Scharlach, A. E., Kellam, R., Ong, N., Baskin, A., Goldstein, C., & Fox, P. J. (2006). Cultural attitudes and caregiver services use: Lessons from focus groups with racially and ethnically diverse family caregivers. *Journal of Gerontological Social Work, 47*(1–2), 133–156.

Schofield, M. J., Powers, J. R., & Loxton, D. (2013). Mortality and disability outcomes of self-reported elder abuse: A 12-year prospective investigation. *Journal of the American Geriatrics Society, 61*(5), 679–685.

Sebastian, D., & Sekher, T. V. (2011). Extent and nature of elder abuse in Indian families: A study in Kerala. *HelpAge India-Research and Development Journal, 17*, 20–28.

Selwood, A., Cooper, C., & Livingston, G. (2007). What is elder abuse-who decides? *International Journal of Geriatric Psychiatry, 22*, 1009–1012.

Skirbekk, V., & James, K. S. (2014). Abuse against elderly in India—The role of education. *BMC Public Health, 14*(1), 1–8.

Spitzer, D., Neufeld, A., Harrison, M., Hughes, K., & Stewart, M. (2003). Caregiving in transnational context: "My wings have been cut; where can I fly?". *Gender & Society, 17*(2), 267–286.

Tam, S., & Neysmith, S. (2006). Disrespect and isolation: Elder abuse in Chinese communities. *Canadian Journal on Aging/La Revue canadienne du vieillissement., 25*(2), 141–151.

U.S. Census Bureau. (2019). *2016–2020 American community survey (ACS) 5-year data products.* https://www.census.gov/en.html

Yan, E. (2014). Elder abuse in Asia – An overview. In R. M. Taylor (Ed.), *Elder abuse and its prevention: Workshop summary.* National Academies Press.

Yon, Y., Mikton, C. R., Gassoumis, Z. D., & Wilber, K. H. (2017). Elder abuse prevalence in community settings: A systematic review and meta-analysis. *The Lancet Global Health, 5*(2), e147–e156.

Yon, Y., Ramiro-Gonzalez, M., Mikton, C. R., Huber, M., & Sethi, D. (2019). The prevalence of elder abuse in institutional settings: A systematic review and meta-analysis. *European Journal of Public Health, 29*(1), 58–67.

CHAPTER 6

Toward a Fuller Understanding of Violence and Trauma Among Sexual- and Gender-Minority Immigrants

Fernando Estrada, Miguel A. Arana, Haleigh Armstrong, and Alison Cerezo

Introduction

In a 2017 study, Cheney et al. (2017) looked at testimonial data from several dozen Mexican transgender women who were applying for asylum in the United States and who ranged in age from 20 to 58. The findings illuminated a need for social protection and better access to mental health, employment, and educational services. Below are excerpts from their testimonies:

F. Estrada (✉)
Department of Specialized Programs in Professional Psychology, Loyola Marymount University, Los Angeles, CA, USA
e-mail: fernando.estrada@lmu.edu

M. A. Arana
Gevirtz School of Education, University of California, Santa Barbara, CA, USA
e-mail: miguel_arana@ucsb.edu

J. S. Hong et al. (eds.), *Violence and Trauma Without Borders*,
https://doi.org/10.1007/978-3-032-29221-6_6

> When my father saw me playing girl games, he beat me. He kicked me and punched me. He said that I was not a *joto* or a *maricon* [derogatory words for gay man], that I was a man. He said that he had not asked for a *joto* son; he had asked for a man. He threatened to send me to a military school, where they would beat me and make me a man. My father threatened to kill me if I turned out to be a faggot.
>
> My brothers beat me a lot, and my father never did anything to protect me. I remember once, my brother A was beating me, and my father, instead of helping me, joined in and began to kick me.
>
> The neighbors got more aggressive and chased me and threw stones at me. If they found me with my transgender friends, they punched us in the face and all over the body while calling us *maricones* and *puto.*
>
> When I went out dressed as a woman, I was often harassed by the police. They often threatened to arrest me for dressing as a woman. They called me faggot. Once, I was talking to another gay in front of a gay bar. I was not cross-dressing at the time. Two police officers approached us and accused us of *faltas a la moral* [moral violations as stated in the Mexican Penal Code]. They threatened to arrest us unless we paid them a bribe.

The research on sexual and gender minority (SGM) immigrants and refugees is steadily growing, with converging findings that suggest a risk of exposure to violence, harassment, and discrimination (Cheney et al., 2017). An investigation into the experiences of 41 individuals who identified as either lesbian, gay, bisexual, transgender, or queer (LGBTQ) and who were detained in jails by US Customs and Border Patrol or Immigration and Customs Enforcement found that one-third of them had experienced physical violence due to their sexual or gender identity, and nearly all of them reported being targets of anti-LGBTQ abuse that included threats of violence and assault (Doubossarskaia et al., 2024). That report, which was a collaborative effort that included the National Immigration Justice Center, Human Rights First, and Immigration

---

H. Armstrong
College of Education, Counseling Psychology, University of Texas, Austin, Austin, TX, USA
e-mail: haa2746@my.utexas.edu

A. Cerezo
Department of Counseling, Clinical, and School Psychology, University of California, Santa Barbara, CA, USA
e-mail: acerezo@ucsb.edu

Equality, also revealed that nearly half of the survey respondents experienced new or increased mental health problems while in detention, including panic attacks, flashbacks, and self-injurious behavior. Such findings help to illustrate some of the vulnerabilities pertaining to sexual and gender minority (SGM) immigrants and refugees and the need to better understand their experiences to be able to respond effectively and comprehensively.

The following sections in this chapter discuss the growing literature that suggests SGM immigrants face amplified risk for exposure to different forms of violence and the adverse impact on their physical and mental health. Also discussed are multilevel responses that can support individual recovery and promote additional resource protections. But first, we examine the diversity of identity-related factors that comprise an increasingly visible population.

Identity and Visibility

In 2013, the Williams Institute published a seminal report that estimated over 900,000 adult immigrants in the United States as identifying as either lesbian, gay, bisexual, transgender, or queer/questioning (LGBTQ). The majority (70%) were considered documented, whereas 30% were undocumented. It is difficult to determine the actual number of adult LGBTQ undocumented immigrants in the United States due to pervasive discrimination after coming out, which may be even more true for LGBTQ immigrants. Nonetheless, the Williams Institute reported at that time that an estimated 267,000, or about 2.7% of the adult undocumented population, were part of the LGBTQ community. In the report, the majority of undocumented LGBTQ immigrants were Latina/o/e (71%), whereas about 15% were individuals of Asian or Pacific Islander descent, Black, or African American individuals made up 6%, and those who were White made up 8%.

Since the publication of that report, there has been a surge of migrants, particularly from Latin America (The Baker Institute, 2023), which would suggest a concomitant rise in the number of LGBTQ immigrants in the United States. Population estimates are also influenced by the use of the "LGBTQ" acronym, which represents a highly diverse array of lived experiences that are informed by factors such as sex, sexuality and sexual orientation, and gender identity and expression (American Psychological Association, 2022). The term "queer," for example, is used by some and broadly describes those whose gender or sexuality falls outside of cisgender and heteronormative standards (Hatzenbuehler & Pachankis, 2021). Moreover, sexuality and gender are nested within varying sociocultural and political milieus, and, therefore, the concepts themselves are expansive, fluid, and deeply personal (Hatzenbuehler & Pachankis, 2021; Killermann, 2017). Further complicating population-level data collection efforts are pervasive anti-LGBTQ sentiments and negative sociopolitical rhetoric that can lead individuals to conceal their identity, such as with recent policy changes in the United States that aim to restrict human rights for SGM communities. For example, Utah schools can now lawfully prohibit flags bearing rainbows and other imagery associated with LGBTQ pride (Whitehurst, 2025). And in Alabama, lawmakers extended the "Don't Say Gay" restrictions to institutions of higher education (Chandler, 2025). These policy shifts seek to silence and intimidate SGM individuals and delegitimize their lived experiences, which warrant concerted efforts to safeguard their visibility and amplify their voices.

A Web of Exposure to Violence

Immigrants and refugees who are also SGM, like non-SGM immigrants, will flee their home country because of war, political and ideological persecution, and economic and financial instability (Alessi et al., 2018). SGM individuals, however, can also be forced to migrate due to violence associated with their perceived or actual sexual orientation or gender identity (Toro-Alfonso et al., 2012). According to the International Lesbian, Gay, Bisexual, Trans, and Intersex Association, there are at least 42 countries that legally restrict freedom of expression on issues related to sexual and gender diversity (Mendos et al., 2020). Additionally, 67 countries have provisions that criminalize LGBTQ-related behavior, such as consensual same-sex sexual acts in private between adults. In six countries, death penalty is the legally prescribed punishment for consensual same-sex relations. Across global regions, the enforcement of sexual- or gender-related violations remains ongoing; however, it is strongly suspected that the actual number of arrests and other forms of punishment is underreported (Botha, 2023).

Anti-SGM legislation increases the risk of encounters with law enforcement and involvement in the criminal justice system, which can force SGM individuals to conceal their identity for fear of persecution and surveillance, as well as acts of discrimination and violence (Redcay et al., 2019).

In the United States, incidents of anti-SGM bias perpetrated by state authorities point to a troubling pattern of institutional violence that can be difficult for victims to publicly report and seek justice (Doubossarskaia et al., 2024). Additionally, by denigrating and repressing diverse sexual and gender identities and expression, anti-SGM legislation, coupled with negative US sociopolitical rhetoric, further reinforces definitions of family that are cisheteronormative (i.e., centering and privileging heterosexuality and cisgender identity) and that are used in immigration proceedings, which often exclude more diverse relationship structures outside of traditional notions of marriage and blood kinship (Chávez, 2011; Card et al., 2022). These systemic forces threaten an immigrant's sense of safety in their host country as well as separate and isolate them from their loved ones and their community, both locally and abroad (Díaz, 2022; da Silva Rebelo et al., 2018).

Pervasive xenophobia and anti-immigrant attitudes in the United States and elsewhere pose a safety threat to all immigrants; however, SGM individuals can also experience violence during the migration journey (Alessi et al., 2021; Estrada et al., 2022). Cis hetero norms and anti-SGM sentiments among fellow migrants can have an isolating effect on SGM individuals and even expose them to physical and sexual harassment (Cerezo et al., 2014). A common occurrence among SGM immigrants traveling northward through Central America and Mexico involves withholding disclosures about their sexual orientation to avoid mockery and taunting, and some transgender women will alter their appearance to evade being spotted, kidnapped, and sexually assaulted by drug cartel members (Hernandez, 2025). The exposure to repeated violence and threats of violence can be especially pronounced for transgender and nonbinary or gender-expansive individuals due to the visibility of their gender expression (Cheney et al., 2017; Gowin et al., 2017), which makes them more likely to be targeted for harassment by their immigrant peers (Alessi, 2016; Alessi et al., 2018; Leyva-Flores et al., 2016, 2019). Such vulnerability can also be experienced while in custody at a US detention center, where transgender individuals have been subjected to repeated acts of discrimination, including being denied access to appropriate medical care (Borges, 2020; Minero, 2020). In a recent study, Bird et al. (2024) interviewed service providers at a specialty refugee mental health clinic, and they found that SGM refugees and asylum seekers, compared to non-SGM immigrants, reported greater childhood trauma exposure, increased isolation, and decreased access to support, further underlining the need to better understand health implications and strategic responses.

Health Considerations

After exposure to trauma, SGM immigrants are at risk for enduring psychological, emotional, and physiological responses that can include interfering thoughts, hypervigilance, and a constant state of heightened arousal, which are symptoms of posttraumatic stress disorder (PTSD; Rasmussen et al., 2012). SGM immigrants who have had prolonged or repeated exposure to trauma are at risk for developing complex or compounded PTSD, characterized by experiences such as amnesia, persistent nightmares, impulsivity, and aggressiveness, as well as difficulties with identity issues and maintaining interpersonal relationships (Alessi et al., 2021; Shidlo & Ahola, 2013). Bodily responses to traumatic stress can also manifest as somatic problems such as headaches and gastrointestinal pain, as has been observed among some Latine SGM immigrants (Estrada et al., 2021). Furthermore, reactions to trauma among SGM immigrants are likely to worsen with the existence of other commonly co-occurring mental health conditions, including anxiety, depression, and the problematic use of substances, including alcohol and narcotics such as methamphetamines and opioids (Cano, 2019).

Understanding the fuller effects of traumatic exposure among SGM immigrants necessitates the consideration of intersecting factors such as the process of social and cultural adaptation and integration, or acculturation, and the stressors involved in that process (Crockett et al., 2007). Adjusting to the United States requires searching for housing and employment and establishing new community networks; however, difficulties can arise concerning individuals who have multiple marginalized identities (Cerezo et al., 2014). Acts of discrimination based on race, language, and sexuality can exacerbate traumatic stress by problematizing aspects of daily living, like securing a stable source of income (Cheney et al., 2017). Among transgender women with a history of sex work, for example, acculturative stress can impair the quality of social connections with peers and also increase the sense of social isolation and symptoms of depression (Nemoto et al., 2011; Rhodes et al., 2013; Yaminis et al., 2018). Among older adults (ages 50 and up), SGM immigrants can face additional stressors related to socioeconomic disadvantages and barriers to independently accessing supportive care (Lee et al., 2020).

Alcohol and other substances may be used to help cope with stress; however, there can be differences in substance use patterns among SGM individuals. African gay and bisexual immigrants, for example, have reported using alcohol as a coping mechanism for traumatic stress that was experienced both pre- and post migration (Ogunbajo et al., 2019). Among Arab immigrants, one study found that sexual minority men used alcohol and marijuana to manage the chronic stress related to being targeted for their cultural and sexual identities (Abboud et al., 2022). Among Latine SGM immigrants, women have reported higher alcohol misuse, whereas men show a tendency for higher levels of drug usage (Cerezo et al., 2024). Additionally, Latine transgender immigrants face higher rates of substance use as a function of acculturative stress when compared to their cisgender peers, suggesting an interplay among stressor factors and marginalized identities that is important to consider (Cerezo et al., 2024). Furthermore, substance use can increase the risk of suicidal thoughts and self-injurious behavior (Leza et al., 2024), which further underscores the need to understand the varying sources of trauma exposure among SGM immigrants and their patterns of response and coping.

Research shows that SGM individuals are vulnerable to suicide ideation due to chronic stressors such as intersectional forms of discrimination and uncertainties surrounding legal protections (Kaniuka et al., 2024; Layland et al., 2020). This can be magnified among those who are immigrants and, thereby, increase their risk for suicide (Kashyap & Joscelyne, 2020). Such a risk can be further intensified for transgender and nonbinary individuals who experience family rejection, sexual violence, and social isolation that often begins in childhood (Hopkinson et al., 2017; Alessi et al., 2016). Yet for some, adversity can also be associated with resilience and perseverance, which among SGM immigrants has been correlated with factors such as community connectedness, spirituality, legal and social support, and opportunities for volunteerism and activism (Alessi, 2016; Kim & Feyissa, 2021; Shaw & Verghese, 2022). Social integration involving activism can help SGM immigrants cultivate a sense of community and belonging, while also actively resisting oppressive power structures in solidarity with others (Solórzano, 2020).

Strategic Care and Response

The trauma-related experiences of SGM immigrants underscore the need for policy reform and culturally informed support services. A decrease in exposure to trauma is possible with advancements in the decriminalization of SGM-related identities, expressions, and behaviors. Fortunately, over the last decade, a positive global trend has been observed relative to countries repealing corporal forms of punishment, including death penalty, as a consequence of engaging in same-sex behavior or conduct (Mendos et al., 2020). Legal protections against discrimination and hate crimes are important for SGM immigrants to feel safe engaging with key industries such as healthcare and housing. To that end, there is a need for more state constitutions that explicitly include the terms "sexual orientation" and "gender identity" in their nondiscrimination clauses, which can have a broad positive impact on SGM immigrants relative to employment, housing, healthcare, and education (Mendos et al., 2020). In addition, transgender immigrants need proper legal gender recognition andprotection from targeted arrests and abuse from the police (Botha, 2023), particularly given a recent US presidential executive order that calls into question the very existence of transgender people (Mulvihill & Hanna, 2025) and that has resulted in some countries warning SGM individuals about travel risks (Associated Press, 2025).

In the United States, over the last two decades, there have been alarming upticks in anti-immigrant sentiments, evidenced by the historic number of deportations that occurred between the years of 2009 to 2016 (US Department of Homeland Security, 2017a) and the executive order mandating that all undocumented immigrants be deported regardless of whether they belonged to a protected class (Department of Homeland Security, 2017b). Such draconian policy is coupled with rapidly increasing sociopolitical rhetoric aimed at thwarting progress on SGM-related issues such as use of pronouns and access to life-saving, gender-affirming care (Argiros et al., 2024). The current and swift rollback of rights and protections for SGM individuals in the United States and abroad greatly increases the risk of experiencing harm and displacement (Johnson et al., 2025; Spike, 2025), and such conditions further perpetuate SGM immigrant vulnerability and underscore the urgent need to better understand effective methods of support. To that end, Chavez (2011) interviewed SGM immigrants in the United States on issues related to healthcare, housing, and legal matters. The findings revealed a pattern of cultural insensitivity from healthcare professionals, suggesting a need for organizational-level interventions to improve service providers' competency relative to their interpersonal communication skills, particularly with sensitive topics such as a person's immigration status and gender identity. Noteworthy here is the research suggesting that cases of cultural insensitivity among service professionals can discourage SGM persons from discussing sensitive healthcare concerns, including HIV status and treatment (Quinn et al., 2015). Chavez (2011) also found that SGM immigrants experienced problems with finding and keeping housing, which is urgent to address, considering national data showing SGM youth face a disproportionate risk for homelessness (Ray, 2006). Improvements can also be made to the intake process that refugees undergo, particularly concerning resettlement organizations and their assumptions of cis heterosexuality that can problematize roommate pairing for SGM refugees and potentially expose them to a hostile and unsafe living environment (Chavez, 2011). Lastly, legal clinics held in the community and with experts who are familiar with SGM identities and topics are vital given the increasing militarization of immigration enforcement and local police that threatens the overall safety of SGM immigrants, especially concerning being apprehended and deported (Chavez, 2011).

Accessible health and mental health services can make a positive impact on the well-being of SGM immigrants, especially when services are rendered by culturally competent professionals (Estrada et al., 2022). For example, knowledge of cultural norms and traditions, a value for sexual and gender diversity, skills as an advocate, and proficiency in a second language are areas of professional competency that can lead to improved patient outcomes with SGM immigrants (Cadenas et al., 2022; Pratt-Chapman et al., 2022). There is an immediate need for health and mental healthcare industry leaders to invest in the professional development of their staff, especially given the persistent gaps in graduate-level training about curricular content focused on multicultural education and biliteracy development (Consoli & Flores, 2021; Rodriguez de los Reyes & Collict, 2022). Additionally, approaching health and mental health services with a trauma-informed lens can lead to sustained positive changes through treatment that is comprehensive. As a framework, trauma-informed care recognizes the widespread impact that traumatic stress has on an individual and espouses the use of whole-person interventions to help clients gain not only a sense of physical and psychological safety but also skills for self-regulating their emotions (Portman-Thompson, 2020). For example, knowing how to engage in belly breathing and visualization can help to calm and ease the nervous system, which helps combat recurrent and distressing thoughts and emotions (Barnes & Andrews, 2019; O'Sullivan et al., 2019). This can be important for SGM immigrants when considering that among individuals with multiple marginalized identities, symptoms of PTSD tend to co-occur or be comorbid with other mood problems associated with anxiety and depression (Navarro Flores et al., 2023). Trauma-informed care also emphasizes treatment that integrates existing social and community resources and that can increase a sense of connectedness and reduce feelings of isolation, which further mitigate the disproportional risk that SGM individuals face compared to non-SGM persons relative to suicide ideation and self-injurious behavior (Harmer et al., 2020; Kaniuka et al., 2024).

Adversity coexists with resilience and wisdom, and affirming and integrating a client's own healing practices can benefit their health and mental health outcomes. For example, studies with Latine SGM individuals have found that management of emotional distress, less substance use, and less sexual risk-taking coincide with counter-hegemonic practices such as interrogating and even rejecting traditional gender norms (Yamasaki & Le, 2022). SGM immigrants might also draw strength from family members who are outwardly accepting of SGM-related issues (Przeworski & Piedra, 2020), as well as a sense of solidarity with other marginal groups (Ayoub & Bauman, 2019).

Conclusion

The compounded adversities faced by SGM immigrants constitute a pressing public health and human rights concern that is intensifying under the current US administration. The multifaceted nature of violence and exclusion experienced by SGM immigrants across the migration journey, within detention systems, and throughout the process of resettlement is the result of entrenched structural inequities that both produce and perpetuate traumatic stress. Interlocking cisheteronormativity, racism, and xenophobia lead to overlapping vulnerabilities across psychological, physical, and social aspects of life that take a pernicious toll on one's quality of life and aggravate posttraumatic stress disorder and other comorbid problems. Yet within these hostile conditions, SGM immigrants continuously assert agency, foster community, and cultivate resilience in ways that demand recognition in research and policy. Addressing their needs requires more than inclusive rhetoric; it warrants intentional, trauma-informed, culturally responsive, and equity-driven approaches in health, legal, and social service sectors. By amplifying the voices of SGM immigrants, we can enact structural reforms that dismantle oppressive systems and foster environments where visibility, safety, dignity, and belonging are not only possible but fiercely protected and promoted.

References

Abboud, S., Veldhuis, C., Ballout, S., Nadeem, F., Nyhan, K., & Hughes, T. (2022). Sexual and gender minority health in the Middle East and North Africa region: A scoping review. *International Journal of Nursing Studies Advances, 4*, 100085.

Alessi, E. J. (2016). Resilience in sexual and gender minority forced migrants: A qualitative exploration. *Traumatology, 22*(3), 203–213.

Alessi, E. J., Kahn, S., & Chatterji, S. (2016). "The darkest times of my life": Recollections of child abuse among forced migrants persecuted because of their sexual orientation and gender identity. *Child Abuse & Neglect, 51*, 93–105.

Alessi, E. J., Kahn, S., Woolner, L., & Van Der Horn, R. (2018). Traumatic stress among sexual and gender minority refugees from the Middle East, North Africa, and Asia who fled to the European Union. *Journal of Traumatic Stress, 31*(6), 805–815.

Alessi, E. J., Cheung, S., Kahn, S., & Yu, M. (2021). A scoping review of the experiences of violence and abuse among sexual and gender minority migrants across the migration trajectory. *Trauma, Violence & Abuse, 22*(5), 1339–1355.

American Psychological Association. (2022). *A guide to sexual orientation and gender diversity terms.* https://www.apa.org/ed/precollege/psychology-teacher-network/introductory-psychology/diversity-terms

Argiros, A., Park, E., Phillips, K., Cyperski, M., & Clark, K. (2024). "It doesn't feel easy at all": Stressors and supports of parenting sexual and gender minority adolescents in the US Southeast. *LGBTQ+ Family: An Interdisciplinary Journal*, 1–22. https://doi.org/10.1080/27703371.2024.2395902

Associated Press. (2025, March 22). *Denmark advises transgender people to contact US Embassy before traveling to the United States.* https://apnews.com/article/denmark-us-transgender-travel-advisory-c0b533a72f2b22b438e6a4077889fefb?utm_source=copy&utm_medium=share

Ayoub, P. M., & Bauman, L. (2019). Migration and queer mobilisations: how migration facilitates cross-border LGBTQ activism. *Journal of Ethnic and Migration Studies, 45*(15), 2758–2778. https://doi.org/10.1080/1369183X.2018.1497955

Baker Institute. (2023). *Expert focus on US immigration: Challenges and possible solutions.* https://www.bakerinstitute.org/research/expert-focus-us-immigration-challenges-and-possible-solutions

Barnes, J. S., & Andrews, M. (2019). Meeting survivors where they are: The vital role of trauma-informed and competent clinicians in primary care. *Journal of Aggression, Maltreatment & Trauma, 28*(5), 601–612. https://doi.org/10.1080/10926771.2019.1587559

Bird, C., Somantri, A. R., Narasimhan, R., Lee, I., Bowers, G., Loo, S., Piwowarczyk, L., & Ng, L. C. (2024). Mental health disparities of sexual minority refugees and asylum seekers: Provider perspectives on trauma exposure, symptom presentation, and treatment approach. *Journal of Counseling Psychology, 71*(4), 229–241.

Borges, S. (2020). "We have to do a lot of healing": LGBTQ migrant Latinas resisting and healing from systemic violence. *Journal of Lesbian Studies, 24*(2), 94–109.

Botha, K. (2023). *Our identities under arrest: A global overview on the enforcement of laws criminalising consensual same-sex sexual acts between adults and diverse gender expressions* (2nd ed.). ILGA, November 2023. https://ilga.org/wp-content/uploads/2024/03/Our_Identities_Under_Arrest_2023.pdf#page=18

Cadenas, G. A., Neimeyer, G., Suro, B., Minero, L. P., Campos, L., Garcini, L. M., Mercado, A., Paris, M., Silva, M., & Domenech Rodríguez, M. M. (2022). Developing cultural competency for providing psychological services with immigrant populations: A cross-level training curriculum. *Training and Education in Professional Psychology, 16*(2), 121–129.

Cano, M. (2019). Prescription opioid misuse among U.S. Hispanics. *Addictive Behaviors, 98*, 106021. https://doi.org/10.1016/j.addbeh.2019.06.010

Card, D., Chang, S., Becker, C., Mendelsohn, J., Voigt, R., Boustan, L., & Jurafsky, D. (2022). Computational analysis of 140 years of U.S. political speeches reveals more positive but increasingly polarized framing of immigration. *Proceedings of the National Academy of Sciences, 119*(31), e2120510119.

Cerezo, A., Morales, A., Quintero, D., & Rothman, S. (2014). Trans migrations: Exploring life at the intersection of transgender identity and immigration. *Psychology of Sexual Orientation and Gender Diversity, 1*(2), 170.

Cerezo, A., Estrada, F., Renteria, R., Rivera, D. B., & Ramirez, A. (2024). Drug use and risk correlates among Latinx sexual and gender minority immigrants. *Journal of Latinx Psychology, 12*(3), 294–310.

Chandler, K. (2025, April 26). *Alabama lawmakers approve expansion of 'Don't Say Gay' to cover public colleges.* Associated Press. https://apnews.com/article/alabama-legislature-dont-say-gay-a47776faa10ce8b1126f3be8fd00e681

Chávez, K. R. (2011). Identifying the needs of LGBTQ immigrants and refugees in Southern Arizona. *Journal of Homosexuality, 58*(2), 189–218.

Cheney, M. K., Gowin, M. J., Taylor, E. L., Frey, M., Dunnington, J., Alshuwaiyer, G., Huber, J. K., Garcia, M. C., & Wray, G. C. (2017). Living outside the gender box in Mexico: Testimony of transgender Mexican asylum seekers. *American Journal of Public Health, 107*(10), 1646–1652. https://doi.org/10.2105/ajph.2017.303961

Consoli, A. J., & Flores, I. (2021). The teaching and training of bilingual (English/Spanish) mental health professionals in the United States. In G. J. Rich, A. Padilla Lopez, L. Ebersöhn, J. Taylor, & S. Morrissey (Eds.), *Teaching psychology around the world* (Vol. #5, pp. 441–454). Cambridge Scholars Publishing.

Crockett, L. J., Iturbide, M. I., Torres Stone, R. A., McGinley, M., Raffaelli, M., & Carlo, G. (2007). Acculturative stress, social support, and coping: Relations to psychological adjustment among Mexican American college students. *Cultural Diversity and Ethnic Minority Psychology, 13*(4), 347–355. https://doi.org/10.1037/1099-9809.13.4.347

da Silva Rebelo, M. J., Fernández, M., & Achotegui, J. (2018). Mistrust, anger, and hostility in refugees, asylum seekers, and immigrants: A systematic review. *Canadian Psychology / Psychologie Canadienne, 59*(3), 239–251.

Díaz McConnell, E. (2022). "It could be 3 million, it could be 30 million": Quantitative misperceptions about undocumented immigration and immigration attitudes in the Trump era. *Latino Studies, 20*(2), 242–279.

Doubossarskaia et al. (2024). *No human being should be held there: The mistreatment of LGBTQ and HIV-positive people in US federal immigration jails.* Immigration Equality.

Estrada, F., Cerezo, A., & Ramirez, A. (2021). An examination of posttraumatic stress disorder–related symptoms among a sample of Latinx sexual- and gender-minority immigrants. *Journal of Traumatic Stress, 34*(5), 967–976.

Estrada, F., Jones, I. J., Rivera, D., Ramirez, A., & Cerezo, A. (2022). Trauma and Latinx sexual- and gender-minority immigrants in the U.S. *Current Opinion in Psychology, 47*, 101439.

Gowin, J. L., Sloan, M. E., Stangl, B. L., Vatsalya, V., & Ramchandani, V. A. (2017). Vulnerability for alcohol use disorder and rate of alcohol consumption. *The American Journal of Psychiatry, 174*(11), 1094–1101.

Harmer, B., Lee, S., Duong, T. V. H., & Saadabadi, A. (2020). Suicidal ideation. In *Acute medicine: A symptom-based approach* (pp. 415–420). https://doi.org/10.1007/9781139600354.061

Hatzenbuehler, M. L., & Pachankis, J. E. (2021). Sexual and gender minority health disparities. In *The science of health disparities research* (pp. 429–444). Wiley.

Hernandez, M. T. (2025, March 26). *How a shelter hit by Trump's aid cuts protects LGBTQ migrants in Mexico.* Associated Press. https://apnews.com/article/mexico-tapachula-lgbtq-migrants-migration-shelter-70b4098111181f7394949c8862d129ced?utm_source=copy&utm_medium=share

Hopkinson, R. A., Keatley, E., Glaeser, E., Erickson-Schroth, L., Fattal, O., & Nicholson Sullivan, M. (2017). Persecution experiences and mental health of LGBT asylum seekers. *Journal of Homosexuality, 64*(12), 1650–1666.

Johnson, C. K., Bose, D., & Bargfeld, L. (2025, January 30). *Some hospitals pause gender-affirming care to evaluate Trump's executive order.* Associated Press. https://apnews.com/article/transgender-trump-executive-order-hormones-hospitals-8d9e6b94b34d2e6f890c06ebeba0fe1d.

Kaniuka, A. R., Nanney, E. M., Robertson, R., Hoff, R., Smith, M., Bowling, J., Basinger, E. D., Dahl, A. A., & Cramer, R. J. (2024). *A grounded theory of sexual and gender minority suicide risk: The sexual and gender minority suicide risk and protection model.* Psychology of Sexual Orientation and Gender Diversity. Advance online publication https://doi.org/10.1037/sgd0000699

Kashyap, S., & Joscelyne, A. (2020). Refugees and suicide: When the quest for a better life becomes thwarted. In *Alternatives to suicide* (pp. 257–297). Academic Press.

Killermann, S. (2017). *A guide to gender: The social justice advocate's handbook.* Impetus Books.

Kim, S., & Feyissa, I. F. (2021). Conceptualizing "family" and the role of "chosen family" within the LGBTQ+ refugee community: A text network graph analysis. *Healthcare, 9*(4), 369.

Layland, E. K., Exten, C., Mallory, A. B., Williams, N. D., & Fish, J. N. (2020). Suicide attempt rates and associations with discrimination are greatest in early adulthood for sexual minority adults across diverse racial and ethnic groups. *LGBT Health, 7*(8), 439–447.

Lee, J. G. L., Shook-Sa, B. E., Gilbert, J., Ranney, L. M., Goldstein, A. O., & Boynton, M. H. (2020). Risk, resilience, and smoking in a national, probability sample of sexual and gender minority adults, 2017, USA. *Health Education & Behavior, 47*(2), 272–283.

Leyva-Flores, R., Infante, C., Servan-Mori, E., Quintino-Pérez, F., & Silverman-Retana, O. (2016). HIV prevalence among Central American migrants in transit through Mexico to the USA, 2009–2013. *Journal of Immigrant and Minority Health, 18*(6), 1482–1488.

Leyva-Flores, R., Infante, C., Gutierrez, J. P., Quintino-Perez, F., Gómez-Saldivar, M., & Torres-Robles, C. (2019). Migrants in transit through Mexico to the US: Experiences with violence and related factors, 2009–2015. *PLoS One, 14*(8), e0220775.

Leza, L., Haro, B., López-Goñi, J. J., & Fernández-Montalvo, J. (2024). Substance use disorder and lifetime suicidal behaviour: A scoping review. *Psychiatry Research, 334*, 115830.

Mendos, L. R., Botha, K., Lelis, R. C., de la Pena, E. L., Savelev, I., & Tan, D. (2020). *State-sponsored homophobia: Global legislation overview update.* International Lesbian, Gay, Bisexual, Trans and Intersex Association.

Minero, L. P. (2020). *The impact of detention proceedings and solitary confinement on Latinx, transgender, undocumented and asylum seeking immigrants* [Doctoral dissertation, University of Wisconsin Madison].

Mulvihill, G., & Hanna, J. (2025, February 8). *The US stopped allowing passport gender marker changes. Here are some of the people affected.* Associated Press. https://apnews.com/article/trump-order-transgender-nonbinary-passport-dd7d25350afea024c0a9de1011174e2c

Navarro Flores, C. M., Vázquez, A. L., Galvan, T., & Garcini, L. M. (2023). Cuento de nunca acabar [never-ending story]: Compounding trauma and mental health among undocumented Latinx immigrants. *Journal of Traumatic Stress, 36*(3), 593–604.

Nemoto, T., Bödeker, B., & Iwamoto, M. (2011). Social support, exposure to violence and transphobia, and correlates of depression among male-to-female transgender women with a history of sex work. *American Journal of Public Health, 101*(10), 1980–1988.

O'Sullivan, D., Watts, J. R., & Strauser, D. (2019). Trauma-sensitive rehabilitation counseling: Paradigms and principles. *Journal of Vocational Rehabilitation, 51*(3), 299–312. https://doi.org/10.3233/JVR-191047

Ogunbajo, A., Anyamele, C., Restar, A. J., Dolezal, C., & Sandfort, T. G. M. (2019). Substance use and depression among recently migrated African gay and bisexual men living in the United States. *Journal of Immigrant and Minority Health, 21*(6), 1224–1232.

Portman-Thompson, K. (2020). Implementing trauma-informed care in mental health services. *Mental Health Practice, 23*, 34–41. https://doi.org/10.7748/mhp.2020.e1443

Pratt-Chapman, M. L., Eckstrand, K., Robinson, A., Beach, L. B., Kamen, C., Keuroghlian, A. S., Cook, S., Radix, A., Bidell, M. P., Bruner, D., & Margolies, L. (2022). Developing standards for cultural competency training for health care providers to care for lesbian, gay, bisexual, transgender, queer, intersex, and asexual persons: Consensus recommendations from a national panel. *LGBT Health, 9*(5), 340–347.

Przeworski, A., & Piedra, A. (2020). The role of the family for sexual minority Latinx individuals: A systematic review and recommendations for clinical practice. *Journal of GLBT Family Studies, 16*(2), 211–240.

Quinn, G. P., Sutton, S. K., Winfield, B., Breen, S., Canales, J., Shetty, G., Sehovic, I., Green, B. L., & Schabath, M. B. (2015). Lesbian, gay, bisexual, transgender, queer/questioning (LGBTQ) perceptions and health care experiences. *Journal of Gay & Lesbian Social Services, 27*(2), 246–261. https://doi.org/10.1080/10538720.2015.1022273

Rasmussen, A., Crager, M., Baser, R. E., Chu, T., & Gany, F. (2012). Onset of posttraumatic stress disorder and major depression among refugees and voluntary migrants to the United States. *Journal of Traumatic Stress, 25*(6), 705–712.

Ray, N. (2006). *Lesbian, gay, bisexual and transgender youth: An epidemic of homelessness.* National Gay and Lesbian Task Force Policy Institute and the National Coalition for the Homeless.

Redcay, A., Luquet, W., & Huggin, M. E. (2019). Immigration and asylum for lesbian, gay, bisexual, and transgender individuals. *Journal of Human Rights and Social Work, 4*(4), 248–256.

Rhodes, S. D., Martinez, O., Song, E.-Y., Daniel, J., Alonzo, J., Eng, E., Duck, S., Downs, M., Bloom, F. R., Allen, A. B., Miller, C., & Reboussin, B. (2013). Depressive symptoms among immigrant Latino sexual minorities. *American Journal of Health Behavior, 37*(3), 404–413.

Rodriguez de los Reyes, G. O., & Collict, D. (2022). 'It's not only about clinical tools but also our role as agents of social change': Implementing a LGBT competency training for future mental health practitioners in Mexico. *Journal of Homosexuality, 69*(2), 230–253. https://doi-org.lmu.idm.oclc.org/10.1080/00918369.2020.1815433

Shidlo, A., & Ahola, J. (2013). Mental health challenges of LGBT forced migrants. *Forced Migration Review*, (42).

Shaw, A., & Verghese, N. (2022). *LGBTQI+ Refugees and Asylum Seekers.* The Williams Institute. https://williamsinstitute.law.ucla.edu/wp-content/uploads/LGBTQI-Refugee-Review-Jul-2022.pdf

Solórzano, R. R. (2020). Welcome to Cuban Miami: Linking place, race, and undocuqueer youth activism. In E. Luibhéid & K. R. Chávez (Eds.), *Queer and trans migrations* (pp. 106–124). University of Illinois Press.

Spike, J. (2025, April 8). *Protesters rally for the fourth week against Hungary's law banning LGBTQ+ Pride events.* Associated Press. https://apnews.com/article/hungary-protests-against-lgbtq-pride-ban-3ea6e7b74008ff472780468319dbe49a

Toro-Alfonso, J., Ortiz, M. L., & Lugo, K. N. (2012). Sexualidades migrantes: La emigración de hombres dominicanos gay. *Caribbean Studies, 40*(1), 59–80.

US Department of Homeland Security. (2017a). *2017 yearbook of immigration statistics.* https://ohss.dhs.gov/sites/default/files/2023-12/yearbook_immigration_statistics_2017_0.pdf

US Department of Homeland Security. (2017b). *Executive order: Enhancing public safety in the interior of the United States.* https://www.dhs.gov/archive/news/2017/02/21/fact-sheet-enhancing-public-safety-interior-united-states

Whitehurst, L. (2025, April 26). *Utah schools can ban pride flags under new law, governor says.* Associated Press. https://apnews.com/article/lgbtq-pride-flag-ban-utah-school-republican-ced0db22bd0ce8d37e010e9a65fec220

Yamanis, T., Malik, M., Del Río-González, A. M., Wirtz, A. L., Cooney, E., Lujan, M., Corado, R., & Poteat, T. (2018). Legal immigration status is associated with depressive symptoms among Latina transgender women in Washington, DC. *International Journal of Environmental Research and Public Health, 15*(6), 6.

Yamasaki, V., & Le, T. P. (2022). Family matters: The impact of traditional and egalitarian gender role messages on sexual and gender minority Latinx adults' alcohol use and sexual risk. *Journal of Sex Research, 59*(5), 652–661.

CHAPTER 7

Violence, Trauma, and Grievability at the US-Mexico Border: A Visual Communication Ethics Analysis

Leandra H. Hernández, Gabrielle Y. Garza, and Marissa Medina

Introduction

In 2019, a photo circulated in mediated spaces that depicted Óscar Alberto Martínez Ramírez and his 23-month-old daughter Valeria, who drowned while attempting to cross the border from Mexico to the United States. Martínez Ramírez and Valeria were traveling from El Salvador to the United States and were found drowned, face down, in the Rio Grande River, with her arm still draped around his neck. Photographer Julia Le Duc took the photo on June 24, 2019, and the photo later circulated on several news outlets and social media accounts. Journalists, podcasters, and scholars have long discussed the impacts of the photo, questioning whether it should have been taken in the first place and whether it should have been published (see Aguilera, 2019; Bogle, 2019; Da Silva, 2019).

Martínez Ramírez's case is one of many recent images of precarity at the US-Mexico border that represent the traumas and horrors that migrants face on their journey from various countries in Latin America to

L. H. Hernández (✉) • G. Y. Garza • M. Medina
Department of Communication, University of Utah, Salt Lake City, UT, USA

J. S. Hong et al. (eds.), *Violence and Trauma Without Borders*,
https://doi.org/10.1007/978-3-032-29221-6_7

the United States. The image also poses significant questions about ethics and consent, given the minor's age and the fact that they are no longer with us to speak about their own experiences. We also situate this case within the scores of migrants who have died either while crossing the US-Mexico border or arriving at the US-Mexico border. According to a recent report by *The Guardian*, over 100 migrants died at the US-Mexico border in 2024, a tenfold increase in the past two years, because of violence and environmental hazards ("More than 100 people died near the New Mexico border in 2024—a tenfold increase in two years," 2024). Thus, in this chapter, building upon concepts of precarity and grievability, we consider the media ethics and visual ethics implications of photovisual and journalistic representations of migration at the US-Mexico border and conclude with implications for journalists and practitioners regarding photovisual documentation of migrant trauma and death.

Literature Review

Mediated Representations of Latin American Migration

Representations of the border in the media have been critiqued by scholars from fields in media, communication, and beyond. Latin American migrants are often framed in negative and pejorative ways. Quinsaat's (2014) analysis of the framing of immigration in policy debates found that immigrants and immigration were often framed in diametrically opposed manners (necessary for nation building, assaults on national sovereignty, and cultural contamination, to name a few). In discourses related to the Border Protection, Anti-terrorism, and Illegal Immigration Control Act of 2005 (H.R. 4437) in 2006 and the Support Our Law Enforcement and Safe Neighborhoods Act or Arizona Senate Bill (S.B.) 1070 in 2010, immigrants were represented in news discourses as citizens integral to the nation, dispensable workers, criminals, invaders, and forever foreigners (Quinsaat, 2014). Ultimately, Quinsaat (2014) concluded that such discourses normalize power structures and fail to challenge historical and normative discourses on nationhood, minorities, social mobility, success, and a national ethos.

Lisa Flores' (2020) scholarship identified four prominent racialized discourses that have been utilized historically to frame Mexican migrants specifically: the illegal alien, the bracero, the zoot suiter, and the wetback. Flores (2020) argues that these four discourses have been deployed strategically at different time points in American history to position Mexican migrants as deportable, disposable, and illegal. Previous critiques of migrant representations in the media also highlight the problems with journalists' approaches to covering the migrant subject. The visuals and images of migrant crossings displayed throughout the news and social media have imminent impacts that *others* the migrant crossing the border in criminalizing and ultimately dehumanizing ways (Campbell, 2015; Jaramillo-Dent & Pérez-Rodríguez, 2021; Paynter & Riva, 2024; Scott, 2024). Alex Scott (2024) discovered that 88.5 percent of images collected by reporters focused more on the "journey" of migrating versus settlement and post-settlement moments of migration. Additionally, 90.4 percent of these "journey" moment images included some sort of authority figure, such as law enforcement and or border patrol agents, in physically dominant positions over the migrant subject, revealing symbolistic power. Scott (2024) found that journalists at the border often need to "embed" themselves with border patrol organizations to get access to certain "hot spots" of the border. In a sense, border patrol agents play the role of public relations practitioners between the media and the public when it comes to border representations. One of Scott's (2024) interviewees even recognizes that border patrol agents and representatives strategize where to take media professionals. The interviewee states, "I tried to keep a really heavy dose of skepticism, keeping in mind where it was they were taking me versus where they weren't taking me, what they were showing me versus what they were trying to keep me from seeing" (2024, p. 209). In this exchange between border patrol agents and the media, scholars in border studies acknowledge the role that law enforcement officials play in the production of the border "crisis" campaign and the imagery media consumers see.

Similar concerns have been raised about the framing of migrants through the lens of the migrant caravan, a discourse that gained prominence during Trump's first presidential administration. Regarding the otherness of migrant and border representation on social media platforms such as Instagram, Rosa and Soto-Vásquez's (2022) analysis of Instagram discourses on the migrant caravan revealed that such discourses were mostly mediated by professionals and organizations interested in promoting their work, not necessarily the migrants themselves. Rosa and Soto-Vásquez (2022) contextualize this finding within the aesthetics of otherness, defined as "the result of the interaction between platform users' selections and platform affordances that creates a gap between the marginalized other and the user" (p. 2). In a similar analysis, Daniela Jaramillo-Dent and María Amor Pérez-Rodríguez (2021) noted that a majority of posts using the hashtags #MigrantCaravan and #CaravanaMigrante were mostly written in English, meaning that a large part of the discourse about the migrant caravan on Instagram was controlled by the English-speaking community, making it possible to position migrants as *others* through language and linguistic choices (Jaramillo-Dent & Pérez-Rodríguez, 2021). Otherness was apparent in both anti- and pro-immigration posts by using words such as criminal, dangerous, victim, helpless, smuggle, gang member, sneak, and illegal immigrants (Jaramillo-Dent & Pérez-Rodríguez, 2021). This type of language on social media feeds border "crisis" campaigns, which keeps behaviors and actions displayed in migrant imagery as uncontrollable and wrong. By constantly positioning migration at the US-Mexico border as wrong, the media also create "migration deterrence campaigns" (Paynters & Riva, 2024). The media's use of metaphors is also used to evoke fear and insecurity about migrants and migration. Such metaphors include natural phenomena, crime, and terrorism to describe migrants, refugees, and the general process of migration (Arcimaviciene & Hamza Baglama, 2018). These rhetorical attempts to frame the dangers of migration across the US-Mexico border aim to dissuade people from migrating across borders around the globe. The violence of migrating across borders is hyper-focused throughout the media on *othering migrants*, which also criminalizes their decision to migrate and their journey. Further, representing migration as a choice negates the realities as to why people make the decision to migrate in the first place.

Further, representing migration as a choice individualizes the migration process, raises the possibility for culpability and blame, and has the potential to lend blame to individual migrants, as opposed fostering space to recognize and address the structural and systemic factors (international foreign policy, national intervention, etc.) that compel communities to migrate. For example, recent scholarship on forced family separation at the US-Mexico border and the border wall has found that negative and stereotypical framing of migrants persists with an individualistic lens to frame their choices. Kang and Yang's (2023) computational study of over 900 news articles identified six dominant news frames of migration and the border wall, with migrants referred to under clusters such as undocumented immigrants, illegal immigration, and voter fraud. Mills et al. (2023) conducted a thematic analysis of news coverage of detained migrants and found that young children were framed as vulnerable and innocent and in much more sympathetic ways. Migrant parents and adults, on the other hand, were framed negatively—news reports framed them as irresponsible parents and burdens on the system. Thus, news representations of Latin American migration work to *other* migrant bodies and exacerbate stereotypical representations of migrant families.

The Ethics of Media Framing of Migration

As we have illustrated thus far, representations of migration at the US-Mexico border highlight concerns associated with inequitable media representation. We assert that such inequities are, through the lens of trauma-informed ethics, foundationally hinged upon concepts of precarity and grievability. Reflecting upon 9/11 and its ensuing events, Butler (2004) considered the relationships among vulnerability, aggression, and precarity for individuals impacted differently on and after September 11, 2001. In theorizing the detainment of prisoners at Guantanamo Bay, Butler (2004) discussed "the normative conceptions of the human, that produce, through an exclusionary process, a host of 'unlivable lives' whose legal and political status is suspended" (p. xv). For Butler (2004), concepts such as "detention" or "indefinite detention" render individuals as dehumanized nonsubjects who fundamentally do not count as human, a concept that is useful for considering ontological and material framings of migrants detained at the US-Mexico border who are separated from family members, subjected to discursive and material violence, and rendered as noncitizens undeserving of justice or humanity. Their precarity and vulnerability are both a cause and outcome of their nonsubject position. As Butler (2004) illustrates:

> This means that each of us is constituted politically in part by virtue of the social vulnerability of our bodies—as a site of desire and physical vulnerability, as a site of publicity at once assertive and exposed. Loss and vulnerability seem to follow from our being socially constituted bodies, attached to others, at risk of losing those attachments, exposed to others, at risk of violence by virtue of that exposure. (p. 20)

Butler's discussions of precarity ultimately highlight the conditions, vulnerabilities, and contexts that render certain individuals more likely to be precarious, vulnerable, or at risk (Kaplan, 2021). The conceptualization of precarity, as Butler (2004) outlines and builds upon Levinas, also seeks to construct a nonviolent ethic based upon an understanding of "how easily human life is annulled," which has significant implications for how photovisual journalists understand and represent trauma at the US-Mexico border (p. xvii). In other words, building upon Levinas, Butler (2004) asks us "how best to depict the human, human grief, and suffering, and how best to admit the 'faces' of those against whom war is waged into public representation" (p. xviii). Thus, building upon concepts of precarity and grievability, we turn to the case of Óscar Alberto Martínez Ramírez and his 23-month-old daughter Valeria. We analyze this case in more detail and complicate the framing of their migration experiences. We explore some of the ethical tensions associated with their cases, the photovisual journalists' reasoning underpinning the taking and publishing of the photos, and conclude with implications for journalists and communication scholars about the precarity of photovisual documentation of the US-Mexico border. We selected this case as the focal point of this chapter because of its recency and its depiction of violence against migrant families, representations of migrants (particularly migrant children) without their consent, and the use of violent state actors to gain access to migrants for journalistic purposes. It was also selected because of the popularity and reach of their story, particularly in terms of the ethical news discourses generated after the dissemination of their photos.

Case Study Analysis

As Butler (2004) explains:

> Many people think that grief is privatizing, that it returns us to a solitary situation and is, in that sense, depoliticizing. But I think it furnishes a sense of political community of a complex order, and it does this first of all by bringing to the fore the relational ties that have implications for theorizing fundamental dependency and ethical responsibility. (p. 22)

In the case of the US-Mexico border, images of Óscar Alberto Martínez Ramírez and his daughter remind larger publics and news consumers of the malleability and social construction of borders in the first place. Given any other time frame, doctrine, treaty, or law, Martínez Ramírez and his daughter could have been anyone else of a different identity constellation, illustrating the ethical responsibility of journalists covering their stories at a microlevel and society's ethical responsibility and moral witnessing at a macrolevel. In highlighting our fundamental dependency on others, their cases also elucidate the precarity of our subject positions at any given moment and the relational ties that connect us through the grief of witnessing their photos. Butler (2004) further states, "If my fate is not originally or finally separable from yours, then the 'we' is traversed by a relationality that we cannot easily argue against; or, rather, we can argue against it, but we would be denying something fundamental about the *social* (emphasis ours) conditions of our very formation" (pp. 22–23).

Case Study: Óscar Alberto Martínez Ramírez and His Daughter, Valeria

The case of Óscar Alberto Martínez Ramírez and his 23-month-old daughter Valeria is an especially poignant look at the harm that the southern border can create. The photo of their drowned bodies on the shores of the Rio Grande River was touted by some as "real" and "raw" depictions of what can happen when people are desperate enough to try and cross. However, others have noted the exploitative and harmful nature of the photos and how sharing the photo is a disservice to the two and their family members, none of whom had a say in the capturing and sharing of the photo itself. As an attempt to demonstrate the reality of the southern border, both deaths are used to send various messages about border crossings; however, there are ethical considerations that must be addressed for taking a photo of dead children and disseminating it to the masses. What factors related to Valeria's dead body and migrant children's dead bodies are more likely to construct them as a media spectacle than other photos of dead children's bodies? This case study exemplifies the symptom of the long historical racial framing of migrants that leads to the racialized othering of the migrant child subject, which explains the media's tendency to publish photos of dead migrant children versus images of White or nonmigrant children's bodies. Therefore, media producers and audiences depend on this historical othering to desensitize themselves from the subject at hand. The othering apparent in this photo could also be understood as representative of Butler's (2004) idea of precarity. Valeria and her father's bodies demonstrate the precarity of migration due to them being concretized as migrants or criminals, limiting them to being seen as fully human.

For those who have had family members or loved ones who have faced harmful circumstances or even death at the southern border, this picture is a further reminder and can trigger some of our most vulnerable in bringing up those specific memories. Although some have argued that sharing the photo humanizes the situation and turns statistics into real people (Aguilera, 2019), others argue that, often due to the current state of our society, many people may see the photo and move on quickly or, in worst-case scenarios, may blame the victims for what happened (Da Silva, 2019). One immigrant organization had the following to say about the photo: "The media wants you to view them as just another tragedy, more [numbers] to rack up migrant deaths. They will show you the graphic image, saying it will make people 'care' or 'move them into action.' We think otherwise" (Da Silva, 2019). Desensitization has become a more common occurrence in our daily lives as people see more and more violent images such as this one over time (Bogle, 2019). Seeing this photo for some will not do any more to move them to action, as they do not associate with or care about migrant lives. Even for those who may also be immigrants, there is often a strong bias in favor of those who migrate "legally," and anyone who did not do so, or those coming from other countries of origin, may not be accepted. Considering the number of Mexican immigrants or those of Mexican descent who were pro-president leading up to the 2020 election (Soto-Vásquez & Hazelton, 2023), it becomes harder to say which audiences are identifying with or empathizing with such photos and stories.

Beyond the photo itself, there are ethical concerns regarding the story and its dissemination. Julie Le Duc, the photographer and journalist who took the photo, shared the context of the photo with several news outlets. However, it is important to note how she talks about getting the information about the deceased and their family. Le Duc mentioned how she happened to overhear the story and details being told to the police by the wife and mother of the two victims. Rather than speaking to the family member herself or getting permission to share the photos and details, she pieced together what she heard and moved forward with the photography process. This action raises significant ethical questions, as one of the victims of this tragedy is facing possible revictimization due to the ways in which Le Duc moved forward with the process. Another issue that arises when reading through articles covering this photo is that there were different accounts of what actually happened and how the two family members passed. The possibility of misinformation in sharing these photos and story raises further ethical questions, given the coverage of the migrants' lived experiences.

As we have discussed thus far, the media's choice to photograph and publish images of the dead is often met with ethical concerns, particularly in migration contexts. While some might justify the need for disseminating these types of traumatic images to show the "reality" of the border, others have criticized the dehumanizing aspects of photos and recommend avoiding sharing the photo for advocacy reasons. A *Newsweek* article written by Chantal Da Silva (2019) reported that the RAICES organization asked the public to "refrain from sharing the other image of their unjust death and instead honor them by sharing this image of this beautiful family in life" (2019, para. 19). The RAICES organization understands the rhetorical effect of the recirculation of the dead father and child as it allows viewers to *other* them as solely dead migrants crossing the border instead of looking at them as full human beings. Given platform affordances and user selection, there is an inevitable gap between the individuals represented in the images and the viewer/user in mediated contexts, allowing for the aesthetic of otherness (Rosa & Soto-Vásquez, 2022). The othering creates a comfortable distance for the viewer, as the subject is somehow less human than them, leading to the lack of grievability (Butler, 2004) of migrant children's bodies. The lack of grievability of migrant children's bodies makes it palatable for viewers and producers, whereas images of White, nonmigrant children receive a more empathetic response, leading to more ethical considerations that migrant children are not privy to. Höijer (2004) argues that we need to view representations of death in the news in their relevant social, historical, and cultural context. Socially, politically, and discursively, the White, nonmigrant child subject is fiercely protected from death in the dominant US cultural context, which is exemplified in the way their death is routinely reported on the media; however, in this case, migrants crossing the U.S.-Mexico border are often viewed as non-grievable because of the framing of their actions.

Further, depicting children in distressed conditions leads to harsh criticism of parents and further feeds the "crossing at the border as a choice" narrative. The first *Guardian* article of the story, reported and written by Julie Le Duc, intended to use the photograph as a visual example to show the dangers and risks of crossing the US-Mexico border. Le Duc writes, "I've been a crime reporter for many years, and I've seen a lot of bodies—and a lot of drownings. The Río Bravo [Rio Grande] is a very strong river: you think it's just shallow, but there are lots of currents and whirlpools" (2019, para 10). Another article published by *The Guardian* titled "Shocking photo of drowned father and daughter highlights migrants' border peril," written by Patrick Timmons, Martin Hodgson, and David Agren (2019), echoed similar concerns about crossing the Rio Grande. They write, "So far this year, dozens of people have died attempting to cross the Rio Grande, where water levels are at their highest levels in 20 years and record levels of snowmelt run-off have transformed the river into a raging torrent" (2019, para. 5). Both messages include rhetorical messages that could be viewed as attempts to dissuade people to cross the river; however, at the same time, using Óscar and Valeria's dead bodies as a representative for dangerous outcomes further positions Óscar's border crossing as a choice. Furthermore, using their bodies to emulate the "border crisis" strips both of their agency, limiting the story of their lives to this devastating moment.

Discussion and Concluding Thoughts

As scholars have long noted, the use of suffering children's photos in larger discourses of trauma, crisis, and war is not new (Mortensen, 2017; Mortensen et al., 2017; Vis & Goriunova, 2015); however, as Berents (2019) illustrates, what is new is the circulation of dead children to report on contexts of trauma and in the pursuit of various outcomes. Our chapter contributes to this growing discussion by interrogating the ethics of one photovisual case study representation of migration at the US-Mexico border: Óscar Alberto Martínez Ramírez and his daughter, Valeria (who passed away before her photo was taken and circulated). Through the lens of precarity and grievability, we explored how this case study framed the violence inflicted upon families during their migration process from Latin America to the United States. In the case of Óscar and his daughter, they died while migrating, and photos of their death continue to circulate in the mass media, thus cementing the memorialization of their lives in the moment of their death. As Berents (2019) notes, scholars must continue to interrogate the circulation of photos of dead bodies—and dead children in particular—because of their cultural impacts on how individuals make sense of cultural others. In other words, as Hallam, Hockey, and Howarth (1999) assert, dead bodies can be "socially alive/biologically dead" (pp. 2–3), with children's bodies and corpses functioning "not as an unfortunate accident of the international system but rather as part of how the international system functions" (Berents, 2019, p. 150). Through a media ethics lens, we are fundamentally concerned with considerations of age, agency, consent, privacy, and memorialization, particularly when photos are taken without migrant consent and then later circulated and detached from the context at hand. In other words, what sorts of telegenic purposes do the photos serve in eliciting some sort of response from viewers or, as Berents (2019) asks us to consider, in consuming photos of dead children, "there is a tension between the real fleshy bodies of deceased children and the symbolism of their circulation" (p. 147). Further, in the instances of photovisual representations of migrant children, the symbolism of their circulation results in a further othering of the migrant child subject. Fishman (2017) asserts that photojournalistic representations of dead children overwhelmingly highlight the deaths of non-American, or "foreign," children, further highlighting both the extreme precarity and lack of grievability of non-American children's lives.

We question what it might look like for journalists to further consider the role of bearing witness when discussing migration from Latin America to the United States. Through the lens of witnessing, framing migrants in a more empathetic and humanizing way raises the potential for readers to (1) become more educated on the subject, (2) connect empathetically with migrant families, and (3) engage in some sort of action, whether that be writing to politicians, talking about it with others, or joining a rally, for example (Hernández, Alvarado, & De Los Santos Upton, forthcoming). Pantti (2020) explains that the cultivation of empathy in journalism, which is essential for mobilizing audiences to action, remains a controversial issue because the call to bear witness to suffering in ways that point audiences toward moral indignation and action also runs counter to the ideals of objectivity and detachment normalized in traditional approaches to journalism. Witnessing is powerful because it can position audiences to speak and intervene in injustice, and it can enable audiences to connect to stories and global injustices in more humane ways (Pantti, 2020).

Moreover, another important component of photovisual documentation of the US-Mexico border that deserves further interrogation is the overrepresentation of trauma and pain and the underrepresentation of joy. The mediated overrepresentation of death essentializes the US-Mexico border and its subjects—migrants, families, and others—within constant hyperviolence and positions its subjects as lacking agency, joy, or any other experience. When images are chosen and circulated with a focus on violence, conflict, and/or destruction, photojournalists and editors "leave behind countless other images that signify what this moment is about for the people who live with oppression every day" (Elian, 2020). By overdetermining representations of trauma, pain, and violence, migrants are essentialized through a matrix of power that restricts the representational possibilities of joy and humanity and obscures the power of the state in constructing contexts that force migrants to flee from their home countries.

Several photographers have sought to counter such representations of migrant violence and death with those of joy, such as Venezuelan journalist Alejandro Cegarra. He won the 2024 World Press Photo contest with his photography of migrants in Mexico, and his photography explores themes of vulnerability and belonging. Working with the *New York Times*, Cegarra's award-winning long-term photography project entitled "Los Dos Muros" (The Two Walls) "documents the vulnerability of migrant communities attempting to make it to the United States across the Mexico border, illustrating the front line of the global migration crisis" (Laksman, 2024, para. 2). One photo in the project documents migrants crossing the river that separates Guatemala and Mexico, and another photo documents the fences in between Mexico and Guatemala and Mexico and the United States. While the aforementioned photos are indeed powerful, two other photos that caught our attention include (1) his photo of young migrant children playing with bubbles and (2) his photo of Rosa Bello and Rubén Soto sitting atop a train car, smiling at each other lovingly. Cegarra described how Bello and Soto fell in love during their journey and later noted that their photo was one that all viewers could identify with (Laksman, 2024). Both photos rehumanize the migrants depicted and also emphasize the joy and humanity that individuals can continue to feel amid sorrow and trauma. Cegarra also noted his personal feelings about photographing migrants in migration, such that he often felt shocked and lonely during the long journey. However, he was encouraged to continue his photography through the connections he developed with fellow migrants: "Alejandro told his own story, and the migrants told him theirs. Photographing gave him a sense of human embrace that both enveloped him and made him feel small. Not only did Alejandro share a seat with the migrants, but land and blood as well" (Laksman, 2024, para. 7). Only when journalists are supported in changing their framing and their approaches can visual representations of the US-Mexico border fully tell humanizing and empathetic stories about migrants and migration.

References

Aguilera, J. (2019, June 27). How controversy over the photo of a drowned migrant father and daughter captured the profound cost of the border crisis. *Time*. https://time.com/5614807/photo-migrant-death-border-crisis/

Arcimaviciene, L., & Baglama, S. H. (2018). Migration, metaphor and myth in media representations: The ideological dichotomy of "Them" and "Us". *SAGE Open*, *8*(2), 2158244018768657. https://doi.org/10.1177/2158244018768657

Berents, H. (2019). Apprehending the "telegenic dead": Considering images of dead children in global politics. *International Political Sociology*, *13*(2), 145–160.

Bogle, E. (2019, June 26). The argument for – And against – Publishing the traumatic photo from Mexican border. *NPR*. https://www.npr.org/sections/pictureshow/2019/06/26/736361547/the-argument-for-and-against-publishing-the-traumatic-photo-from-mexican-border

Butler, J. (2004). *Precarious life: The powers of mourning and violence*. Verso.

Campbell, K. M. (2015). Dry hate: White supremacy and anti-immigrant rhetoric in the humanitarian crisis on the U.S.-Mexico border. *West Virginia Law Review*, *117*(3), 1081–1130.

Da Silva, C. (2019, June 27). Stop sharing 'Dehumanizing' photo of drowned migrant father and daughter, immigration groups say: 'Before they were migrants, they were a family'. *Newsweek*. https://www.newsweek.com/father-child-rio-grande-deaths-photo-oscar-alberto-martinez-ramirez-valeria-1446238

Elian, M. B. (2020). In photographing social justice protests, respect means 'looking again'." *Niemanreports.org*. https://niemanreports.org/articles/inphotographing-social-justice-protests-respect-means-looking-again/

Fishman, J. M. (2017). *Death makes the news: How the media censor and display the dead*. NYU Press.

Flores, L. A. (2020). *Deportable and disposable: Public rhetoric and the making of the "illegal" immigrant*. Penn State Press.

Höijer, B. (2004). The discourse of global compassion: The audience and media reporting of human suffering. *Media, Culture & Society*, *26*(4), 513–531.

Jaramillo-Dent, D., & Pérez-Rodríguez, M. A. (2021). #MigrantCaravan: The border wall and the establishment of otherness on Instagram. *New Media & Society*, *23*(1), 121–141.

Kang, Y., & Yang, K. C. (2023). Communicating racism and xenophobia in the era of Donald Trump: A computational framing analysis of the US-Mexico cross-border wall discourses. In C. Onwumechili (Ed.), *Donald J. Trump's presidency* (pp. 26–45). Routledge.

Kaplan, H. (2021). Framing precarity through images of the grievable life of children. *Studies in Art Education*, *62*(4), 325–338.

Laksman, M. (2024, July 10). Alejandro Cegarra's haunting photos of migrants in Mexico: 2024 World Press photo contest winner. *Orato*. https://orato.world/2024/07/10/alejandro-cegarras-haunting-photos-of-migrants-in-mexico-2024-world-press-photo-contest-winner/

Mills, J., Oliveira, R., & Gomes, S. (2022). Lives in cages: A media analysis of incarceration experiences across generations on the US-Mexico border. In *Incarceration and generation, volume II: Challenging generational relations* (pp. 227–272).

Mills, J. M., Gomes, S., & Walzak, J. (2023). "The press has gone crazy": Online media and political rhetoric of immigrants in the USA. *International Journal of Migration and Border Studies, 7*(3), 215–238. https://doi.org/10.1504/IJMBS.2023.130741

"More than 100 people died near the New Mexico border in 2024 – a tenfold increase in two years." (2024, October 15). *The Guardian*. https://www.theguardian.com/us-news/2024/oct/15/deaths-new-mexico-border-immigration

Mortensen, M. (2017). Constructing, confirming, and contesting icons: The Alan Kurdi imagery appropriated by #humanitywashedashore, Ai Weiwei, and Charlie Hebdo. *Media, Culture & Society, 39*(8), 1142–1161.

Mortensen, M., Allan, S., & Peters, C. (2017). The iconic image in a digital age: Editorial mediations over the Alan Kurdi photographs. *Nordicom Review, 38*(s2), 71–86.

Pantti, M. (2020). Journalism and witnessing. In K. Wahl-Jorgensen & T. Hanitzsch (Eds.), *The handbook of journalism studies*. Routledge.

Paynter, E., & Riva, S. (2024). Performing border externalisation: Media deterrence campaigns and neoliberal belonging. *Geopolitics, 29*(4), 1272–1296. https://doi.org/10.1080/14650045.2023.2234826

Quinsaat, S. (2014). Competing news frames and hegemonic discourses in the construction of contemporary immigration and immigrants in the United States. *Mass Communication and Society, 17*(4), 573–596.

Rosa, F. R., & Soto-Vásquez, A. D. (2022). Aesthetics of otherness: Representation of #migrantcaravan and #caravanamigrante on Instagram. *Social Media + Society, 8*(1), 20563051221087623.

Scott, A. (2024). Visions of migration: News images and the production of knowledge on the U.S. Southern Border. *Journalism & Communication Monographs, 26*(3), 176–247.

Soto-Vásquez, A. D., & Hazelton, A. J. (2023). Latinos for Trump: 2020 US election results: Why did so many Latinos back Trump?. In The perils of populism: The end of the American century? (pp. 221–238). Cham: Springer Nature Switzerland.

Vis, F., & Goriunova, O. (Eds.). (2015). *The iconic image on social media: A rapid research response to the death of Aylan Kurdi*. Visual Social Media Lab.

CHAPTER 8

Child Maltreatment in Immigrant Families

Jun Sung Hong and Mijin Choi

Introduction

Maltreatment, which includes physical abuse, sexual abuse, emotional abuse, and neglect (Fortson et al., 2016), continues to be a pressing concern despite countless efforts that have been made to stop the abuse and protect children and adolescents. According to the World Health Organization (2024), nearly 3 in 4 children, or 300 million children (age 2–4 years), experience physical violence and/or psychological violence by their caregivers. In the United States, 7,176,600 children were referred for alleged child maltreatment in 2021, according to the US Department of Health and Human Services (2023). For the survivors of child maltreatment, there are numerous health, mental health, social, and educational consequences (Fitton et al., 2020; Jonson-Reid et al., 2012; Kaplow & Widom, 2007; Romano et al., 2015). Survivors of maltreatment are at an increased risk of internalizing and externalizing mental health problems

J. S. Hong (✉)
School of Social Work, Wayne State University, Detroit, MI, USA
e-mail: fl4684@wayne.edu

M. Choi
School of Social Work, Texas State University, San Marcos, TX, USA
e-mail: m_c951@txstate.edu

J. S. Hong et al. (eds.), *Violence and Trauma Without Borders*,
https://doi.org/10.1007/978-3-032-29221-6_8

(Vilariño et al., 2022), PTSD in adulthood (Rameckers et al., 2021), sleep disturbances (Brown et al., 2022), school maladaptation (Zhang et al., 2025), low life success (Najman et al., 2023), and suicidal ideation (Berardelli et al., 2022).

Although maltreatment affects all children, for some children, their risk of maltreatment may be even higher. Children in immigrant families, for example, are especially at risk of abuse, which tends to go unreported. Over the past few decades, there has been a dramatic increase in the number of children of immigrants, migrants, and refugees in the United States (Migration Policy Institute, n.d.). Despite the increasing presence of children of immigrants, information on the maltreatment of these children has been severely limited, as research focusing on the experiences of children in immigrant families is scant (Seon, 2021). However, understanding the experiences in maltreatment of children in immigrant families is critical, since the child welfare system and child protective service workers are increasingly called upon to provide culturally competent social services for children and families of immigrant backgrounds. Children in immigrant families are vulnerable to maltreatment at home. Many immigrants reside in impoverished and disorganized neighborhoods; experience racial discrimination, microaggressions, and xenophobia; live in fear of arrests and deportation; and experience a vast assortment of additional stressors (Dettlaff & Earner, 2012; Kohli & Fineran, 2020; Rasmussen et al., 2012), which could exacerbate physical and psychological aggression resulting in child abuse. The aim of this chapter is to expand our understanding of abuse in immigrant families by providing an overview of maltreatment in four major immigrant communities (African/Black, Latina/o/x/e, Asian, and Muslim), which is followed by a discussion of implications for research, practice, and policy.

Maltreatment in Immigrant Communities

African/Black Immigrants

The Pew Research Center found that the number of Black immigrants in the United States, which includes immigrants from Africa and the Caribbean, reached 4.6 million in 2019 (Tamir, 2022). Also, according to the Migration Policy Institute (2022), the prevalence of the sub-Saharan African immigrant population is small but growing substantially. In 2019, approximately 2.1 million sub-Saharan Africans were living in the United

States. Sub-Saharan African migrants bring with them their traditional cultural beliefs, values, attitudes, and practices when it comes to parenting (Mugadza et al., 2019). Collectivist cultural values have been the reference for parenting among sub-Saharan African parents who commonly employ an authoritarian parenting style, which is characterized by high demands and low responsiveness (Mugadza et al., 2019). Sub-Saharan African parents also have very high expectations of their children and display a low level of nurturance. Many expect obedience and respect for elders from their children, and using corporal punishment as a disciplinary method is common (Mugadza et al., 2019). Due to a lack of understanding and training regarding cultural differences, their risk of being involved in the US child welfare system is high.

In general, research studies on maltreatment experienced by sub-Saharan African migrant children are limited. However, one study qualitatively explored sub-Saharan African immigrant parents' involvement in the US child welfare system. The study found that child abuse was one of the most common reasons sub-Saharan Africans get involved in the US child welfare system (Deedat et al., 2023). According to one study participant, "…as Africans we perceive to be minor, you can end up losing your child for something as simple as caning a child…." (Deedat et al., 2023, p. 29). The study participants also stated that neglect was the most frequently discussed reason for becoming entangled with the child welfare system. Another study participant said, "you are a SSA [sub-Saharan African] immigrant parent and you don't bring your child to school, neglect your child, don't feed your child, then you will become involved with the child welfare system" (Deedat et al., 2023, p. 30).

In Palm Beach County, Florida, which consists of more than 100 ethnicities, Haitians are the largest group of immigrants (LaFalaise, 2017). The rate of abuse allegations was reported to be significantly higher for this group compared to other cultures (LaFalaise, 2017). However, it is important to note that in the Haitian American community, parenting is influenced by Haitian culture and the American surroundings, resulting in the complex interplay of traditional practices and the pursuit of effective childrearing (Domond, 2024).

Latina/o/x/e Immigrants

In 2021, close to 20 million Latino immigrants resided in the United States, accounting for one-third (31.8%) of the nation's total population

(Haner & Lopez, 2023). Of these, approximately 2.6 million immigrants arrived in the United States five years before 2021 (Haner & Lopez, 2023). Being a parent is highly valued in Latina/o/x/e cultures (Fontes, 2002), and many Hispanics/Latinos value closeness and interconnectedness among family and extended family members (*familismo*). For Latina/o/x/e families, children are expected to be well behaved (*bien educado*), as it is a reflection on them; as a result, when a Latina/o/x/e parent observes their child misbehaving, they are likely to respond immediately, which can place them at risk for involvement in the child welfare system (Fontes, 2002). Latina/o/x/e children are the fastest-growing ethnic minority group in the United States, and the proportion of reported maltreatment among Latina/o/x/e children has also been increasing (Dettlaff & Johnson, 2011). Interestingly, immigrant children are slightly underrepresented among children who enter the child welfare system in comparison to the general population (Dettlaff & Johnson, 2011). A study using a nationally representative sample concluded that children with foreign-born parents consisted of 8.6% of all children who entered the child welfare system compared to 23% of the overall population (Dettlaff & Earner, 2009).

Several studies have investigated the antecedents of maltreatment among Latina/o/x/e immigrant families. One study, which estimated the proportion of Latino children with noncitizen parents in the child welfare system, identified several risks facing noncitizen parents, including financial difficulties, low educational attainment, and neighborhood disorganization (Cardoso et al., 2014). Despite these risks, children of noncitizen parents did not have a higher rate of substantiated maltreatment than those with US-born parents (Cardoso et al., 2014). Another study, which identified predictors of child maltreatment among migrant and nonmigrant Puerto Rican children, also reported that poverty was among the most salient predictors of maltreatment for migrant and nonmigrant families (Sledjeski et al., 2009). However, the association between poverty and child maltreatment is complex and may vary by ethnic group. For instance, Johnson-Motoyama et al.'s (2015) study explored whether maternal foreign-born status conferred a protective advantage against maltreatment among the Hispanic-origin group. The study found that the risk of substantiation among infants of Mexican and Central/South American mothers was lower than that of the Puerto Rican and Cuban mothers, despite being economically disadvantaged.

Over the years, risk factors that increase the odds of maltreatment have been documented in the research literature. In comparison, research on the protective factors is limited, although growing. Scholars have come to recognize the importance of identifying protective factors that could decrease the risks and the detrimental outcomes of maltreatment. Scholars have observed that not every child who is maltreated has poor outcomes; some children may cope successfully with maltreatment and have positive outcomes (see Crouch et al., 2019). Some studies have examined protective factors that are associated with lower risks of maltreatment among Latina/o/x/e immigrant families, such as social support (Bailey et al., 2015). Two studies also explored the protective effect of a large presence of foreign-born immigrants (Kim & Kim, 2023; Tejeda et al., 2024) in maltreatment among Latina/o/x/e children. In recent years, the "Hispanic paradox" has been applied to explain better-than-expected health, educational, and social outcomes of children in Hispanic immigrant families. According to the Hispanic paradox, many Hispanic immigrants encounter several risks, such as poverty and racism, for example. However, they tend to have better than expected outcomes, especially compared to US-born Hispanics or the general US population (Tejeda et al., 2024). Certain cultural values (e.g., familism), strong social supports within the Latina/o/x/e community, and healthy habits (e.g., high consumption of legumes) might protect Latina/o/x/es from negative outcomes of the various risks they encounter (Abraído-Lanza et al., 2016; Young & Hopkins, 2014). One study, which used national child maltreatment and census data to explore the protective effects of the Hispanic paradox, reported that counties with a higher percentage of foreign-born Hispanics have lower rates of child maltreatment; however, the protective effects of the Hispanic paradox may diminish generationally (Tejeda et al., 2024).

Asian Immigrants

Asian Americans are one of the fastest-growing groups in the United States. Over the past two decades, the number of Asian Americans has increased by 88% from 11.9 million in 2000 to 22.4 million by 2019, accounting for approximately 7 percent in the United States (Pew Research Center, 2021). Additionally, according to the Pew Research Center (2024a), Asian Americans are the racial or ethnic group in the United

States with the highest proportion of immigrants. As of 2022, of the 24 million Asian Americans, 54% are immigrants.

Asian American children have consistently been reported to experience lower rates of child maltreatment compared to other racial and ethnic groups in the United States (Zhai & Gao, 2009). In 2023, they had the lowest rates of maltreatment among all racial and ethnic groups, at 1.2 per 1000 children, compared to the national rate of 7.4 per 1000 children (U.S. Department of Health & Human Services, 2025). In addition, Asian children are disproportionately underrepresented among maltreated children, accounting for 5.6% of the child population in the USA, but only 0.9% of all maltreated children.

It is reported that Asian American children have a high rate of physical abuse and a low rate of neglect compared to the national averages (Zhai & Gao, 2009). A study analyzing Korean maltreatment incident reports revealed that physical abuse was the most common form of maltreatment, followed by neglect and emotional abuse (Chang et al., 2006). Furthermore, one-fourth of the victims experienced multiple forms of maltreatment, with the most frequent combinations being physical abuse paired with emotional abuse or neglect. Compared to other racial and ethnic groups in the same region, Korean immigrant families were more likely to be charged with physical abuse and less likely to be charged with neglect. Similarly, in a study of Vietnamese child maltreatment case files, Rhee et al. (2012) reported that the most prevalent type of maltreatment was physical abuse, followed by neglect and sexual abuse. This high incidence of physical abuse has been consistently observed across diverse subgroups of Asian Americans (Rhee et al., 2008; Tajima & Harachi, 2010), suggesting that it may be linked to cultural approval of corporal discipline and the practice of corporal punishment (Rhee et al., 2012; Segal, 2000).

Traditionally, American parents, especially White middle-class parents, have emphasized the importance of an authoritative parenting style, which strikes a balance between structure and nurture. According to Baumrind (2013), parents who employ an authoritative parenting style set clear boundaries for their children but also provide the support they need. In contrast, Asian parents have upheld filial piety and familism, based on Confucian philosophy, emphasizing a hierarchical family structure, respect for elders, male-dominated patriarchal authority (Chang et al., 2006; Zhai & Gao, 2009), and the importance of an authoritarian parenting style. Although these values have gradually shifted among immigrant parents—shaped by the dominant US culture and evolving societal norms in South

Korea—they continue to influence child-rearing practices, interparental relationships, and parent-child dynamics. In particular, differences in culturally expected behavioral norms between Asian immigrant families and American culture may lead to the use of traditionally accepted discipline, such as corporal punishment.

While child maltreatment among Asian immigrants is an underexplored area of research (Yoon et al., 2023), several studies have documented the antecedents and protective factors of child maltreatment within these communities. A study with first-generation Asian immigrants revealed that higher levels of parenting stress are associated with an increased risk of child maltreatment (Yoon et al., 2023). The study highlighted how parenting stress is associated with negative parenting behaviors, the use of strict discipline, an authoritarian parenting style, and disruptions in parents' cognitive-emotional processes, all of which may contribute to child maltreatment. Furthermore, new immigrants and refugees often face environmental challenges such as isolation from support systems, communication barriers, financial difficulties, and feelings of powerlessness. These challenges may prompt some parents to use traditional forms of punishment as a way to shield their children from the influences of US culture they view as unfavorable (Zhai & Gao, 2009).

Another study identified several contributing factors to the occurrence of child maltreatment among Korean immigrant families, including excessive discipline through corporal punishment, family conflicts stemming from parental relationship issues, inadequate parenting skills, inability to provide appropriate care, and parental mental health. Additionally, emotional abuse was most reported in circumstances where children were exposed to spousal domestic violence, inferring the need for a holistic approach to preventing spouse abuse and child abuse (Chang et al., 2006).

At the same time, Zhai and colleagues (2009) highlighted that the Asian culture's emphasis on indulging and protecting infants and toddlers may function as a protective factor against maltreatment in young children, noting the lower maltreatment reports for younger children in this group compared to other racial/ethnic groups, which reported higher maltreatment rates for younger children. Furthermore, the cultural taboos surrounding sexuality and incest in many Asian cultures may act as protective factors in preventing potential perpetrators from committing sexual abuse due to the fear of losing face.

In addition, studies have focused on specific groups of Asian immigrant families to identify the antecedents and protective factors of child maltreatment. A study, which was grounded in an ecological perspective, examined various factors influencing Korean mothers' beliefs in the use of physical punishment and perceptions regarding physical abuse (Park, 2001). At the microsystem level, mothers who experienced higher levels of family acculturation conflicts were more likely to report positive beliefs about the use of physical punishment. However, mothers who had been physically punished as children were less likely to hold positive beliefs about physical punishment. At the exosystem level, mothers with higher levels of education are less likely to hold positive perceptions of physical abuse. Lastly, at the macrosystem level, higher levels of perceived discrimination as immigrants and positive societal attitudes toward corporal punishment were identified as influential factors for positive belief in the use of physical punishment (Park, 2001). Similarly, parents' unfamiliarity with mainstream American cultural norms regarding child discipline and child protection laws, as well as acculturation stress—stemming from limited social interaction with other ethnic groups, limited education, and lack of English fluency—has been noted as a potential contributing factor to child welfare involvement among Vietnamese families (Rhee et al., 2012).

Notably, despite several studies on factors influencing child maltreatment, it remains unclear whether the disproportionately low occurrence of child maltreatment among immigrant families reflects an actual lower incidence or underreporting. Such underreporting may be influenced by cultural values, including reluctance to report incidents involving family members, unwillingness to disclose stigmatized behaviors, or unfamiliarity with US child welfare laws and systems (Larsen et al., 2008; Lau et al., 2006).

Muslim Immigrants

Muslims are the fastest-growing population in the world (Park et al., 2012). In the United States, the Muslim population is diverse and growing, estimated at 3.45 million people (Pew Research Center, 2024b). The Muslim community comprises immigrants and the children of immigrants (Pew Research Center, 2024b) from countries with a high prevalence of Muslims (e.g., the Middle East). Like parents of other racial and religious groups, parents in Muslim societies are strictly responsible for providing for their children's material needs (e.g., housing). However, Muslim parents also assume the responsibility of ensuring that their children's spiritual needs are being met (Akin, 2012).

However, Muslim immigrants, who are typically Arab, Middle Eastern, and North African, experience various types of traumas in the United States, including historical and intergenerational trauma (Atari-Khan et al., 2024) due to terrorist attacks or wars in the homeland, which could undermine their parenting practices. They are also at an elevated risk of other forms of stressors, most notably, Islamophobia, which stems from misunderstanding and negative public perceptions of the Islamic faith. The prevalence of Islamophobia and hate crimes against Muslims, as well as those perceived as Muslims (e.g., South Asians), skyrocketed after 9/11 in 2001 (Al Atom, 2014). These stressors can negatively affect relationships in the family and possibly reinforce domestic violence. However, it is important to recognize that trauma and stressors affect everyone differently, and some may try to alleviate trauma and stressors through self-medicating (e.g., alcohol use), compulsive (e.g., overeating), impulsive, and/or self-harm behaviors (Center for Substance Abuse Treatment, 2014). For others, trauma could trigger a violent response, which may be due to disruptions in brain development, such as changes in the structure and function of multiple stress-sensitive areas, such as the hippocampus, prefrontal cortex, and the amygdala (Cross et al., 2017). Disruptions in brain development could lead to changes in emotional regulation and impulse control, making it difficult to control anger and frustration, leading to increased odds of developing abusive and violent behaviors. Also, although Islamic teachings of childcare in the Muslim world overlap with child protection in the Western world, there are some contested positions, which could result in the involvement of child protection services (O'Leary et al., 2020). To date, empirical studies on child maltreatment in Muslim immigrant families are limited. However, one study examined the prevalence, beliefs, and demographic predictors of parent-to-child physical violence among South Asian, Middle Eastern, East Asian, and Latina women in the United States (Maker et al., 2005). The study found that 73% of the South Asian and Middle Eastern sample reported experiencing at least one type of physical abuse.

Implications for Research

Although studies have documented the prevalence of child maltreatment and its antecedents among specific racial and ethnic immigrant families, the within-group variability among diverse subgroups in patterns of child maltreatment has not been fully studied. Additionally, within a group, specific subgroups may be over- or under-represented, as differences exist across subgroups (Pelczarski & Kemp, 2006). This should be considered when collecting and interpreting data. In addition, future studies with more representative samples are recommended.

Second, despite the importance of cultural factors among immigrant families in influencing the incidence of child maltreatment (Yoon et al., 2023), studies examining the trajectories of acculturation and their link to child maltreatment are limited. Longitudinal studies are recommended to identify how cultural factors within immigrant families impact child maltreatment as the acculturation process progresses. Additionally, considering the intersection of multiple factors and cultural influences, culturally grounded qualitative methods are recommended (Schwartz et al., 2015).

Third, immigrants vary in legal status, age, length of stay in the United States, number of generations, reasons for migration, socioeconomic conditions in their country of origin, linguistic backgrounds, and cultural perceptions regarding child maltreatment (Kuper, 2023). These heterogeneous factors should be considered in future research to identify elements impacting child maltreatment.

Barriers and Implications for Practice and Policy

Although empirical evidence on child maltreatment in immigrant communities is limited, maltreatment is a major concern. However, the importance of expanding maltreatment prevention and intervention was acknowledged by the government, resulting in the passage of the Family First Prevention Services Act (FFPSA) in 2018. The FFPSA expanded the breadth of federally reimbursable evidence-based programs that are designed to prevent entry into the child welfare system (Finno-Velasquez et al., 2023). Although this is a step in a positive direction, there are numerous challenges for both child welfare and legal systems, according to Dettlaff and Finno-Velasquez (2013). Most child welfare systems do not have sufficient information or knowledge of immigrant policies and are ill-equipped to assist immigrant children or parents in addressing these issues. The higher risk of involvement in the child welfare system among certain immigrant groups, such as Sub-Saharan Africans, is likely due to cultural differences. Certain aspects of the parenting practices of immigrants may be misconstrued as abuse in the mainstream society. Also, due to racial bias in the US child welfare system (Ellis, 2019), a disproportionate number of racial minority and immigrant children have been removed from their homes and placed in foster care—a phenomenon that prompted the abolitionist movement, a collaborative movement aimed at abolishing the child welfare system (Dettlaff et al., 2020).

Moreover, a dearth of culturally or linguistically relevant social services is another major concern, resulting in miscommunication and misunderstandings, which could affect families' participation in the intervention. For immigrant children in the child welfare system due to maltreatment, a lack of culturally or linguistically relevant services could limit them from receiving the needed services to address physical and mental health needs (Finno-Velasquez et al., 2023). Thus, increasing culturally or linguistically relevant social services is warranted and could potentially be achieved by increasing culturally and linguistically competent training in social work. With an increased recognition of racial/ethnic disparities in social services, culturally competent services have increased over the years, which may be important for acceptability, initial engagement, and retention in services (Beasley et al., 2014).

Additionally, research and practice in child maltreatment have concentrated largely on identifying and intervening in risk and protective factors at the individual and family levels (Molnar et al., 2016). It is important to assess community-level factors, such as disorganized neighborhoods, for example, and consider community-based programs aimed at preventing maltreatment (see McLeigh et al., 2017).

Finally, child and immigrant advocates need to consider how the current immigration policies, including policing of and raiding immigrant and refugee communities, potentially impact children's experiences with maltreatment or entering the child welfare systems. Such policies are likely to result in lower reporting of incidents of maltreatment due to fear of deportation. Ultimately, the victims will continue to suffer as their cries will likely go unheeded.

References

Abraído-Lanza, A. F., Echeverría, S. E., & Flórez, K. R. (2016). Latino immigrants, acculturation, and health: Promising new directions in research. *Annual Review of Public Health, 37*(1), 219–236.

Akin, M. (2012). *Exploring theology and practice in Islamic parenting* [unpublished master's thesis]. University of Central Florida. ProQuest.

Al Atom, B. (2014). Examining the trends of islamophobia Western public attitudes since 9/11. *Studies in Sociology of Science, 5*(3), 83–88.

Atari-Khan, R., Alshabani, N., Rabgay, S. D., Elhedk, F. R., Clifford, A., Gomariz, S., & Sahib, W. (2024). *Understanding intergenerational trauma among Arab, Middle Eastern, and North African (Arab/MENA) Americans.* Qualitative Psychology. Advanced online publication. https://doi.org/10.1037/qup0000310

Bailey, A. M., Brazil, A. M., Conrad-Hiebner, A., & Counts, J. (2015). Protective factors among Latino families involved with child welfare: A review of Spanish protective factor research on child maltreatment prevention in seven countries. *Children and Youth Services Review, 55*, 93–102.

Baumrind, D. (2013). Authoritative parenting revisited: History and current status. In R. E. Larzelere, A. S. Morris, & A. W. Harrist (Eds.), *Authoritative parenting: Synthesizing nurturance and discipline for optimal child development* (pp. 11–34). American Psychological Association.

Beasley, L. O., Silovsky, J. F., Owora, A., Burris, L., Hecht, D., DeMoraes-Huffine, P., Cruz, I., & Tolma, E. (2014). Mixed-methods feasibility study on the cultural adaptation of a child abuse prevention model. *Child Abuse & Neglect, 38*(9), 1496–1507.

Berardelli, I., Sarubbi, S., Rogante, E., Erbuto, D., Giuliani, C., Lamis, D. A., Pompili, M., et al. (2022). Association between childhood maltreatment and suicidal ideation: A path analysis study. *Journal of Clinical Medicine, 11*(8), 2179.

Brown, S. M., Rodriguez, K. E., Smith, A. D., Ricker, A., & Williamson, A. A. (2022). Associations between childhood maltreatment and behavioral sleep disturbances across the lifespan: A systematic review. *Sleep Medicine Reviews, 64*, 101621.

Cardoso, J. B., Dettlaff, A. J., Finno-Velasquez, M., Scott, J., & Faulkner, M. (2014). Nativity and immigration status among Latino families involved in the child welfare system: Characteristics, risk, and maltreatment. *Children and Youth Services Review, 44*, 189–200.

Center for Substance Abuse Treatment. (2014). *Trauma-informed care in behavioral health services* (Treatment Improvement Protocol Series, No. 57). Substance Abuse and Mental Health Services Administration. https://www.ncbi.nlm.nih.gov/book/NBK207201/

Chang, J., Rhee, S., & Weaver, D. (2006). Characteristics of child abuse in immigrant Korean families and correlates of placement decisions. *Child Abuse & Neglect, 30*, 881–891.

Cross, D., Fani, N., Powers, A., & Bradley, B. (2017). Neurobiological development in the context of childhood trauma. *Clinical Psychology: Science and Practice, 24*(2), 111–124.

Crouch, E., Radcliff, E., Strompolis, M., & Srivastav, A. (2019). Safe, stable, and nurtured: Protective factors against poor physical and mental health outcomes following exposure to adverse childhood experiences (ACEs). *Journal of Child & Adolescent Trauma, 12*, 165–173.

Deedat, H. A., Baba, Z., & Faye, P. (2023). Sub-Saharan African immigrant parents and child protection in the United States: Considerations for the US child welfare system. *APSAC Advisor, 36*(2), 25–39.

Dettlaff, A. J., & Earner, I. (2009). *Children of immigrants in the child welfare system: Findings from the national survey of child and adolescent well-being*. Migration and Child Welfare National Network. https://cimmcw.org/wp-content/uploads/pc-childofimmigrant.pdf

Dettlaff, A. J., & Earner, L. (2012). Children of immigrants in the child welfare system: Characteristics, risk, and maltreatment. *The Journal of Contemporary Social Services, 93*(4), 295–303.

Dettlaff, A. J., & Finno-Velasquez, M. (2013). Child maltreatment and immigration enforcement: Considerations for child welfare and legal systems working with immigrant families. *Children's Legal Rights Journal, 33*(1), 37–63.

Dettlaff, A. J., & Johnson, M. A. (2011). Child maltreatment dynamics among immigrant and U.S. born Latino children: Findings from the National Survey of Child and Adolescent Well-Being (NSCAW). *Children and Youth Services Review, 33*(6), 936–944.

Dettlaff, A. J., Weber, K., Pendleton, M., Boyd, R., Bettencourt, B., & Burton, L. (2020). It is not a broken system, it is a system that needs to be broken: The upEND movement to abolish the child welfare system. *Journal of Public Child Welfare, 14*(5), 500–517.

Domond, R. (2024). *First generation Haitian American women parenting styles: A qualitative study* [Unpublished doctoral dissertation, Capella University]. ProQuest.

Ellis, K. (2019, December 17). Race and poverty bias in the child welfare system: Strategies for child welfare practitioners. *ABA Groups*. https://www.americanbar.org/groups/public_interest/child_law/resources/child_law_practiceonline/january%2D%2D-december-2019/race-and-poverty-bias-in-the-child-welfare-system%2D%2D-strategies-f/

Finno-Velasquez, M., Sepp, S. M., Lopez, A., Aquino, E., Cherie, N., & Ortiz-Upston, M. (2023). Child maltreatment prevention interventions for Latinx immigrant populations: A systematic review. *Journal of Public Child Welfare, 17*(4), 845–878.

Fitton, L., Yu, R., & Fazel, S. (2020). Childhood maltreatment and violent outcomes: A systematic review and meta-analysis of prospective studies. *Trauma, Violence, & Abuse, 21*(4), 754–768.

Fontes, L. A. (2002). Child discipline and physical abuse in immigrant Latino families: Reducing violence and misunderstanding. *Journal of Counseling & Development, 80*, 31–40.

Fortson, B. L., Klevens, J., Merrick, M. T., Gilbert, L. K., & Alexander, S. P. (2016). *Child abuse and neglect prevention resource for action: A compilation of the best available evidence*. National Center for Injury Prevention and Control, Centers for Disease Control and Prevention.

Haner, J., & Lopez, M. H. (2023, September 28). *8 facts about recent Latino immigrants to the U.S.* Pew Research Center. 8 facts about recent Hispanic immigrants to the US | Pew Research Center.

Johnson-Motoyama, M., Putnam-Hornstein, E., Dettlaff, A. J., Zhao, K., Finno-Velasquez, M., & Needell, B. (2015). Disparities in reported and substantiated infant maltreatment by maternal Hispanic origin and nativity: A birth cohort study. *Maternal and Child Health Journal, 19*, 958–968.

Jonson-Reid, M., Kohl, P. L., & Drake, B. (2012). Child and adult outcomes of chronic child maltreatment. *Pediatrics, 129*(5), 839–845.

Kaplow, J. B., & Widom, C. S. (2007). Age of onset of child maltreatment predicts long-term mental health outcomes. *Journal of Abnormal Psychology, 116*(1), 176–187.

Kim, H. J., & Kim, H. (2023). County-level relationships between foreign-born residents, Latinos, immigration enforcement, and child maltreatment report rates in the United States, 2015–2018. *Journal of Interpersonal Violence, 38*(17–18), 10309–10332.

Kohli, H. K., & Fineran, S. (2020). Immigrant Latino fathers' perceptions of child abuse and neglect. *Critical Social Work, 21*(2), 1–17.

Kuper, J. L. (2023). Weaving culture with consequence: Immigrant status and child maltreatment outcomes in early adulthood. *Child Abuse & Neglect, 146*. https://doi.org/10.1016/j.chiabu.2023.106451

LaFalaise, M. E. (2017). *Exploring child abuse prevention methods in Palm Beach County's Haitian community* [Unpublished doctoral dissertation, Walden University]. ProQuest.

Larsen, S., Kim-Goh, M., & Nguyen, T. D. (2008). Asian American immigrant families and child abuse: Cultural considerations. *Journal of Systemic Therapies, 27*(1), 16–29. https://doi.org/10.1521/jsyt.2008.27.1.16

Lau, A. S., Takeuchi, D. T., & Alegría, M. (2006). Parent-to-child aggression among Asian American parents: Culture, context, and vulnerability. *Journal of Marriage and Family, 68*(5), 1261–1275. https://doi.org/10.1111/j.1741-3737.2006.00327.x

Maker, A. H., Shah, P. V., & Agha, Z. (2005). Child physical abuse: Prevalence, characteristics, predictors, and beliefs about parent-child violence in South Asian, Middle Eastern, East Asian, and Latina women in the United States. *Journal of Interpersonal Violence, 20*(11), 1406–1428.

McLeigh, J. D., Katz, C., Davidson-Arad, B., & Ben-Arieh, A. (2017). The cultural adaptation of a community-based child maltreatment prevention initiative. *Family Process, 56*(2), 393–407.

Migration Policy Institute. (n.d.). *Children in U.S. immigrant families.* https://www.migrationpolicy.org/programs/data-hub/charts/children-immigrant-families

Migration Policy Institute. (2022, May 11). *Sub-Saharan African immigrants in the United States.* https://www.migrationpolicy.org/article/sub-saharan-african-immigrants-united-states

Molnar, B. E., Beatriz, E. D., & Beardslee, W. R. (2016). Community-level approaches to child maltreatment prevention. *Trauma, Violence, & Abuse, 17*(4), 387–397.

Mugadza, H. T., Mujeyi, B., Stout, B., Wali, N., & Renzaho, A. M. N. (2019). Childrearing practices among Sub-Saharan African migrants in Australia: A systematic review. *Journal of Child and Family Studies, 28*, 2927–2941.

Najman, J. M., Scott, J. G., Farrington, D. P., Clavarino, A. M., Williams, G. M., McGee, T. R., & Kisely, S. (2023). Does childhood maltreatment lead to low life success? Comparing agency and self-reports. *Journal of Interpersonal Violence, 38*(1–2), 1320–1342.

O'Leary, P., Abdalla, M., Hutchinson, A., Squire, J., & Young, A. (2020). Child protection with Muslim communities: Considerations for non-Muslim-based orthodoxies/paradigms in child welfare and social work. *The British Journal of Social Work, 50*(4), 1201–1218.

Park, H. J., Yi, S. H., Lee, K. Y., Kim, B. K., & Park, S. R. (2012). Parenting values and practices among Muslim parents in Indonesia. *Child Studies in Diverse Contexts, 2*(2), 109–122.

Park, M. S. (2001). The factors of child physical abuse in Korean immigrant families. *Child Abuse & Neglect, 25*(7), 945–958. https://doi.org/10.1016/S0145-2134(01)00248-4

Pelczarski, Y., & Kemp, S. (2006). Patterns of child maltreatment referrals among Asian and Pacific Islander families. *Child Welfare, 85*(1), 5–31.

Pew Research Center. (2021). *Key facts about Asian Americans, a diverse and growing population.* https://www.pewresearch.org/short-reads/2021/04/29/key-facts-about-asian-americans/

Pew Research Center. (2024a). *Why Asian immigrants come to the U.S. and how they view life here.* https://www.pewresearch.org/race-and-ethnicity/2024/10/09/why-asian-immigrants-come-to-the-u-s-and-how-they-view-life-here/#fn-188479-1

Pew Research Center. (2024b). 1. *Demographic portrait of Muslim Americans.* Pew Research Center. Demographic portrait of Muslim Americans.

Rameckers, S. A., van Emmerik, A. A., Bachrach, N., Lee, C. W., Morina, N., & Arntz, A. (2021). The impact of childhood maltreatment on the severity of childhood-related posttraumatic stress disorder in adults. *Child Abuse & Neglect, 120*, 105208.

Rasmussen, A., Smith, A. A., Chu, T., & Keatley, E. (2012). "911" among West African immigrants in New York City: A qualitative study of parents' disciplinary practices and their perceptions of child welfare authorities. *Social Science & Medicine, 75*(3), 516–525.

Rhee, S., Chang, J., Berthold, S., & Mar, G. (2012). Child maltreatment among immigrant Vietnamese families: Characteristics and implications for practice. *Child & Adolescent Social Work Journal, 29*(2), 85–101.

Rhee, S., Chang, J., Weaver, D., & Wong, D. (2008). Child maltreatment among immigrant Chinese families: Characteristics and patterns of placement. *Child Maltreatment, 13*(3), 269–279.

Romano, E., Babchishin, L., Marquis, R., & Fréchette, S. (2015). Childhood maltreatment and educational outcomes. *Trauma, Violence, & Abuse, 16*(4), 418–437.

Schwartz, S. J., Unger, J. B., Zamboanga, B. L., Córdova, D., Mason, C. A., Huang, S., Baezconde-Garbanati, L., Lorenzo-Blanco, E. I., Des Rosiers, S. E., Soto, D. W., Villamar, J. A., Pattarroyo, M., Lizzi, K. M., & Szapocznik, J. (2015). Developmental trajectories of acculturation: Links with family functioning and mental health in recent-immigrant Hispanic adolescents. *Child Development, 86*(3), 726–748. https://doi.org/10.1111/cdev.12341

Segal, U. A. (2000). Exploring child abuse among Vietnamese refugees. *Journal of Multicultural Social Work, 8*(3–4), 159–191.

Seon, J. (2021). How does neighborhood affect child maltreatment among immigrant families? *Child Abuse & Neglect, 122*, 105300.

Sledjeski, E. M., Dierker, L. C., Bird, H. R., & Canino, G. (2009). Predicting child maltreatment among Puerto Rican children from migrant and non-migrant families. *Child Abuse & Neglect, 33*(6), 382–392.

Tajima, E. A., & Harachi, T. W. (2010). Parenting beliefs and physical discipline practices among Southeast Asian immigrants: Parenting in the context of cultural adaptation to the United States. *Journal of Cross-Cultural Psychology, 41*(2), 212–235.

Tamir, C. (2022, January 27). *Key findings about Black immigrants in the U.S. Pew Research Center.* Key findings about Black immigrants in the U.S. | Pew Research Center.

Tejeda, Y., Jones, D., & Drake, B. (2024). The Hispanic paradox in child maltreatment: Does it fade over time? *Child Abuse & Neglect, 156*, 107007.

U.S. Department of Health and Human Services. (2023). *Child maltreatment 2021.*

U.S. Department of Health & Human Services, Administration for Children and Families, Administration of Children, Youth and Families, Children's Bureau. (2025). *Child maltreatment 2023.* https://www.acf.hhs.gov/cb/data-research/child-maltreatment

Viláriño, M., Amado, B. G., Seijo, D., Selaya, A., & Arce, R. (2022). Consequences of child maltreatment victimisation in internalising and externalising mental health problems. *Legal and Criminological Psychology, 27*(2), 182–193.

World Health Organization. (2024). *The child maltreatment.* Child maltreatment.

Yoon, A. S., Zhai, F., Gao, Q., & Solomon, P. (2023). Parenting stress and risks of child maltreatment among Asian immigrant parents: Does social support moderate the effects? *Asian American Journal of Psychology, 14*(1), 28–35. https://doi.org/10.1037/aap0000251

Young, R. P., & Hopkins, R. J. (2014). A review of the Hispanic paradox: Time to spill the beans? *European Respiratory Review, 23*(134), 439–449.

Zhai, F., & Gao, Q. (2009). Child maltreatment among Asian Americans: Characteristics and explanatory framework. *Child Maltreatment, 14*(2), 207–224. https://doi.org/10.1177/1077559508326286

Zhang, Z., Xiang, Y., & Li, X. (2025). Effects of parental childhood maltreatment on children's school adaptation: An intergenerational perspective based on envy. *Journal of Interpersonal Violence, 40*(7–8), 1571–1596.

CHAPTER 9

Vietnamese Youth Gangs in the USA: Background, Theories, and Future Directions

Jun Sung Hong, James Diego Vigil, and Hassan Arab

Introduction

On April 4, 1991, 41 people at a Good Guys electronic store in Sacramento were taken hostage by three brothers—Loi Nguyen, 21, Pham Nguyen, 19, and Long Nguyen, 17—along with their friend Tran, 17. The youths began shooting the hostages, killing two employees and a customer and wounding eleven people. After a long standoff, Pham, Long, and Tran died in the shootout with deputies. It had been reported that the youths were members of an Asian gang, the Oriental Boys (Paddock & Dizon,

J. S. Hong (✉)
School of Social Work, Wayne State University, Detroit, MI, USA
e-mail: fl4684@wayne.edu

J. D. Vigil
School of Social Ecology, Department of Criminology, Law and Society, University of California, Irvine, CA, USA
e-mail: vigil@exchange.uci.edu

H. Arab
College of Social Science, Department of Sociology and Social Work, Kuwait University, Safat, Kuwait City, Kuwait
e-mail: hassan.arab@ku.edu.kw

J. S. Hong et al. (eds.), *Violence and Trauma Without Borders*,
https://doi.org/10.1007/978-3-032-29221-6_9

1991). Bim Khac Nguyen, father of Loi, Pham, and Long, sadly recalled that his sons were well behaved at home and always listened to him. Outside the school, others saw them as "troubled" teens who were struggling to adapt to their new life in the United States (Paddock & Dizon, 1991). This case demonstrates that Asian immigrants' adaptation to the USA sometimes involves problems with youth groups, especially street gangs.

The authors will address the subject of Vietnamese American youth gangs with an emphasis on causation and developments in the USA. In addition to assessing the research findings on street gangs in this population, we have drawn from firsthand accounts of individual life histories to contextualize our interpretations within the particular social experiences and cultural realities of gang youth. The Asian American street gang problem has mushroomed since the immigrant community attained critical mass after 1965. Although still a minuscule portion of all street gangs nationwide (for example, Vietnamese and Cambodian gang members account for only 1.6% to 2.2% of the gang population, respectively), research on Asian American groups has offered important insights into the causative factors of this phenomenon (Hunt et al., 1997; Long, 1996, 1997; Nguyen & Henkin, 1982; Vigil & Yun, 1990). In the works that focus on prevention and intervention strategies (see, e.g., Clarke, 1995; Goldstein & Huff; Gottfredson, 1986; Rosenbaum, 1992; Tolan & Gorman-Smith, 1997), none of them considered the particular characteristics of the Asian American, much less the Vietnamese American youths' experiences in gang activities. To address this notable gap in the research literature on Vietnamese American youth gangs, this chapter provides an overview of Vietnamese immigration to the USA by first including a historical overview of Vietnamese immigration, which is followed by a discussion of motivations for joining a gang, how Vietnamese American youth gangs compare with youth gangs of other ethnic groups, methodological limitations of current research, and implications for practice and advocacy.

A Historical Overview of Vietnamese Immigration to the United States

The evolution and formation of Vietnamese youth gangs are rooted in the sociohistorical backdrop of immigration, poverty, and racism, which are commonly experienced by Vietnamese immigrants in the United States. Many Asians, particularly Chinese and Japanese, have been immigrating to the USA since the nineteenth century. In comparison, Vietnamese immigration history became prominent in the 1970s. Most immigrants from Asian countries immigrated to the USA for economic reasons (Kula et al., 2021). Before the fall of Saigon, Vietnamese Americans from 1945 to 1975 were of a small number of high social, political, or economic standing whose goal for immigrating was to obtain educational training in the USA and return to Vietnam to be a part of the country's development (Pham, 2002). Since 1975, however, Vietnamese immigration to the USA has been primarily a result of US involvement in the Vietnam War. Many Indochinese refugees, i.e., those from Vietnam, Cambodia, and Laos, fled their countries in 1975 during the fall of Saigon and resettled in the United States by boat (Pew Research Center, 2023). Between 10,000 and 15,000 Vietnamese were evacuated (Kula et al., 2021). Approximately 130,000 refugees were granted asylum in the USA and placed in camps in US military bases (Takaki, 1998). Refugees in the first wave (1975–1978) were educated and had some financial stability in their home country; they were somewhat familiar with Western culture and values as they had been exposed to French colonization in South Vietnam in the past (Kula et al., 2021). Among the first wave of refugees were many South Vietnamese soldiers who returned home after the Vietnam War. Because they had no place to go and no place to live, they organized gangs of young criminals by enticing them with money and drugs to survive (Long & Ricard, 1996). From 1975 to 1977, the first wave of refugees, as well as the soldiers, went to the USA. The soldiers continued to recruit young people into a life of crime. Over time, the soldiers passed their skills onto other Vietnamese youth who became gang leaders themselves (Long & Ricard, 1996).

The subsequent refugee groups were primarily less educated and possessed fewer skills because of poverty, strict government control, and food shortages due to the trade embargoes and agricultural problems under the socialist regime (Harjanto & Batalova, 2021). Refugees who arrived between 1979 and 1982 were regarded as the second wave of refugees who experienced trauma, which stemmed from escaping from Vietnam and leaving their families behind, feelings of uncertainty about their future, and language and cultural barriers (Kula et al., 2021).

The third wave of immigrants was those who entered the USA in the 1980s and 1990s, and unlike the earlier arrivals, the third wave of immigrants was mostly composed of Amerasians (offspring of US servicemen and Vietnamese mothers who are referred to as *bui doi* in Vietnam) and political prisoners (Rkasnuam & Batalova, 2014). Although some US servicemen married Vietnamese women who bore their children, only a handful brought their brides to the USA (Long & Ricard, 1996). Policies, such as the Amerasian Homecoming Act, Orderly Departure Program, and Humanitarian Operations, were aimed at bringing the remaining victims of the Vietnam War to the USA (Kula et al., 2021). Amerasian children were victimized, exploited, and abandoned in Vietnam, which fueled their desire to come to the USA to reunite with their fathers; however, less than 1% were reunited with their fathers (Long & Ricard, 1996). Moreover, many Amerasians are exploited by the Vietnamese, who perceive them as a one-way ticket to the USA. They were promised marriage-related cash donations to their mother or guardians, financial assistance on arrival, college education, and a car. But soon after they arrived, they were abandoned (Long & Ricard, 1996). Many Americans ended up in US urban ghettos and lived in abject poverty; they run the risk of joining Vietnamese gangs, especially when they run out of welfare assistance and are actively recruited into gangs (Long & Ricard, 1996).

Although many in the third wave were classified as refugees, an increasing number of subsequent arrivals came to the USA as family-sponsored immigrants. However, according to Zhou and Bankston (2000), from 1988 to 1992, the influx of refugees rose sharply, and from 1990, political prisoners were the largest category of refugees who were admitted to the USA. However, the Vietnamese immigration population declined in the 1990s, and the growth rate fell from 26% between 2000 and 2010 to 12% between 2010 and 2019 (Harjanto & Batalova, 2021). By 2019, 1.4 million Vietnamese had immigrated to the USA, which accounts for approximately 3% of the overall 44.5 million immigrants (Harjanto & Batalova, 2021).

Motivations for Joining a Gang Among Vietnamese Youth

Although Vietnamese and Southeast Asian youth gangs are not as well known as African American and Latino youth gangs, Vietnamese gang leaders have been working with other Vietnamese criminals in the United States and abroad to recruit juveniles into gang activities. Similar to other racial and ethnic groups, many Vietnamese youths are motivated to join a gang for several reasons, such as feeling alienated from their home, school, and society (Long, 1997).

Social and Cultural Explanations

There is a distinct pattern of cultural and social problems that motivates Vietnamese youth to join a gang. In their report, Kent and Felkenes (1998) identified several reasons Vietnamese youth may join a gang, such as low self-concept (due to low social status as a refugee), conflict between parents and youth on cultural orientation (e.g., maintaining the Vietnamese language and culture versus using English only and adopting American culture), barriers to acquiring an American identity, and perceived benefits of gang membership (e.g., social support, financial gain, and protection). According to Kent and Felkenes (1998), an individual who had worked with Vietnamese and Southeast Asian youth in juvenile facilities in Santa Clara County described several factors that had the greatest influence on participating in gang activities (Kent & Felkenes, 1998). Factors identified were problems in the home environment, alienation from school, feeling estranged from the US culture, and peer pressure. Contrary to these findings, however, Wyrick's (2000) study found that Vietnamese youth who rejected their Vietnamese identity but found it difficult to adopt an American identity were not more likely than others to become involved in gangs. Instead, factors that predicted youth gang involvement are the development of a pro-gang attitude, a negative attitude toward school, conflict with family, low level of social integration, and perceived benefits of joining a gang (Wyrick, 2000).

Gang members are predominantly males; however, like other ethnic groups, an increasing number of Vietnamese female youths are targeted by gangs. Although the prevalence of female gang members is difficult to ascertain, their numbers were significant (Moore & Hagedorn, 2001). Some females might join a gang due to coercion. Kidnapping of young girls and forcing them to be involved in a gang lifestyle is frequent among Vietnamese youth gangs (Krott, 2001).

Structural Explanations

Vietnamese youth gang identities are inextricably linked to racism and labor migration (Darder & Torres, 2004; Lam, 2015), which can be traced to the 1965 Immigration and Nationality Act and has affected the way Asian Americans are perceived in the United States (Lam, 2019a). Also, as argued by Lam (2019b), structural forces, for example, political unrest, economic instability, the role of the US military, and migration patterns and trends, can shape the particularities of youth gang subculture, including protection and self-preservation, ethnic pride, seeking family, having to navigate youth identities, and the desire to achieve status, power, and wealth.

Are Vietnamese Youth Gangs Similar to Other Ethnic Groups?

Historically, youth gangs emerged in urban areas in the early twentieth century and consisted mainly of newly arrived immigrants (Tobin, 2024). Youth gangs in the United States are multiracial in terms of membership (Tobin, 2024). According to the National Gang Center (n.d.), law enforcement agencies report that the majority of the documented youth gangs are African Americans and Latina/o/x/es. In comparison, the size of Asian youth gangs is much smaller, although the presence of several organized Asian gangs, such as the Asian Boyz (mostly Cambodians), Santanas (Ese Te Ese; Filipinos), Menace of Destruction (Hmong), Fullerton Boys (Koreans), and Tokyo Boys (Japanese), is found in San Francisco, Los Angeles, Orange County, and New York City. Various Asian groups yield different types of youth gangs. Unlike other groups, community disorganization due to lack of control by families, schools, etc., as well as internalization of criminal subcultural values, does not sufficiently explain the formation of Asian youth gangs (Song & Dombrink, 1992). Among Asian youth gangs is the inability to cope satisfactorily with identity and their reaction to law enforcement (Song & Dombrink, 1992).

Compared to gangs of other races and ethnicities, including Blacks and Latinos, Vietnamese youth gangs are less known, and many are refugees who, along with their families, experienced a great deal of trauma (Kent & Felkenes, 1998). The most frequent crime perpetrated by Vietnamese gangs, notably Born to Kill, is home invasion robbery (Krott, 2001). Home invasion robberies are carefully planned, and the victims are typically Vietnamese or other Asian refugee families who, due to fear of retaliation and fear of law enforcement, rarely report the crime despite experiencing violence. Unlike other racial and ethnic groups, including Chinese gangs, who typically have a long family tradition of gang membership (Kent & Felkenes, 1998), some Vietnamese youth may have older brothers who were involved in gangs, but they do not have fathers or uncles in a gang (Kent & Felkenes, 1998). Vietnamese do not have a long history of ties to organized crimes, although many youth gang members transition to more organized crimes when they become adults. Organized crimes may include racketeering, prostitution, and narcotics, and extreme violence is central to their activities (Krott, 2001).

Research Shortcomings: What Gang Researchers Should Consider

It has been argued that Asian, including Vietnamese, criminal activities have been increasing in the United Kingdom, Canada, Australia, and the United States (Long & Ricard, 1996), and cooperation among these countries to exchange information and resources to more effectively address gang activities has been suggested (Long & Ricard, 1996). However, research on Vietnamese youth gangs has been and continues to be limited, which is likely due to substantially less attention given to Vietnamese immigrant youths, especially in comparison to gangs of other ethnic groups. The scant research attention to Vietnamese youth gangs is likely due to the small Vietnamese population size, as well as being primarily concentrated in metropolitan areas, such as Los Angeles and Sacramento (Lam, 2019a).

Nevertheless, extant research studies on Vietnamese youth gangs have mainly focused on relational-level factors, such as parental conflict or feeling disengaged from school, or cultural-level factors, such as acculturation. Research to date has rarely considered Vietnamese youth gangs within the context of racism (e.g., racial profiling) or other potentially relevant factors, such as neighborhood composition and mass incarceration. Likewise, many studies to date have overly relied on the deficit model to identify risk factors rather than a model that emphasizes strengths and resilience to identify protective and promotive factors of these youths.

Practice and Advocacy for Vietnamese Youth

Vietnamese youth gangs tend to be not only overlooked but also misunderstood. However, there is a crucial need for more rigorous research to better understand Vietnamese youth gangs, which potentially translates into more effective and culturally relevant interventions. The first step for practice with Vietnamese youth who are identified as a gang is a thorough assessment of the youth by identifying not only the risk factors, but also protective and promotive factors, which the practitioner could later home in on during the intervention stage. For instance, a strong sense of familism has been identified as an important protective factor for many minority adolescents, as studies show that racial minority adolescents with a strong connection with their family tend to exhibit fewer problematic behaviors and better outcomes (e.g., school performance) (e.g., Stein et al., 2013) even under adverse conditions (e.g., frequent encounters with deviant and delinquent peers) (Germán et al., 2008).

More importantly, youth advocates have a significant role in addressing broader issues, such as racism, which is prevalent in several institutions, such as schools and law enforcement. Racism and xenophobia in the classroom, which may be perpetrated not only by students but also by teachers and staff in some cases, could alienate Vietnamese immigrant youth and prevent them from fully participating in the classroom and school. Racial profiling by law enforcement is another concern, as minority adolescents are significantly more likely to be profiled and raise questions about the legitimacy and the procedural fairness of the law enforcement (Engel & Johnson, 2006). Youth advocates who work with Vietnamese youth are strongly encouraged to work closely with grassroots organizations that fight for social justice, such as Black Lives Matter, a Holistic Approach to Social Justice, and Color of Change, to address how racism and racial profiling have an impact on youth.

Conclusion

Many aspects of the gang functioning of Vietnamese youth are a mystery due to relatively few studies. However, Asians, including Vietnamese, continue to be among the fastest-growing populations in the United States

(Im, 2025). Effectively addressing problematic behaviors, which could lead to the development of delinquent activities (e.g., gang activities), requires evidence-based intervention programs that are developmentally appropriate and culturally relevant. Moreover, lawmakers need to also consider developing policies to dismantle racism that exists in existing institutions, such as law enforcement, that may trigger psychological distress and trauma, among these youth. For Vietnamese immigrant youth, these programs and policies are more important than ever.

References

Clarke, R. V. (1995). Situational crime prevention. In M. Tonry & D. P. Farrington (Eds.), *Strategic approaches to crime prevention: Building a safer society* (pp. 91–150). University of Chicago Press.

Darder, A., & Torres, R. (2004). *After race: Racism after multiculturalism*. New York University Press.

Engel, R. S., & Johnson, R. (2006). Toward a better understanding of racial and ethnic disparities in search and seizure rates. *Journal of Criminal Justice, 34*, 605–617.

Germán, M., Gonzales, N. A., & Dumka, L. (2008). Familism values as a protective factor for Mexican-origin adolescents exposed to deviant peers. *The Journal of Early Adolescence, 29*(1), 16–42. https://doi.org/10.1177/0272431608324475

Gottfredson, D. C. (1986). An empirical test of school-based environmental and individual interventions to reduce risk of delinquent behavior. *Criminology, 24*(4), 705–731.

Harjanto, L., & Batalova, J. (2021). *Vietnamese immigrants in the United States*. Migration Policy Institute. https://www.migrationpolicy.org/article/vietnamese-immigrants-united-states

Hunt, G., Joe, K., & Waldorf, D. (1997). Culture and ethnic identity among southeast Asian gang members. *Free Inquiry: Gangs, Drugs, and Violence, 25*(1), 9–21.

Im, C. (2025, May 1). *Facts about Asians in the U.S.* Pew Research Center. https://www.pewresearch.org/race-and-ethnicity/fact-sheet/asian-americans-in-the-u-s/

Kent, D. R., & Felkenes, G. T. (1998). *Cultural explanations for Vietnamese youth involvement in street gangs*. U.S. Department of Justice, Office of Justice Programs, & Office of Juvenile Justice and Delinquency Prevention.

Krott, R. (2001). Vietnamese gangs in America. *Law and Order, 49*(5), 100–104.

Kula, S. M., Tran, V. Q., Garcia, I., Saito, E., & Paik, S. J. (2021). Vietnamese Americans: History, education, and societal context. *Journal of Southeast Asian American Education and Advancement, 16*(1), 1–22.

Lam, K. D. (2015). *Youth gangs, racism, and schooling: Vietnamese American youth in a postcolonial context*. Palgrave Macmillan.

Lam, K. D. (2019a). Asian American youth violence as genocide: A critical appraisal and its pedagogical significance. *Equity & Excellence in Education, 52*(2–3), 255–270.

Lam, K. D. (2019b). Critical perspectives in youth gang formation in the United States. In G. Noblit (Ed.), *Oxford research encyclopedia of education* (pp. 1–20). Oxford University Press.

Long, P. D. P. (1997). Cultural and social factors and Vietnamese gangs. *Journal of Contemporary Criminal Justice, 13*(4), 331–339.

Long, P. D. P., & Ricard, L. (1996). *The dream shattered: Vietnamese gangs in America*. Northeastern University Press.

Moore, J., & Hagedorn, J. (2001). *Female gangs: A focus on research*. Office of Juvenile Justice and Delinquency Prevention. https://www.ojp.gov/pdffiles1/ojjdp/186159.pdf

National Gang Center. (n.d.). *National youth gang survey analysis: Demographics*. https://nationalgangcenter.ojp.gov/survey-analysis/demographics

Nguyen, L. T., & Henkin, A. B. (1982). Vietnamese refugees in the United States: Adaptation and transitional status. *The Journal of Ethnic Studies, 9*(4), 101–116.

Paddock, R. C., & Dizon, L. (1991, April 21). 3 brothers in shootout led dual lives. *Los Angeles Times*. https://archive.seattletimes.com/archive/19910421/1278606/3-brothers-in-shootout-led-dual-lives

Pew Research Center. (2023). *Vietnamese Americans*. https://www.pewresearch.org/social-trends/rise-of-asian-americans-2012-analysis/Vietnamese/

Pham, V. H. (2002). *Beyond and before boat people: Vietnamese American history before* 1975. [Doctoral dissertation, Cornell University]. ProQuest Dissertation and Theses database.

Rkasnuam, H., & Batalova, J. (2014). *Vietnamese immigrants in the United States*. Migration Policy Institute. https://www.migrationpolicy.org/article/vietnamese-immigrants-united-states-2012

Rosenbaum, J. E. (1992). Black pioneers: Do their moves to the suburbs increase economic opportunity for mothers and children? *Housing Policy Debate, 2*, 1179–1213.

Song, J. H., & Dombrink, J. (1992). Lost in the melting pot: Asian youth gangs in the United States. *Gang Journal, 1*(1), 1–12.

Stein, G. L., Gonzalez, L. M., Cupito, A. M., Kiang, L., & Supple, A. J. (2013). The protective role of familism in the lives of Latino adolescents. *Journal of Family Issues, 36*(10), 1255–1273. https://doi.org/10.1177/0192513X13502480

Takaki, R. (1998). *Strangers from a different shore: A history of Asian Americans*. First Back Bay.

Tobin, K. (2024). *Youth gangs*. EBSCO Research Starters. https://www.ebsco.com/research-starters/social-sciences-and-humanities/youth-gangs

Tolan, P. H., & Gorman-Smith, D. (1997). Treatment of juvenile delinquency: Between therapy and punishment. In D. Stoff, J. Brieling, & J. Maser (Eds.), *Handbook of antisocial behavior* (pp. 405–415). Wiley.

Vigil, J. D., & Yun, S. C. (1990). Vietnamese youth gangs in Southern California. In C. R. Huff (Ed.), *Gangs in America* (2nd ed., pp. 146–162). Sage.

Wyrick, P. A. (2000). *Vietnamese youth gang involvement. US Department of Justice, Office of Justice Programs, Office of Juvenile Justice and Delinquency Prevention.*

Zhou, M., & Bankston, C. L. (2000). *Straddling two social worlds: The experience of Vietnamese refugee children in the United States* (ED-99-CO-0035). ERIC. https://files.eric.ed.gov/fulltext/ED439180.pdf

CHAPTER 10

Monstrous Heathens: Asians as Targets of Hate and Violence

Rose M. Kim

Introduction

The outbreak of the COVID-19 pandemic in the United States in March 2020 ignited a sharp rise in anti-Asian hate crimes, many rising to criminal levels, and raised great concern about violence against Asians and Asian Americans. The scapegoating of Asians, specifically the Chinese, as the source of the virus that had emerged in Wuhan, China, began just days after the federal declaration of a national emergency. On March 16, the president of the United States led the assault on *Twitter*, calling the coronavirus "the Chinese virus," despite public health experts who warned against naming a disease after a place or group of people. Despite the public criticism that followed, the president doubled down on the rhetoric, also calling it the "Asian virus" and "kung flu." Within two weeks, more than 1100 incidents, including verbal and physical assaults, were reported by the Stop AAPIT Hate Reporting Center, opened by civil rights groups in San Francisco. Personally, I experienced several attacks,

R. M. Kim (✉)
Social Sciences, Human Services and Criminal Justice, Borough of Manhattan Community College, New York, NY, USA
e-mail: rkim@bmcc.cuny.edu

J. S. Hong et al. (eds.), *Violence and Trauma Without Borders*,
https://doi.org/10.1007/978-3-032-29221-6_10

including by a White man, seemingly in his early 70s, who yelled at me in a Long Island beach parking lot, "It's because of *you* we have this virus." A year later, a study of nearly 700,000 tweets containing nearly 1.3 million hashtags, the week before and after the president's first tweet, found those who typed *#chinese virus*—rather than *#covid 19*—were doubly more likely to express anti-Asian bias (Hswen et al., 2021).

The digitally organized attack on the US Capitol on January 6, 2021, following the electoral defeat of the president, marked an escalation of White supremacist violence in the USA, toppling longstanding norms of law and order and "political correctness." Rioters, bearing racist and White supremacist imagery and armed with handguns and other weapons, violently assaulted police and stormed the Capitol building, leading legislators to flee in fear for their lives. That day, one participant, Ashli Babbitt, was fatally shot by a Capitol police officer, and three other supporters of the president died from natural or drug-induced causes. Then, two months later, Robert Aaron Long, a 21-year-old White man, who police said claimed to suffer from a sexual addiction, attacked two spas in Georgia, fatally shooting eight people, six of whom were women of Asian descent. The mass killing galvanized the Asian American community, calling attention to the troubling spike in anti-Asian hate and the historical and ongoing sexual objectification of Asian women, as well as internal biases within the AAPI (Asian American Pacific Islander) community toward women associated with spa, massage, and sex work.

The sharp rise in anti-Asian hate crimes, an increase of more than 70 percent in 2020, led the United States Commission on Civil Rights to study the issue, marking only the second time in its 65-year history that it had examined anti-Asian racism and discrimination. In its 2023 report, "The Federal Response to Anti-Asian Racism in the United States," the commission noted how the scapegoating of Asian communities had a long history, stretching back to the nineteenth century when Asian immigrants were labeled the "Yellow Peril." The report blamed the lack of awareness about the problem on an absence of comprehensive data and recommended various solutions, such as vigorously prosecuting hate crimes and educating first responders on what constituted a hate crime. It further encouraged federal, state, and local law enforcement agencies and victim services "to identify critical deficiencies in Limited English Proficient (LEP) programs for individuals who need language assistance" (USCCR, 2023, p. 195). However, the report significantly failed to recognize the longstanding role of the state itself in manufacturing and perpetuating anti-Asian hate. This power dynamic was obvious in the president's racist narrative about the origins of the COVID-19 pandemic (2020 to 2022), as well as during the 2016 campaign when he attacked China for currency manipulation, saying, "We can't continue to allow China to rape our country, and that's what's they're doing" (*BBC News*, 2016). But anti-Chinese rhetoric stretches even further back to the origins of this nation as a White settler colonial society, constructing a stratified, global race framework, a paradigm that persists to this day.

Rather than viewing anti-Asian violence as an individualized, subjective bias against Asians and Asian Americans that can be remedied through policing and behavioral conditioning, this essay is a theoretical consideration of how the state has systematically manufactured anti-Asian hate, even as it has historically, simultaneously, purported to be a force for racial equality and racial justice, domestically and internationally; this contradiction is rooted in this nation's identity as an imperialist, White supremacist, capitalist patriarchy, a term coined by bell hooks (Yancy & hooks, 2015). One key way this contradiction is obscured is through systematic distortions and erasures of the Asian American experience in the dominant, collective US history, a process experienced by other racialized minorities, as well. Due to the lack of a critical self-awareness as a nation, for Asian Americans (and other racialized minority groups), the process of assimilation into the (White) American imaginary can be akin to cultural genocide, for truly, it is impossible to tell the story of the USA without understanding how the USA has interacted with nations beyond its borders. What happens "inside" the USA is inextricably linked to what happens "outside" it. As Viet Thanh Nguyen noted in *The Nation* (1/29/24), "[W]hat happens inside America's pluralistic society, often posed as a problem of race and racism, cannot be separated from war and colonialism."

The comparison of assimilation to cultural genocide is reflected in my own history. I grew up knowing virtually nothing about the Korean War (1950 to 1953), even though my parents were refugees of this very war. My parents never spoke about their lives in Korea, and I was never taught about the war in school. I only began learning about this conflagration in my mid-30 s, while in graduate school studying sociology. When I later asked my mother about her wartime experiences, I learned that my paternal grandmother and uncle had been killed by US pilots who had bombed their home. If I hadn't attended graduate school, I might never have learned this personal history. Truly, it is impossible to understand modern

US-South/North Korean relations without a knowledge of this history, yet so few Americans know about this war that it is widely called the "forgotten war."

Indeed, there is a longstanding history of state violence against Asian Americans. This history includes the Page Act of 1875 that restricted the immigration of Chinese women, the Chinese Exclusion Act of 1882 that banned Chinese laborers and also denied them citizenship, the Immigration Act of 1917 that barred entry to the USA to those from the Asiatic Barred Zone, the Immigration Act of 1924 that imposed quotas that favored northern and western Europeans, and Executive Order 90666 that forced persons of Japanese descent to relocate to concentration camps during World War II. At various times and places in US history, Asians have been unable to testify in court, marry Whites, and live in certain neighborhoods. Anti-Asian violence also has been manifested in social upheavals, such as the hostility toward Japanese car makers in the 1970s, epitomized in the murder of Vincent Chin; the 1992 LA riots/insurrection/*saigu* and the targeting of Korean merchants, following the acquittal of the four police officers charged in the violent assault on Rodney King, a Black motorist; and, most recently, during the COVID-19 pandemic. Meanwhile, the "Asian" countries that the USA has been at war with, from the twentieth century to the present day, include Japan, Korea, Vietnam, Cambodia, Laos, Afghanistan, and Iraq. Beth Lew-Williams (2018) describes the connection between these two realms as one of shifting scales:

> Though they shared a similar belief in white supremacy, those who dreamed of overseas expansion saw its fruition in opening China for exploitation, while others invested in white settler colonialism saw its culmination in Chinese exclusion. How white Americans viewed Chinese migration depended, in part, on the scale they used to imagine their world. (p. 20)

This chapter applies the concept of racial capitalism, as defined by Cedric Robinson, to make sense of these events and their historical erasures. Robinson conceptualizes *racial capitalism* as a social ideology that links modern racism, nationalism, and global capitalism. Robinson argues that race did not emerge as a concept due to the European encounter with non-European people, but that its genesis was "in the 'internal' relations of European peoples" and that racialism permeated "the social structures emergent from capitalism" (1983/2000, p. 3). He argues that "racialized" differences constructed labor relations and social hierarchies in the

Middle Ages and that these ideas continued to develop with the rise of European "free trade" and colonization:

> The tendency of European civilization through capitalism was thus not to homogenize but to differentiate—to exaggerate regional, subcultural, and dialectical differences into "racial" ones…so at the systematic interlocking of capitalism in the sixteenth century, the people of the Third World began to fill this expanding category of a civilization reproduced by capitalism. (p. 26)

Robinson describes racialism as a force that enforced "on a scale beyond previous human experience—the brutal degradations of life and the most acute violations of human destiny" (1983/2000, p. 308). He describes race as the rationale and mechanism of domination: "Race was its epistemology, its ordering principle, its organizing structure, its moral authority, its economy of justice, commerce, and power" (Robinson 1983/2000, p. xxxi).

Robinson discusses how the end of slave systems of production in the nineteenth century led to a massive reorganization of the capitalist world system and the rise of modern nations. The colonization of Africa and Asia led to the end of slavery, but also to the rise of "cheap labor powered by peasants and migrant laborers" (Robinson, 1983/2000, p. 312). He writes that "the 'new imperialism' of monopoly capitalism demanded a more destructive form of appropriation and exploitation" and that the colonial state had "parasitized the peasants…transforming traditional economic sectors from the project of reproduction into the source and support of forcibly recruited labor and the sites of cash-crop monoculture and the extraction of minerals and raw materials" (1983/2000, p. 312). These practices are in full swing today, with mono-crop plantation economies, such as for the cultivation of coffee, palm oil, and beef, or the rapacious excavation for rare earth minerals used in the manufacture of electronic devices, in countries across Latin America, Africa, and Asia.

Forever, Forever Foreign

When Mia Tuan's *Forever Foreigners or Honorary Whites? The Asian American Experience Today* (1998) was published on the cusp of a new millennium, it posed the question of whether Asian Americans would ever be considered as "true" Americans or, instead, always as alien and "other": "Will we be able, decades from now, to look back at the current experiences of Asian ethnics as but a rite of passage, a period of momentary social exclusion experienced by virtually all groups as they enter the final stages in the assimilation process?" (p. 167). Twenty-four years later, we have the answer, having experienced the worst explosion of anti-Asian violence in the USA in the twenty-first century. A key social force in manufacturing the perception of Asians as foreigners is historical, governmental, and other dominant social discourses that prescribe stereotypes of "Asians" as fundamentally foreign and different from "Americans," a process that can be understood as "orientalism." Edward Said described Orientalism as "the corporate institution for dealing with the Orient—dealing with it by making statements about it, authorizing views of it, describing it. By teaching it, settling it, ruling over it: in short, Orientalism as a Western style for dominating, restructuring, and having authority over the Orient" (1978, p. 3). Or, as Viet Thanh Nguyen recently wrote in *The Nation* (1/29/2024), "the Oriental is an object and an opportunity manufactured by the Occident, a fantasy with very real consequences." Michael Omi and Howard Winant (1986/1994) used the term "racial formation" to describe "the sociohistorical process by which racial categories are created, inhabited, transformed, and destroyed." Omi and Winant explain that racial formation is linked to "historically situated projects in which human bodies and social structures are represented and organized," in "an effort to reorganize and redistribute resources along particular racial lines" (p. 56).

One of the most enduring Asian American tropes, still today, is the "coolie," i.e., an indentured laborer from China or India who was contracted to work on colonial plantations across North America, Latin America, Southeast Asia, the Caribbean, and Oceania. Following the abolition of slavery in Great Britain, France, and Spain in the nineteenth century, these colonial powers sought to replace formerly enslaved people with "coolies." This phantasmagoric construct of a "non-free" laborer fueled the idea that Asians were antithetical to the American spirit of entrepreneurial capitalism and, thus, foreign (Chang, 2015, p. 37). However, the Chinese emigrants, who came to the American West, following the discovery of gold in California in 1848, were not as poor as the plantation indentures who were shipped to work in Cuba or Peru: They were "farmers, rural workers, artisans, mechanics, and merchants who, in many respects, were just like other people from around the world who came seeking gold" (Ngai, 2021, p. 34). However, in time, US politicians began mischaracterizing all Chinese as coolies, using them as a scapegoat for economic woes, and deflecting the resentments of White laborers toward "foreign" competition; the term was formally enshrined in legislation as California's Anti-Coolie Act of 1862. It is important to note that the act applied only to the importation of workers to destinations *outside the USA* (my italics), "thereby classifying the Chinese of the American West as free rather than involuntary immigrants" (Kenny, 2021, p. 362). However, as time passed, critics of Chinese immigration gradually applied the term "coolie" to *all* Chinese laborers, including those in the USA, casting them as inherently incompatible with the "free" European immigrant.

More recently, Moon-Ho Jung has argued that the distinction between free vs. indentured labor is a red herring, distracting us from its real purpose: "My contention is that no one was ever really a 'coolie.' 'Coolies' proliferated worldwide in the era of slave emancipation, a product of the imagineers, not of the imagined" (2017, p. 3). Alternatively, Jung proposes that the "coolie question" be considered "first and foremost as a heuristic, a means to deconstruct race and empire" (2017, p. 3). To this end, Jung argues that the idea of the "coolie" served as a mechanism to exclude and expel the Chinese from the USA, while simultaneously arguing it was being done benevolently to fight slavery and to defend universal freedom: "Like their British counterparts, US government officials claimed the power to monitor and control the movements of Asian workers, all under the banner of abolishing slavery and advancing freedom" (2017, p. 5); more concisely, "(a) vote for Chinese exclusion was cast as a vote against slavery" (2017, p. 6). The trope of the Asiatic coolie was "asserted over and over to exclude and to exploit Asian workers, while simultaneously making whiteness a racial prerequisite to full citizenship"; this happened in various White settler colonial societies, such as in the USA (1882), Canada (1885), New Zealand (1881), and Australia (1901).

Decades after the abolition of slavery in the USA, the reason for excluding the Chinese pivoted from barring exploited, indentured labor to the issue of national security, as reflected in the 1889 US Supreme Court decision, upholding the Chinese Exclusion Act. In *Chae Chan Ping v. U.S.*, the court ruled that if

> the government of the United States…considers the presence of foreigners of a different race in this country, who will not assimilate with us, to be dangerous to its peace and security, their exclusion is not to be stayed

> because at the time there are no actual hostilities with the nation to which the foreigners are subjects.

Thus, whether at war or not, the Chinese—foreigners of "a different race"—were, inherently, a threat to the dominantly White US society, especially as it impacted its economic interests.

The court's decision included a brief history of Chinese emigration to the USA, which is quite informative. The narrative begins with the discovery of gold in California in 1848 (U.S. Supreme Court, 1889):

> The news of the discovery penetrated China, and laborers came from there in great numbers...These laborers readily secured employment, and, as domestic servants, and in various kinds of outdoor work, proved to be exceedingly useful. For some years little opposition was made to them except when they sought to work in the mines, but, as their numbers increased, they began to engage in various mechanical pursuits and trades, and thus came in competition with our artisans and mechanics, as well as our laborers in the field.

According to the court's narrative, the Chinese were not considered a problem when they worked as domestic servants or field workers. However, when they ventured beyond subservient niches into profitable enterprises, such as gold mining or skilled industrial labor, they were seen as unwelcome competitors to White laborers ("our laborers") and, thus, a national economic threat. The Chinese were the first and only ethnic group to be barred from entering the USA by federal law. There was a place for Asians, but it was *not* as full-fledged citizens entitled to the rights granted to the White settler majority.

Furthermore, the court's claim that "(f)or some years little opposition was made except when they sought to work in the mines" falsely represents the violence and hostility Chinese emigrants experienced, quite soon after they arrived in the state. In *Driven Out: The Forgotten War Against Chinese Americans* (2008), Jean Pfaelzer uncovered how thousands of Chinese Americans had been rounded up and driven out of approximately 200 communities in California and the Pacific Northwest from 1850 to 1906. Chinatowns were burned down, and Chinese men and women were forced onto trains and ships or killed. One of the most violent events occurred in Los Angeles, CA, on the night of October 24, 1871, when about 500 Californios, Mexicans, and Whites, angered by the killing of a

White man by alleged Chinese gang members, attacked Chinese residents, killing at least 18 people, of whom 15 were lynched. In Rock Springs, Wyoming, on September 2, 1885, a mob of White coal miners, angry over the lower wages paid to the Chinese workers, killed at least 28 Chinese Americans and burned down the town's Chinese quarter, home to around 500 to 600 residents. In the Hells Canyon Massacre of 1887, a gang of seven White men murdered 34 Chinese gold miners, and no one was ever found guilty of the crimes. Pfalzer describes the racialized violence, which Chinese Americans call *pai hua* (the Driven Out), as an "ethnic cleansing": "(T)he term expulsion doesn't fully represent the rage and violence of these purges. What occurred along the Pacific coast, from the gold rush through the turn of the century, was ethnic cleansing." (2008, p. xxix)

The reasons for opposing the importation of Chinese "cooleys" were varied and not necessarily always anti-Chinese (Ngai, 2021); initially, the debate focused on the difference between Chinese laborers who were "free" or "unfree," as discussed earlier. But then, California's first governor, John Bigler, began blurring that difference in public addresses. In an official speech before the state legislature, he decried "nearly all were being hired by 'Chinese masters' to mine for gold at pitiable wages, while their families were being held hostage for the faithful performance of their contracts" (Ngai, 2021, p. 85). Bigler alleged they "dug up gold and removed it from the country; they had no interest in becoming citizens, caring not to 'avail themselves of the blessings of free government'; and they were a menace to public safety" (Ngai, 2021, p. 85). Bigler's demonization of the Chinese was fueled by his own political interests: "(b)y tarring all Chinese workers as 'coolies,' Bigler found a racial trope that compared Chinese to Black slaves, the antithesis of free labor, and thereby cast them as a threat to white miners' independence" (Ngai, 2021, p. 86). Over time, this narrative of the Chinese "threat" would be routinely deployed, as needed, to serve as a convenient scapegoat: "Bigler's success in tarring the Chinese as a 'coolie race' gave California politicians a convenient trope that could be trotted out whenever conditions called for a racial scapegoat" (Ngai, 2021, p. 87). Since these rank charges persist today, I feel a need to say that, indeed, many Chinese migrants did assimilate and settle in the USA and fight for the right to remain. The Chinese took up arms, carried out strikes, and turned to the nation's courts for legal intervention; more than 100,000 Chinese participated in a mass civil disobedience against the Geary Act of 1892 that required Chinese residents to report themselves to government officials by refusing to carry photo identity cards (Pfaelzer, 2008; Hernandez, 2017).

It is important to understand how the inaccurate "coolie" trope served to help construct a "White" settler identity: "But more than a political tool, anticoolieism became a kind of protean racism among Whites on the Pacific coast" (Ngai, 2021, p. 87). This racial trope of the enslaved, foreign coolie continued to gain force and evolved into a political-economic theory that argued that "Asian" workers, if incorporated into the US economy, would detrimentally drag down wages for White workers. Ngai cites the 1902 publication of *Meat* vs. *Rice: American Manhood against Asian Coolieism, Which Shall Survive?* by labor leader Samuel Gompers as an example of how race, class, and gender were bound together and pitted against "free labor." Ngai concludes, "Both in the United States and in the British dominions, anticoolieism was foundational to identities of class, nation, and empire. The American and Australian working classes created identity and interests bounded by race, boundaries sharpened on the knife edge of anticoolieism" (2021, p. 184). This racialization also had a gendered aspect, as manifested in the Page Act of 1875 that barred Chinese women from entering the country, due to charges they engaged in prostitution, whether or not they actually did. While the law generally addressed "unfree laborers and women" engaged in "immoral purposes," the law was primarily targeted against Chinese women (Loh-Hagan et al., 2022). The court described Asian women as "obnoxious persons" and described them as "lewd" and corrupting blood.

Although the Chinese constituted only a small fraction of the total immigration flow, i.e., less than 5 percent of the total number of arrivals from 1870 to 1880, they became the focus of disproportionate hatred. Historically, the gold rush in California brought together an unprecedented number of Chinese and Euro-Americans on a mass scale, as reflected in immigration numbers. Ngai cites the arrivals recorded by the San Francisco Customs Office: 325 in 1849, 450 in 1850, 2700 in 1851, and 20,000 in 1852 (2021, p. 36). Only 1 percent of California's mining population in 1850, the Chinese grew to represent 10 percent of the total population by the late 1850s and upwards of 20 to 25 percent of the mining population. By 1860, nearly 35,000 Chinese lived in California; by 1880, more than 75,000 lived in the USA, mostly in California (Hernandez, pp. 65–66).

Nowadays, after decades of scholarly and community activism, Chinese migrants are commonly associated with the building of the transpacific railroad, a role that historians previously had erased. Two photographs mark the change in this historical narrative. In 1869, Andrew J. Russell marked the completion of the first transcontinental railroad with a photograph that showed two White male engineers shaking their hands, amid a crowd of White male workers, at Promontory Point, Utah. In 2014, Corky Lee took the second photograph at the same site, with scores of descendants of the Chinese railroad workers who supplied the actual, material labor. The two contrasting photographs vividly illustrate the erasure of race in dominant historical narratives and the collective, intergenerational efforts required to correct history. This revised history is still inaccurate since the Chinese actually had arrived more than a decade earlier, following the news of "Gam Saan" ("Gold Mountain") in 1849; work on the first transcontinental railroad started more than a decade later in 1863 and was completed in 1869.

Despite the historical corrections by scholars such as Kelly Lyle Hernandez, Mae Ngai, and Jean Pfaelzer, there is still a widespread lack of awareness. On March 11, 2025, as I was completing this essay, I saw an interview with David Baluarte, a professor of law at CUNY Law School, on "Asian American Life," a monthly, half-hour TV program. The episode was on birthright citizenship and discussed the case of *United States v. Wong Kim Ark* (1898). For historical background, Baluarte said, "Large groups of Chinese immigrants had come to the US to help build the railroads," bypassing the gold miners who had come a decade earlier. This inaccurate statement, made by a law professor who works on immigrant issues and broadcast by an award-nominated program that specializes in Asian American issues, illustrates how pervasive these racialized misconceptions still are.

Robinson's theory of racial capitalism can help explain the false narratives and disproportionate hatred toward Chinese immigrants, as well as the court's narrative of Chinese emigration and the perceived role of the Chinese in US society. The historiography of the "coolie" illustrates how the Chinese were constructed as an alien "other" and thereby pushed out of the USA through multiple legislative acts, with the support of violent mobs, to construct and enforce a global, racialized order. This history illustrates how information is distorted and/or erased to serve the interests and aims of an imperialist, White supremacist, capitalist, patriarchal state. However, thanks to the work of innumerable ethnic studies scholars, this history has been excavated and recovered.

In the next section, I highlight other examples of historical erasures that do not serve the narrative of the USA as a righteous, heroic nation. These critical reassessments of "commonsense" historical narratives are the fruition of intergenerational efforts to diversify the academy and its work of producing knowledge. Today, these fields of scholarship are under attack, as reflected in the federal government's various assaults on critical race theory; diversity, equity, and inclusion (DEI) programs; and the federal Department of Education. Yet it is essential for the critiques to continue if we are to grow more self-conscious as a nation; the only path to a future that includes us all requires an honest, critical assessment of our collective past.

Assimilation as Cultural Genocide

So far, this chapter has argued that the formation of an American identity is linked to a collective consciousness of this nation's history, while also pointing out that this history is often obscured or rewritten to serve the nation's dominant political and economic interests. An example of such an obscured event is the US-Korean War, the cataclysmic event that caused my parents to migrate to the United States. The US-Korean War is an event so foggy in the American collective consciousness that the US Department of Defense continues to call it the "Forgotten War" (Vergun, August 4, 2023). But even more obscure is the first Korean War in 1871; it deserves the title of the "Unknown War." I only learned about it a few years ago, on my own. In 1871, the USA sent a company of five battleships and about 600 men to Korea, on a mission to follow up on a missing ship, the USS *General Sherman*, as well as to survey the territory and to open up trade. Despite repeated calls by Korean officials to respect their wishes not to meet with the USA, the US forces sailed up the Han River and, as a result, were fired upon by the Koreans. After demanding an apology and not receiving it, on June 10, the US forces attacked several Korean fortresses, leading to the death of an estimated 243 to 350 Koreans and three Americans. The disproportionate number of Koreans killed reflected the greater firepower of the USA's gunnery.

The Philippine-American War is another conflict that is obscure in the collective US memory. Many Americans are unaware of its occurrence or that, as a result, the Philippines became a colony of the USA from 1898 to 1946. Historian Daniel Immerwahr admitted to having missed this history, as well: "Though I studied U.S. foreign relations as a doctoral student and read countless books about 'American Empire'—the wars, the coups, the meddling in foreign affairs—nobody ever expected me to know even the most elementary facts about the territories. They didn't feel important" (2019, p. 15). The US takeover of the Philippines started with the US intervention into the island nation's fight for independence from Spain. After giving the impression that it was helping the Philippines in its fight for independence, the USA installed itself as the new colonial power upon the defeat of Spain. With the transfer of power, Spain ended its presence in the Americas, Asia, and Africa, and the USA gained control over Puerto Rico, Guam, and the Philippines and established a protectorate over Cuba.

Although the war is officially understood as having ended in 1902, following the US declaration of victory, recent scholarship has highlighted how the war continued for at least a decade longer and was much more violent than remembered. In *Massacre in the Clouds: An American Atrocity and the Erasure of History* (2024), historian Kim A. Wagner wrote of "Bud Dajo," the worst civilian massacre carried out by the US military in the Philippines in March 1906. Although the death toll reached nearly 1000—a greater number than the estimated 350 to 500 unarmed villagers killed in My Lai during the Vietnam War (1955 to 1975)—the event virtually disappeared from the USA's collective conscience until Wagner's book. Wagner argues that such forgetting was a deliberate effort: After failing to present the massacre as a "civilizing mission," the decision was to cover it up. Scholars have also uncovered how it was in the Philippines that the USA first carried out "scorched earth" policies, decimating mass populations, their possessions, and surroundings, a military strategy later widely executed during the Korean and Vietnam Wars: "Outside of designated 'reconcentration camps,' US troops torched crops and residences, to cut off the guerillas' food supply and to punish their supporters, and fired upon anyone they came across" (Jung, 2022, p. 35). Or consider the Vietnam War, which, just with its name, erases the equally horrific violence unleashed by the USA in Cambodia (1965 to 1973) and Laos (1964 to 1973). It is worth noting that "scorched earth" policies that indiscriminately killed noncombatants were finally banned in the 1977 Geneva Conventions. While the bombing of Dresden, Germany, in 1945 has been held up as a potentially immoral assault on a civilian population, the mass carpet bombings of Asian nations—whether in the Philippines, Japan, Korea, Vietnam, Cambodia, Laos, Iraq, or Afghanistan—have not received the same consideration. The same is true today in Gaza. Is it because these wars involved Asian—rather than European or White—bodies? Which bodies matter?

Anti-Asian hate and xenophobia, generally, are recurring patterns in this nation's history; the tradition is rooted in the scapegoating of immigrants for economic troubles affecting American laborers, as well as racialized hatred fueled by this nation's international wars and conflicts (Kim, 2008). Erika Lee calls xenophobia "a constant and defining feature of American life. It is deeply embedded in our society, economy, and politics…It has shaped American foreign relations and justified American imperialism" (2019/2021, p. 7). She writes that it has endured because "it has been an indelible part of American racism, white supremacy, and nationalism, and because it has been supported by American capitalism and democracy" (2019/2021, p. 7).

Today, scholars are still uncovering and critically analyzing this history, in an effort to better understand our collective past and to chart and imagine our collective future. Every day we continue to uncover the frighteningly broad history of human experience, whether considering Cold War–era state terror tactics that subverted mass democratic movements abroad, such as in postwar Korea, DR Congo, or Chile, or that shattered multiracial alliances at home, whether through illegal government surveillance and infiltration of activist groups or outright violence, such as in the Greensboro Massacre of 1979 (Bermanzohn, 2003). Nearly 70 years ago, C. Wright Mills called for the need for the public-at-large to understand the connections between individual lives/minds with larger sociohistorical forces to resolve "urgent public issues and insistent human troubles" (1959, p. 21). This need is just as urgent today, if not more than ever, and it is the aim of liberatory public scholarship.

Efforts to Shut Down Critical Race Theory

This chapter was slow in emerging because it required a reimagining of the dominant, prevailing historical narratives of this nation, traditions in which I'm deeply steeped. Having grown up in the 1970s, I was schooled to believe that the USA was a democratic republic, in which supreme power was held by the people through their elected representatives. Today, that seems not quite true with the disproportionate influence of wealthy donors and corporations in the electoral process. The claim of being a republic is also troubled by the possession of fourteen overseas territories, five of which (American Samoa, Guam, the Northern Mariana Islands, Puerto

Rico, and the US Virgin Islands) have permanent inhabitants who lack full political representation; the USA also has nearly 800 military bases in other countries and territories (Vine, 2015). These existential contradictions have been highlighted by the work of scholars who have studied the ongoing imperial history of the USA; this group includes Greg Grandin (2019), Daniel Immerwahr (2019), Moon-Ho Jung (2022), and Lisa Lowe (2015). However, much work still needs to be done. To truly understand the intersecting roles of race and empire in US society, a further de-structuring of "Western" historiography is required, as Cedric Robinson noted, "For the realization of a new theory we require new history" (1983/2000, p. 307).

In *Black Marxism* (1983/2000), Robinson offers the "Black radical tradition" as an alternative guiding ideology in imagining the social world. He describes it as "a world-historical consciousness" that opposes "the systemic privations of racial capitalism": "Ideologically, it cements pain to purpose, experience to expectation, consciousness to collective action. It deepens with each disappointment at false mediation and reconciliation and is crystallized into ever-increasing cores by betrayal and repression" (1983/2000, p. 317). Robinson's ideas have decentered European discourses of freedom and liberty by focusing instead on strategies of resistance and survival developed by those who were oppressed by European and American colonization. His ideas have been foundational for innumerable Black liberation scholars, including Robin D.G. Kelley and Ruth Wilson Gilmore, his former students, and have led to a flourishing of critical race scholarship in Black studies, ethnic studies, and gender studies, fields of study which are troublingly under direct attack today by the administration.

All the historical contradictions discussed in this chapter still exist. We are supposed to be a nation where everyone is "equal" and "free," yet we live in an imperialist, White supremacist, capitalistic, patriarchal society where class, race, and gender unjustly structure people's daily lives. We are supposed to be a nation of "law and order," yet we live at a time when the US judicial system is seen as highly politicized, whether due to politicians who manipulate the judicial nomination process or, more recently, the president's sweeping pardons of the January 6 protestors. We also see the anti-Asian and White supremacist hate that has long permeated this nation. In 2023, a conservative law professor at the University of Pennsylvania drew the ire of administrators and students there for opining, among other things, that the United States would be "better off with fewer Asians and less Asian immigration" and that Black people felt "resentment and shame and envy" over the "Western peoples' outsized achievements and contributions" (Confessore, 2024). Since assuming the presidency in January 2025, the president has escalated his anti-Chinese rhetoric, starting a trade war with China. Meanwhile, the recent arrest and threatened deportation of Mahmoud Khalil, an activist for Palestinian rights at Columbia University, who is a legal resident, raises questions about fundamental rights to free speech, protest, and freedom of assembly. All these contradictions and tensions are central to the origins of this nation, a White settler society founded on principles of freedom and democracy for a privileged elite minority. American democracy was never for "all."

The critics of teaching an honest, critical history of the USA argue that such a curriculum is divisive and demoralizing. In June 2021, the Florida Board of Education unanimously voted to ban teaching "critical race theory" in K to Grade 12; the term, which originated as a legal theory focusing on structural racism in social institutions, has been appropriated by its opponents to refer to anything making race salient to discussions on history or current events. Gov. Ron DeSantis (R-FL), in supporting the ban, said, "I think it's going to cause a lot of divisions. I think it'll cause people to think of themselves more as a member of a particular race based on skin color, rather than based on the content of their character and based on their hard work and what they're trying to accomplish in life" (Ali & AP, 2021). However, I disagree. I don't believe that critical awareness of this nation's history will have deleterious effects. Self-awareness—not self-glorification—is essential if we want to create a more just and equitable society. With a spirit of humility, we can learn more about ourselves and the rest of the world. In this collective search for a coherent national identity and a just society, the work of independent, critical scholarship is essential. In my classrooms, I've seen the positive impact of diversifying the academic canon. My students are inspired by the writings of W.E.B. DuBois, bell hooks, and other thinkers whose perspectives were missing from the college curriculum until after the modern civil rights movement. I remember feeling the same way, myself, almost 30 years ago, when I was a graduate student.

The US Commission on Civil Rights' recommendation to fight anti-Asian hate by pursuing and prosecuting anti-Asian crimes that were cited at the start of this chapter is like the distinction between "free" and "coolie" labor, another red herring that falsely presents criminalization as a social solution, when, in fact, it serves to exacerbate social divides and to worsen racial hostilities. To learn more about anti-Asian hate, the government should reflect on itself. In its January 5, 2022, report on the January 6 assault on the US Capitol, Human Rights Watch, the nongovernmental organization that conducts research and advocacy on human rights, urged political leaders and Americans, collectively, to recognize the role of racism in the attack, as well as the president's attempt to halt certification of the 2020 election results, generally. Racism, the group said, was "in the roots of, and remains embedded in this movement":

> Rioters blatantly and proudly hurled racial slurs against Capitol Police officers. Many waved the Confederate battle flag, long a symbol for southern states that supported slavery and those promoting post-Civil War racist policies. Gallows and nooses that recalled the lynching of Black people appeared on and around the Capitol grounds—so many symbols of hatred that the Washington Post compiled a list of many that were witnessed that day. Taken together, they lead to one overarching conclusion: that the January 6 attacks had much to do with race in America. (Stang, 2022)

Despite these findings, the president has been re-elected. On his first day in office, he granted clemency to every person charged or convicted for their participation in the January 6 insurrection. He has also made it a top priority to attack DEI programs and critical race theory. The president's systemic attacks on immigrants and Black and Brown people are deeply troubling and threaten the USA's most fundamental values of equality of opportunity and of proudly being a nation of immigrants.

Some analysts see the current backlash against racialized minorities as a retreat on racial progress. But as Erika Lee noted, progress and retreat are not mutually exclusive: "(J)ust as racial progress and racist progress can happen at the same time, Americans' embrace of immigrants and their fear and hatred of them have coexisted as equally strong forces shaping the United States" (Lee, 2019/2021, p. 324). She discusses the long history of xenophobia in the United States:

> [X]enophobia is a form of racism. It defines certain groups as racial and religious others who are inherently inferior or dangerous—or both—and demonizes them as a group based on these presumptions. Xenophobia has also been an inextricable part of race making in America: it has shaped how Americans classify people by race and rank them in America's racial hierarchy. (Lee, 2019/2021, p. 9)

Lee argues that xenophobia persists in the USA for many reasons, including the multiple ways it serves capitalism:

> The US economy has flourished by exploiting workers, especially those whom American society has already defined as dangerous, "illegal," and unworthy of protection or equal rights. These workers become a permanent class of deportable immigrants who remain socially marginal and economically exploitable even as they continue to serve American economic interests. (Lee, 2019/2021, p. 13)

She also describes its function in the practice of this nation's international relations, as well as how it impacts domestic policies regarding migrants from certain countries, even their descendants:

> The United States built its empire of territory, trade, and power by disparaging foreign countries and their peoples as racially inferior, backward, and conquerable…Our treatment of specific immigrants in the United States has also been determined by our nation's relationships with foreign countries. This pattern has repeated itself time and time again, in the anti-German hysteria that accompanied US involvement in World War I, the incarceration of Japanese Americans during World War II, and the rise of Islamophobia during the war on terror. (Lee, 2019/2021, p. 15)

As Lee concludes her book, she reflects on "Americans' willful and purposeful historical amnesia" of this nation's xenophobic history and its consequences (p. 324): "It has real repercussions. By ignoring the deep roots of xenophobia in the past, we ignore the deep hold that xenophobia has on our present" (Lee, 2019/2021, p. 327).

With the installation of the current presidency's second term, we see the rise of widespread xenophobia in the demonization of immigrants. We see how undocumented immigrants, some of the most poor, vulnerable, and hard-working people in our society, a mere 13 million people in a nation of 330 million, are blamed for the gaping wealth inequalities that exist, rather than the billionaires and corporations who have been raking in record profits. We see the "real repercussions" everywhere, as migrants are being deported without due process. We see it in the separation of migrant families; a practice started in the president's first term that resulted in 1500 children who were permanently separated from their families. I see it in the widespread fear of immigrants and their children in my classrooms and across the city. Cedric Robinson described the systemic ranking of people based on racialized differences as the product of "a civilization maddened by its own perverse assumptions and contradictions" (Robinson, 1983/2000, p. 318). This deranged, dehumanizing vision can never serve the humane and inclusive ideals we espouse as a society. It only serves the imperial, White supremacist, capitalist patriarchal system and those who profit from it—not the whole people, not the totality.

The history of anti-Chinese violence discussed in this chapter is evidence of how race has been used to exploit workers and to pit workers of different races against each other to extract greater profits for the capitalists. Today, as in the past, racial categories construct a racial hierarchy that allows certain groups to be denied the rights granted to citizens, to be deported in times of economic crisis, and to be used as a scapegoat for social problems, as needed. We see this in the daily news. This is harmful statecraft, for empire and democracy can never coexist. The solution to this longstanding problem cannot rest on the importance of honoring the USA's so-called "time-honored" values of freedom and equality, since those values were never extended to all, universally. For real change in US society, perhaps we should turn, instead, to the "Black radical tradition" that has historically been committed to "the continuing development of a collective conscience informed by the historical struggles for liberation and motivated by the shared obligation to preserve the collective being, the ontological totality" (Robinson, 1983/2000, p. 171).

References

Ali, S. S., & The Associated Press. (2021, June 10). *Florida Board of Education passes rule banning critical race theory in classrooms.* https://www.nbcnews.com/news/us-news/florida-board-education-passes-rule-banning-critical-race-theory-classrooms-n1270363

Bermanzohn, S. A. (2003). *Through survivors' eyes: From the sixties to the Greensboro Massacre.* Vanderbilt University Press.

BBC News. (2016, May 2). *Trump accuses China of 'raping' US with unfair trade policy.* https://www.bbc.com/news/election-us-2016-36185012

Chang, K. (2015). *Keywords for Asian American studies.* NYU Press.

Confessore, N. (2024, January 20). "America is under attack": Inside the anti-D.E.I. crusade. *The New York Times.*

Grandin, G. (2019). *The end of the myth: From the frontier to the border wall in the mind of America.* Metropolitan Books.

Hernandez, K. L. (2017). *City of inmates: Conquest, rebellion, and the rise of human caging in Los Angeles, 1771–1965.* University of North Carolina Press.

Hswen, Y., Xu, X., Hing, A., Hawkins, J. B., Brownstein, J. S., & Gee, G. (2021). Association of "#covid19" versus "#chinesevirus" with anti-Asian sentiments on Twitter: March 9–23, 2020. *American Journal of Public Health, 111*(5), 956–964.

Immerwahn, D. (2019). *How to hide an empire: A history of the greater United States.* Farrar.

Jung, M. H. (2017). What is the "coolie question"? *Labour History, 113*, 1–8.

Jung, M. H. (2022). *Menace to empire: Anticolonial solidarities and the transpacific origins of the US security state.* University of California Press.

Kenny, K. (2021). The antislavery origins of US immigration policy. *Journal of the Civil War Era, 11*(3), 361–381.

Kim, N. Y. (2008). *Imperial citizens: Koreans and race from Seoul to LA.* Stanford University Press.

Lee, E. (2019/2021). *America for Americans: A history of xenophobia in the United States.* Basic Books.

Lew-Williams, B. (2018). *The Chinese must go: Violence, exclusion, and the making of the alien in America.* Harvard University Press.

Loh-Hagan, V., Kwoh, J., Chang, J., & Kwoh, P. (2022). Excluded from history: The Page Act of 1875. *Social Education, 86*(2), 73–78.

Lowe, L. (2015). *The intimacies of four continents.* Duke University Press.

Ngai, M. (2021). *The Chinese question: The gold rushes, Chinese migration, and global politics.* W.W. Norton & Company.

Nguyen, V. T. (2024, January 29). Palestine is in Asia: An Asian American argument for solidarity. *The Nation Magazine.*

Pfaelzer, J. (2008). *Driven out: The forgotten war against Chinese Americans.* University of California Press.

Robinson, C. (1983/2000). *Black Marxism: The making of the Black radical tradition.* The University of North Carolina Press.

Said, E. (1978). *Orientalism.* Vintage Books.

Stang, V. (2022, January 5). Racism's prominent role in January 6 US Capitol attack. *Human Rights Watch.* Racism's Prominent Role in January 6 US Capitol Attack | Human Rights Watch.

Tuan, M. (1998). *Forever foreigners or honorary whites? The Asian ethnic experience today.* Rutgers University Press.

United States Commission on Civil Rights. (2023, September 27). *The federal response to anti-Asian racism in the United States.* https://www.usccr.gov/files/2023-09/fy-2023-se-report_0.pdf

U.S. Supreme Court. (1889, May 13). *Chae Chan Ping v. U.S. (Chinese exclusion case).* 130 U.S. 581.

Vergun, D. (2023, August 3). Five Korean War "Firsts" had lasting impacts. *DOD News.*

Vine, D. (2015). *Base nation: How US military bases abroad harm America and the world*. Metropolitan Books.

Wagner, K. A. (2024). *Massacre in the clouds: An American atrocity and the erasure of history*. PublicAffairs.

Yancy, G., & hooks, b. (2015, December 10). bell hooks: Buddhism, the beats and loving blackness. *The New York Times*. https://archive.nytimes.com/opinionator.blogs.nytimes.com/author/bell-hooks/?ref=rootschangemedia.com

CHAPTER 11

"They Even Took My Child Away From Me": Muslim Refugee Mothers' Mistrust Toward the Police and Social Service Providers

Hermeet K. Kohli, Ragini S. Malhotra, and Ashlee Jensen

Introduction

In this chapter, we examine how Muslim refugee women experience surveillance as they raise their children in the United States. We draw on previous participatory action research with Muslim refugee women in the northeastern United States, highlighting how parenting struggles

H. K. Kohli (✉)
Department of Social Work, University of North Carolina, Greensboro, NC, USA
e-mail: HKKOHLI@uncg.edu

R. S. Malhotra
Department of Sociology, University of Southern Maine, Portland, ME, USA
e-mail: ragini.malhotra@maine.edu

A. Jensen
College of Health and Human Services, University of North Carolina Wilmington, Wilmington, NC, USA
e-mail: aejensen@uncg.edu

J. S. Hong et al. (eds.), *Violence and Trauma Without Borders*,
https://doi.org/10.1007/978-3-032-29221-6_11

transcend heterogeneity across country-of-origin differences for Muslim refugee women (Kohli & Fineran, 2020a, 2020b). We focus specifically on the mistrust they expressed toward police and social service providers. Recognizing that Muslim refugee women hold diverse intersecting identities when it comes to religion, geography, citizenship status, country of birth, refugee journeys, ethnicity, and race, we take an intersectional approach. We examine some key factors that account for women's feelings of mistrust toward both the police and social service providers.

We find that systemic racism operates in Muslim refugee women's everyday lives. Specifically, we demonstrate how xenophobia and Islamophobia intersect to shape women's experiences of surveillance within their communities and the criminal legal system and child welfare system. This leads to feelings of fear, anxiety, and isolation. These feelings of distrust create difficult resettlement circumstances for Muslim refugee women who have to negotiate multiple obstacles and barriers in everyday life while raising their children. We end the chapter with trauma-informed and community-oriented recommendations for service providers and police officials so they may work to support refugee Muslim women and their families.

Literature Review

There are currently an unprecedented 122.6 million people around the globe who have been forced from home (UNCHR, 2024a). Among them are nearly 38 million refugees, 41% of whom are under the age of 18 (UNCHR, 2024b). Women and their dependent children are commonly estimated to be 70–80% of the displaced population worldwide (UNHCR, 2024b). In the United States, there are 435,333 refugees and 3,184,161 asylum seekers (UNCHR, 2024a). Of the 60,050 newly admitted refugees to the United States in 2023, as reported by the United States Department of Homeland Security, 49.6 percent were female, 45 percent were children under 18 years of age, and nearly 64% of the refugees newly admitted to the United States in 2023 arrived as dependent family members (Schofield & Yap, 2024).

Refugee families face unique barriers as they try to access government services and systems, including mistrust toward institutions and social service providers. In the following literature review, we examine the pervasive distrust of institutions among refugee populations, including social service providers, medical providers, and criminal legal systems. We explore the factors contributing to this mistrust with social service providers and law enforcement, structural and cultural barriers to help-seeking that exacerbate mistrust, and the impact of mistrust on help-seeking behavior. These factors are discussed in the context of the intersectional identities of Muslim refugee mothers making continuous efforts to integrate into the host country.

Mistrust Toward Systems

Understanding mistrust is essential for comprehending refugee families' interactions with authorities. Fear and distrust are often rooted in concerns about deportation and child separation and can be exacerbated by experiences of government corruption in their home countries (Merken et al., 2023). These feelings of mistrust and the fear of systems of authority can also lead to other forms of exclusion. We know that negative experiences and mistrust in institutions such as law enforcement can decrease trust in other institutions, including those in the medical field (Alang et al., 2020). These experiences can, in turn, impact healthcare-seeking behavior among refugees, for instance (Haider et al., 2023).

Interactions with refugee communities, therefore, require close consideration of how complex identities and experiences intersect in people's everyday lives (Alsaidi et al., 2023; Critelli & Yalim, 2021; Ellis et al., 2020). It is also important to exercise procedural justice, which emphasizes fairness and transparency in processes (Ali et al., 2022) and to treat refugees as knowledgeable individuals capable of acquiring further knowledge (Sundbäck, 2024). These overarching strategies provide practice frameworks for serving refugee populations in ways that foster trust and improve relationships with authorities and service providers.

Lack of trust in institutions and government systems can lead to difficulty engaging Muslim refugees across many different settings, including counter-terrorism efforts (Ali et al., 2022), intimate partner violence services (Merken et al., 2023), police and judicial system interactions (Ellis et al., 2020), resettlement (Shaw et al., 2021), and other social service settings. Police officers, social workers, teachers, and public health workers make decisions that directly impact the lives of those they serve, playing a complex and sometimes harmful role in the trust of government systems (Monish, 2020).

Social Service Providers

Providers acting on behalf of the state can cause harm to refugees and asylum seekers through their actions or inactions, exacerbating their psychological distress and creating an environment of mistrust and vulnerability (Monish, 2020). Social workers, community leaders, NGOs, and other support personnel in assisting migrants have a significant role in influencing their trust in institutions (Sundbäck, 2024). Even negative experiences with interpreters can erode refugees' trust in government systems (Jiménez-Ivars & León-Pinilla, 2018), highlighting the need for competent individuals to serve as frontline service providers.

Social service providers need to build trust with refugee families by demonstrating that they are culturally competent and able to generate conditions that are nonpunitive and conducive to safety (Kohli & Fineran, 2020b). The failure to do this can lead to feelings of mistrust among refugee service users; these feelings of mistrust can be exacerbated by other areas in which institutional distrust exists (Holtmann & Rickards, 2018). Providers note that immigrant women are particularly fearful of authorities like ICE and Children's Services (Merken et al., 2023). Immigrant women experiencing intimate partner violence face specific fear and mistrust toward law enforcement and social services (Critelli & Yalim, 2021). Trauma-informed approaches are essential for creating trust and improving access to domestic violence services for immigrant and refugee women (Critelli & Yalim, 2021).

Police and Law Enforcement

Surveillance using the criminal legal system is deeply seated in the child welfare system and documented by the seminal works of Roberts (2002). Roberts and others have continually called attention to how women of color have been historically policed as mothers, and this criminalization of Black mothers continues, especially as it intersects with poverty (Bach, 2022; Bezusko, 2013; Goodwin, 2020; Miller, 2024; Roberts, 2002, 2014, 2021). These mechanisms of policing have been rooted in the history of slavery itself, and today, we see them operating through everyday interactions with the police, healthcare, and social workers, as well as public school representatives and those working in the foster care system (Holtmann & Rickards, 2018; Monish, 2020).

Fear of detention and persecution is also listed as a barrier to trust and engagement between refugees and police (Ali et al., 2022). Procedural justice and acting within appropriate power limits (bounded authority) are crucial for enhancing cooperation with police (Chenane & Pryce, 2024) and police legitimacy among immigrant and Muslim populations (Ali et al., 2022). Studies show that measures perceived as fair and inclusive promote positive perceptions of police, while violations of bounded authority damage trust (Ali et al., 2022). Deviations in procedural justice lead to mistrust and cause refugees to receive harsher and more frequent policing (Ellis et al., 2020). Concerns about representativeness in policing also influence perceptions of police legitimacy among Muslim populations (Ali et al., 2022). Muslim refugees often face discrimination and profiling, which exacerbates their mistrust toward police and other authorities.

Additionally, studies show that Muslims who are more religious or racially marginalized feel more targeted and less cooperative with police; profiling, combined with the broader context of discrimination and surveillance, significantly impacts their willingness to engage with authorities (Khan, 2023). Congolese women refugees experience challenges raising their children as potential targets of police discrimination (Saksena & McMorrow, 2021). Male Somali refugees in the United States and Canada also report harsher and more frequent policing due to their multiple marginalized (Black, immigrant, and Muslim) statuses (Ellis et al., 2020). The perception of police biases and tiered systems of justice impacts the view of refugees on the trustworthiness of law enforcement.

Barriers to Help-Seeking that Exacerbate Mistrust

Much of the mistrust transcribed to frontline service providers happens because of systemic and cultural barriers. Considering these barriers to trust can help determine where to intervene within systems of care to engender more confident relationships between providers and Muslim refugee clients.

Structural Barriers The structural barriers within sociocultural structures and government bureaucracies that exacerbate the mistrust between Muslim refugees and providers include immigration status, financial strain, language barriers, housing instability, lack of trust in authority figures, concerns about confidentiality, and lack of clarity for accessing or navigating services (Byrow et al., 2020; Holtmann & Rickards, 2018; Shaw et al.,

2021). The ability of service providers to competently empower refugees to successfully overcome such barriers is often seen as a reflection of the service institutions and can engender or damage trust (Sundbäck, 2024). As representatives of the government, trust in service providers may evolve within the context of changing political and social perspectives toward refugee resettlement (Shaw et al., 2021). Abroad, hostile immigration policies in Britain have also exacerbated psychological distress and mistrust among refugees and asylum seekers (Monish, 2020). In the United States, it is important to understand mistrust toward police among marginalized groups within the context of sociopolitical influences such as the impact of historic discrimination and systemic oppression of people of color (Malik, 2023); this includes the political policies of the current president's era (Saksena & McMorrow, 2021) and the impact of racism on perspectives across the United States in the wake of events such as George Floyd's murder and Muslim perceptions post-9/11 (Khan, 2023).

Cultural Barriers Mental health literacy and stigma around help-seeking are cultural barriers that impede trust in service providers and help-seeking among refugees (Byrow et al., 2020). These beliefs, stigmas, and levels of trust vary according to intersections of religion, race, gender, and refugee status. Immigrants' reluctance to seek professional mental health services can be influenced by beliefs about illness, recovery, and well-being; cultural beliefs, religion, and spirituality; language and educational barriers; lack of trust in providers; stigma; and the quality of previous care and understanding of disease (Mohammadifirouzeh et al., 2023; Haider et al., 2023).

Impact of Mistrust on Help-Seeking Behavior

The intersection of gender, race, and refugee status positions Muslim mothers as particularly vulnerable to state surveillance. Their parenting practices are often scrutinized through a White, middle-class lens that fails to account for diverse experiences, cultural differences, histories of trauma, or structural inequities (Saksena & McMorrow, 2021). This scrutiny is not neutral; it is shaped by a long history of racialized family separation policies that continue to echo in modern child protective services practices (Saksena & McMorrow, 2021). Muslim refugee women may avoid seeking help from police or social services not because of cultural resistance, but because of mistrust that is rooted in experiences of racial profiling, over-policing, and the criminalization of their communities (Yazdiha, 2023; Ellis et al., 2020). Gendered Islamophobia also plays a role, as Muslim women are often seen as either helpless victims or dangerous outsiders, both of which can justify state control over their families (Alimahomed-Wilson, 2020).

Barriers like language differences, lack of interpreters, and unfamiliarity with United States laws reflect how systems are designed for dominant groups and systematically exclude marginalized others, including Muslim refugee women. These challenges are further shaped by race, gender, religion, and class; for example, women who wear hijabs or have darker skin may be more visible and thus more vulnerable to discrimination (Mahmood, 2024). As Saksena and McMorrow (2021) note, mistrust of social services is not simply a matter of cultural misunderstanding but is rooted in systemic racism and Islamophobia that shape how refugee women are treated by institutions.

Refugees, especially women, do not engage with service providers and criminal legal systems due to many of the above barriers as well as an absence of social support, fear of consequences, and powerlessness (Al-Shdayfat & Hatamleh, 2017; Fineran & Kohli, 2020; Haider et al., 2023; Tekeste, 2022). By offering acceptance, creating safety, and providing support and empowerment, trust can be established, and these barriers to help-seeking can be overcome (Al-Shdayfat & Hatamleh, 2017). Creating a sense of safety and trustworthiness in service provision is essential for encouraging reporting (Critelli & Yalim, 2021). Attending events related to their culture, language, or religion and more frequent home visits were also associated with higher levels of perceived safety (Shaw et al., 2021). We will now discuss the intersectionality and other conceptual frameworks that guided our study.

Conceptual Framework

There are many frameworks for understanding the unique experiences of oppression and privilege among marginalized groups and how those experiences build or damage institutional trust. Minority stress theory, cultural mistrust theory, and intersectionality can be applied to understand the unique experiences of Muslim refugee women and the formation of mistrust of law enforcement and social service providers.

Minority Stress Theory

Minority stress theory (MST) offers a valuable lens for understanding the chronic stress experienced by marginalized groups due to their stigmatized identities (Meyer, 2003). Meyer (2003) defines minority stress as the additional burden of stigma, prejudice, discrimination, and structural exclusion from resources that exacerbate general life stressors, fostering mistrust and detachment from the dominant culture (Meyer, 2003). Originally developed to explain health disparities among sexual minorities, MST has since been applied to a range of populations, including Muslim Americans (Ashai, 2021). This framework is particularly relevant for Muslim refugee women, who face multiple, intersecting forms of oppression.

Using the framework of MST, recent studies have found that stigmatized status greatly affects trust and vigilance among Muslim refugee women. Chaudhry et al. (2024) further emphasize that both premigration trauma and postmigration discrimination contribute to institutional mistrust among first-generation sexual and gender minority migrant women. Societal Islamophobia was significantly associated with anxiety and high levels of vigilance (Ashai, 2021). Similarly, Di Giuseppe (2021) found that asylum seekers experience chronic environmental stressors due to their stigmatized status and that trust was more easily built with group service providers with shared identities. These findings underscore the need for trauma-informed, culturally affirming, and intersectionally aware approaches to working with refugee families.

Cultural Mistrust Theory

Cultural mistrust theory addresses the historical and systemic roots of mistrust among marginalized groups toward dominant institutions. This framework is particularly relevant for understanding the mistrust Muslim refugee women may feel toward police and social service providers due to similar dynamics of fear and institutional mistrust, rooted in past trauma and cultural disconnect. Francis Terrell's foundational work demonstrated that cultural mistrust significantly influences whether Black individuals engage with US institutional support systems in the context of historical injustices and systemic racism (Terrell, 1984). In his study, Black clients with higher levels of institutional mistrust were more likely to discontinue counseling when paired with White counselors, highlighting the importance of cultural congruence and safety in service provision (Terrell, 1984). These findings suggest that institutional trust is not solely about access but also about the quality of interaction and representation among frontline service providers (Terrell, 1984). Langlois (2025) expands this framework by linking cultural mistrust to historical and intergenerational trauma. While the historical context of these authors differs, Muslim refugee women also carry compounded racial and systemic trauma: war, displacement, and Islamophobia, which shapes their perceptions of institutions as agents of surveillance rather than support (Langlois, 2025). Reframing mistrust as a rational response to systemic harm underscores the need for culturally responsive, trauma-informed care.

Intersectionality

The concept of intersectionality, coined by legal scholar Kimberle Crenshaw (1989), has since been central to transdisciplinary feminist scholarship, including Black feminist thought (Collins, 2000, 2009, 2015; Lorde, 1984). The intersectional frameworks help us understand and analyze how one's social location and varying identities can intersect and interact with each other to create overlapping disadvantages and oppressions. Intersecting forms of disadvantage can thus compound themselves, resulting in unique obstacles for every individual depending on their social location.

We utilize this framework, recognizing that Muslim refugee women hold intersecting identities and that these vary within the Muslim immigrant community. Drawing upon existing scholarship, we frame Islamophobia as an intersectional phenomenon that is representative of systemic racism (Ansari & Patel, 2024; Mahadevan & Mayer, 2017; Mirza, 2013). Specifically, we recognize how Muslim women have been ascribed limiting labels that often obscure their agency based on assumptions about their faith (e.g., choice of dress).

Muslim women's experiences are not homogenous (Ansari & Patel, 2024). Factors such as country of origin, race, ethnicity, religion, linguistic background, refugee status, and histories of dispossession all intersect with gender in unique ways to create distinct experiences of marginality and discrimination. We recognize, for instance, the application of intersectional frameworks to an understanding of Muslim women's diverse experiences. Studies, for instance, apply an intersectional lens to Muslim women's embodied practices, like choosing (or not choosing) to wear hijab (Mirza, 2013).

The diverse experiences that Muslim women have, in turn, shape Muslim attitudes toward institutions, communities, and the criminal legal system (Khan, 2023). In cases where there is a lack of trust in institutions and their representatives (e.g., police and service providers), Muslim refugee women may face additional barriers as they resist seeking assistance. Here, unique vulnerabilities due to gender norms, for instance, can further compound the effects of such mistrust. For example, Syrian refugee women often do not report violence due to fear of repercussions such as arrest or deportation, divorce, lack of income, stigma, fear of blame, and lack of social support (Al-Shdayfat & Hatamleh, 2017).

Experiences can also vary according to other intersecting identities, for instance, country of national origin (Shaw et al., 2021). Additionally, identity centrality can significantly predict help-seeking intentions, as the value placed on ethnic identity can influence alignment with culturally normative beliefs, attitudes, and behaviors around help-seeking and treatment engagement (Sadek & Hashem, 2024). Social and cultural discrimination, particularly racism, may be more astutely experienced by Muslim women who are also Black (Saksena & McMorrow, 2021). Incidents of colorism (discrimination or prejudice against individuals with a darker skin tone within the same ethnic group) and within-group discrimination also vary among Muslim individuals (Alsaidi et al., 2023). Muslims who were more aware of discrimination and proud of their identity felt more negatively about the police, while those who engaged in religious rituals and felt important to society were more acquiescent (Khan, 2023). Mistrust, fear, and resulting hesitancy to seek support from the state are outcomes of discrimination experienced among Muslim American women and act as barriers to help-seeking (Alsaidi et al., 2023). Experiencing discrimination has been associated with lower levels of perceived safety (Shaw et al., 2021). Discrimination affects the ability to establish trust; understanding these dynamics is crucial for developing effective interventions that build trust with Muslim women (Alsaidi et al., 2023).

Together, these theories highlight the importance of culturally competent, trauma-informed approaches. By integrating these perspectives, we can better understand systemic barriers and develop more effective, trust-building interventions for Muslim refugee women. MST, cultural mistrust theory, and intersectionality are interwoven and interconnected frameworks, and the authors utilized the intersectionality framework to guide their research, as intersectionality helps us see that mistrust is a structural outcome of overlapping systems of exclusion (Mahmood, 2024).

Methodology

Data

The data for this chapter emerged from the research conducted by the authors to document the narratives of refugee women regarding child-rearing as well as child abuse and neglect (Kohli & Fineran, 2020a; Kohli & Fineran, 2020b). Even though the focus of the primary research was on studying child-rearing and child abuse and neglect, major themes emerged that focused on mistrust toward police and social service providers, which is the focus of the chapter. This research project was approved by the University of Southern Maine's Institutional Review Board. We designed a semi-structured interview guide that gave women the opportunity to tell their stories while guiding them with thematic follow-up questions. Some examples of questions in the interview guide were the following: What are parents' responsibilities in raising children? Are there any gender differences in raising children in your culture? How do they define child abuse and neglect? The focus was not on their stories of trauma and flight but on their experiences of parenting and family life post-migration. Each of the co-authors came to the project with personal and professional contacts in the immigrant and refugee communities, which facilitated the trust-building process. Refugee women were initially identified through contact with social service agencies serving refugees in Maine, that is, Maine Immigrant and Refugee Services, Gateway Community Services, and Catholic charities in Maine. Snowball sampling was most appropriate given the sensitive nature of the topic and the importance of our work being "vetted" by someone in a position of trust in the refugee/asylum-seeking community in Greater Portland. We made efforts to deliberately work predominantly with women who are often not tapped for their knowledge and opinions and visited them in their homes for the interviews. Our methodology was based on participatory action research (PAR), whereby participants have an active role in shaping research questions as well as in the analysis and verification of research findings. PAR "... includes the subjects as co-creators of the research...the ethos of PAR is based on inclusion, participation, respecting all local voices, and community-driven sustainable outcomes" (O'Neill & Harindranath, 2006, p. 46).

We consulted with refugee women in the community before data collection to get feedback on the interview guide and facilitated their participation in generating and analyzing data after data collection and transcription. We worked with trusted interpreters who were connected with service organizations and informed about the research process. After preliminary analysis, we shared the emerging themes with the participants during a focus group luncheon. All participants attended the focus group luncheon and signed informed consent to maintain confidentiality. We used thematic analysis to code and analyze the transcripts from the interviews and focus groups. After careful and repeated examination of the transcripts, categories and subcategories of analysis were developed and defined. The categories of themes evolved during the analysis as more patterns, variations, and concepts were identified.

Participant Profile

Out of the 17 women who were interviewed for this research, 15 were refugees, and two were asylees living in the Greater Portland Region in Maine. Seven of the women had fled from Somalia, six had come from Iraq, and one each from Burundi, Jordan, Morocco, and Sudan. All but one woman practiced Islam and wore a *hijab* (a veil or headscarf), and 11 of the 17 women only spoke the language from their country of origin and needed interpreters. Six women were multilingual and could converse in Arabic, Somali, and French. In the context of their educational qualifications, two participants had professional degrees, two had bachelor's degrees, one had an associate degree in arts, five completed high school, two completed middle or elementary school, and five reported having no formal education. Eight of them were working outside of the house to support their families, and nine were homemakers. Their ages ranged from 23 to 73 years, with an average of 39 years and a median of 37. They had been in the United States from 1 to 26 years, with an average stay of 8.95 years and a median of 8 years. Their household size ranged from one to 12 people, with a mean of 5.75, and there were one to ten children in the household, with an average of 4.41 children per home. Two participants were widowed, and all others were married and living with their spouses (Table 11.1).

All transcripts were analyzed together as there were no differences across ethnicities. Even though the range of time that the participants had been in the United States was quite large, only two women had been here for a long time (over 20 years), and the rest of the participants were recent immigrants. The women, on average, were raising four to five children,

Table 11.1 Demographic profile of the study participants

	n	*Mean*	*Median*	*Range*
Age		39	37	27–73
Country of origin				
Burundi	1			
Iraq	6			
Jordan	1			
Morocco	1			
Somalia	7			
Sudan	1			
Education				
No formal education	5			
Middle or elementary school	2			
High school	5			
Associates in arts	1			
Bachelor's degrees	2			
Professional	2			
Employment status				
Employed outside the house	8			
Homemaker	9			
Marital status				
Married	15			
Widowed	2			
Children per family		4.41		1–10
Household size		5.75		1–12
Immigrant status				
Asylum seeking	2			
Refugee	15			
Language spoken				
Multilingual	6			
Spoke only the language of the country of origin	11			
Religious affiliation				
Christianity	1			
Islam	16			

and in the large households, the older siblings supported the mothers in household work.

Analyses and Findings

Notably, although this study was focused on understanding experiences of raising children, refugee women's narratives about the latter were consistently intertwined with narratives about their experiences of surveillance by state actors (and within communities). More specifically, the women whose voices make this chapter demonstrate a clear sense of mistrust and distrust toward both law enforcement and social services. Their narratives reflected "… a form of resistance, challenging the formation of dominant narratives which have been told for and about people seeking asylum and refugee status" (Smith, 2015, p. 463).

In this section, we examine women's narratives as they pertain to the following two categories: (1) mistrust in (and fear of) police and White neighbors and (2) mistrust toward social service providers (and the child welfare system). Within the first of these two broad thematic categories, we found that policing by White neighbors leads to (a) general fear of the police, with the fear of neighbors and police co-existing, and (b) mistrust toward the police in connection with fears around child removal. In the case of the second category (mistrust in social service providers), women expressed (a) mistrust due to experiences of child removal and their narratives reflected a resulting culture of fear, (b) mistrust due to cultural incompetence, and (c) mistrust due to an intersection between cultures of fear and experiences of social isolation in the United States. We discuss these themes below using pseudonyms to protect participants' privacy.

Mistrust in (and Fear of) Police and White Neighbors

The sub-themes in this section are both distinct and interrelated. We see women's fear of their White neighbors and police co-existing together with racialized double standards. Women's mistrust toward police is also connected to fears around child removal. We begin by discussing the first theme: Muslim refugee women's experiences of policing by their White neighbors. These experiences were inseparable from women's mistrust of the police. For example, Yasmin, a woman in her 30 s, originally from Somalia, feared her White neighbors. She believed her parenting practices, indigenous to Somalia, would be interpreted as harmful and that her neighbors would call the police on her. Elaborating on this, Yasmin noted, *"So we're scared we cannot discipline our children outside because you say that the white people they just call police on us."* In using the word "we," Yasmin speaks not simply on behalf of herself, but on behalf of other women in her community.

Yasmin also points to racialized double standards, highlighting the fact that when White mothers discipline their children, they are not policed and under surveillance in the same way. For instance, Yasmin notes

> I saw just white woman when they are getting their children, they were beating them...I saw yesterday even in the playground. White woman she's beating her child...but for us we afraid maybe we are told that they call police on us....

This statement demonstrates that women like Yasemin feel that there is a clear double standard: that they are vulnerable to punishment for engaging in parenting practices that White women also engage in. However, in the latter case, these practices are not viewed as forms of misconduct; instead, in the case of White women, mothers' autonomy and right to decide how to parent their children remain protected and viewed in good faith. Moreover, Yasmin speaks to the existence of constant anxiety and the sense that women like her are under surveillance by their White neighbors for the same behaviors that they exhibit.

The fear that women faced was not limited to the domestic realm alone. Muslim refugee women also expressed feeling fearful more generally, about how their lifestyles and ways of life were being perceived and monitored by their White neighbors. As Fauzia, a young woman in her twenties, originally from Iraq, noted

> It's definitely different, it's very different here than my country, but our neighbor here, for some reason, the first day we arrived they called police on us, because we made a lot of noise, like putting things, it was so noisy...my grandson is always scared.

Fauzia's account exemplifies how refugee women and their families experience the policing of their everyday ways of living. The surveillance that Yasmin and Fauzia experience from White neighbors points to xenophobic and Islamophobic ideas about Muslim women and their families. Although they did not mention this explicitly, it is widely documented that the hijab has become a symbol of Islam that has evoked widespread Islamophobia globally (Hagan, 2021; Saleh et al., 2022). Most women in this study, irrespective of their country of origin, wore the hijab and would have thus been perceived not only as visibly foreign but also Muslim. Both Islamophobia and xenophobia thus operate in connection with one another to shape Muslim women's experiences of systemic racism.

The instinctive tendency on the part of White neighbors to call the police demonstrates a disregard for the vulnerability of refugee women. These experiences of surveillance can cause harm to children like Fauzia's grandchild. Moreover, such experiences of policing are not limited to women from particular countries of origin; instead, we see similar experiences shared by women from differing countries of origin.

Refugee women also developed a mistrust of the police because of their experiences of child removal. Raiza, a woman in her fifties, originally from Somalia, recounted an incident in which she experienced intimate partner violence and then called the police:

> He hit me one time, I remember. And I called the police and then [he] go to jail. And they even took my child away from me. So I have that experience. I didn't see my child for three weeks.

Here, Raiza was not accorded full protection. Instead, she also faced punitive repercussions that led to the removal of her child. Her attempt to protect herself from intimate partner violence, thus, led to other harms. Although the logic behind child removal is not discussed, given that law enforcement had removed Raiza's husband from the familial space, their child's exposure to intimate partner violence could not be cited as a reason for their removal.

This incident, therefore, points to paternalism on the part of the state. This would be consistent with historical examples in which native/indigenous and Black women in the United States, at different periods in history, had their children removed from them in the name of "child protection." In such instances, White middle-class notions of parenting and motherhood were privileged as "ideal." Women who didn't fit this standard were thus deemed "unfit" mothers. Here are some quotes that speak to this inability to meet the standards put in place by the systems of the criminal legal system:

> In America when you call police, they ask you a lot of questions [00:44:00] that you are not able to answer. I have seen a lot of them. I was sick last time I called call police, you are sick and you can't talk and they ask you several questions. That's not a good even.
>
> Yes. The white people, they just hear something and they call 911. But we don't...we can get judged.

Scholars have long argued that White supremacist, classist, and racist ideologies have driven these narratives, which are inseparable from histories of settler colonialism and slavery in the United States narratives (Duvenage, 2024; Mazo & Smith, 2018; Roberts 2002, 2021). In sum, then, the state punished Raiza for her efforts to protect herself (and also arguably her child) from violence, rather than offering her protection. This, in turn, can create a cycle in which women like her are subject to heightened vulnerability. As mistrust in the police develops due to such incidents, women are likely to be increasingly hesitant to reach out to the police for support, further intensifying their vulnerability to intimate partner violence. Because women cannot trust that law enforcement will offer them unconditional protection, without also placing them (and arguably, their children) in conditions of harm, women like Raiza are likely to forgo seeking out protection from intimate partner violence in the future. To guard against the forced removal of their children, then, women remain unprotected from continued harm in their intimate partnerships. We discuss these dynamics further in the next section.

Mistrust Toward Social Service Providers

Women expressed a deep sense of mistrust toward social service providers due to their experiences of child removal. A culture of fear stemmed from this; specifically, mothers appeared to live in perpetual fear of being questioned about their capacity to parent. Aliyah, a woman in her late fifties, who was originally from Sudan, spoke to this:

> ...if children are involved, if she [the mother] doesn't want people to come into the household, question her and potentially have the children removed. So fear of not knowing the rules of social service, fear of not knowing resources, language barrier, cultural barrier, religious barrier. So there's many barriers.

Here, Aliyah demonstrates that the culture of fear that shapes refugee women's experiences is tied to the sense that the state—in this case, social services—may at any point choose to investigate their families and even remove their children. This fear, Aliyah notes, is tied to women's lack of familiarity with cultural norms and their inability to access appropriate linguistic and cultural capital. Women indicate that because they do not know the "rules," they must operate under conditions of uncertainty and fear. As Aliyah notes, there is, therefore, a range of intersecting "barriers" that women face. This narrative is echoed by others like Astur, a fifty-seven-year-old woman, originally from Somalia:

> …you don't want your child to be removed out of your home and put in somebody else's with a different religion, different culture -- so they, really, are very vocal about it, and they do not trust the department.

Astur's statement reflects how women resist both forced removal and forced assimilation. The fear of both these things results in a lack of trust in the state, in this case, the social services department. The statement is revealing and points to the importance of a historical reading. It is well established that the United States child welfare system has been complicit in the forced removal and forced assimilation of native/indigenous children from their families (Mazo & Smith, 2018, Roberts 2021). Although those in social services and the child welfare system have acknowledged this fact (Mazo & Smith, 2018), through their narratives about mistrust and fear, Muslim women refugees reveal the ways in which this state entity continues to take on an assimilationist and interventionist role, in this case, in the context of (Muslim) refugee communities.

In discussing these dynamics, Astur elaborated further, recounting a story that reflected how deeply entrenched feelings of mistrust (toward social services) and the subsequent culture of fear had become in her community. She noted that

> Back in 1990…There was a child that was removed from the home. Very small baby. What happened was mom said the baby fall off the bed and broke a leg. There was not enough culture brokers, there were not enough interpreters, there was a lot of misunderstanding within that case at the time. So that child was taken away from mom, and mom become very mentally disabled and sick. And people are reminded by that woman when they see her. So every year she deteriorated, her mental health, and she's still in

> the community, and she's still talking about her daughter every single day, so people are really scared. They say that if it happened to this woman, it can happen to us.

This particular story, shared by more than one participant, demonstrates how widespread the fear of child removal is in Astur's community. It is clear that this incident left its mark on many and that it continues to evoke fear in the community and shape perceptions—specifically, mistrust—toward social services. The layers of this story are also notable. The child who was removed was a baby, and the mother in question suffered greatly because of this decision by the state. She was, therefore, not offered protection, and her child was taken from her, due to what appeared to be some fundamental cultural and linguistic barriers. The fact that such a significant decision was made by social services, in the absence of adequate cultural competency or linguistic support services, points to a clear disregard for the rights and capacity of the mother. Instead, once again, it appears that an underlying paternalism was motivating the state's decision to remove the infant/young child from their mother. The deep distrust stemming from this story, which was retold in the community, continued to permeate the community even decades after the incident that was referenced.

This lack of cultural competency on the part of social services emerged as a theme in other contexts, too. As Aliyah (53), a social service worker herself who is originally from Sudan and in her profession, noted, cultural incompetence manifested in the lack of attentiveness to issues of language and translation in matters as basic as nutrition requirements. She explained this clearly, saying

> ...one of the children was supposed to be eating gluten-free food. That's when I found out what gluten is. I didn't even know. Imagine if somebody who doesn't even speak the language, someone like me, didn't know that. I can see the kids' worker for the department just being so angry. 'You're supposed to be getting this food for this child. She's getting sick all the time or whatever. And, I was like, 'Hold on a minute. What is gluten-free?'...So I asked the woman, 'Do you know?' and she's like, 'I have no idea what it is...So cases like that, people don't know what it is, you cannot hold that against them....

Again, the glaring cultural incompetence on the part of social services signals a lack of interest in providing services that are supportive and culturally sensitive. Instead, social services appeared to operate in a manner that only served to reinforce anxieties and fear. Instead of being offered support, women experienced punishment that seemed to be rooted in frustrations stemming, once again, from deep-seated xenophobia. These dynamics not only left women fearful but also socially isolated. This was another theme that emerged in conversation with women, which we discuss further below.

Aliyah herself noted that

> …people here in the United States…most people don't trust each other. There's fear from the police. There's fear from social service departments. People are not connected as much as they should, so the families are most often feel alone. Even when they really need help they don't readily come out and ask for help. When we go into some households they suspect us in the beginning. They don't trust us.

Here, Aliya speaks to a larger culture in the United States of individualism and arguably also social disconnection and isolation. She speaks to the absence of community and neighborly support—which of course is consistent with Muslim refugee women's experiences of policing by their White neighbors. These dynamics of social isolation and the absence of a sense of community exacerbate the broader cultures of fear and mistrust associated with social services and the police. That is, these dynamics intersect to deepen feelings of isolation, reproducing a sense within refugee families that they are alone and without support when it comes to protecting their families against surveillance and punishment by the state.

Echoing this sentiment, Britta, a woman from Somalia in Africa, who was in her forties, said

> In this country mostly, most people, they live lonely. When we come here from Africa, I have been here 10 years in America, I say today if I could change it, I would go back.… This country, I swear to God, everyone is alone.

Britta's comment speaks to the intensity of such feelings of isolation and how these experiences may stand in contrast to experiences that women had in their home countries. The notion that social isolation is so heightened that "everyone is alone" raises important questions about how cultural tendencies might intersect with state policy to heighten feelings and experiences of vulnerability and exclusion among Muslim refugee women.

Discussion and Recommendations for Practice

Perceptions of Muslim refugee mothers we interviewed regarding mistrust toward police and social service providers resonate with the reflections of refugees from diverse ethnocultural backgrounds. The women expressed mistrust in and fear of the police and White neighbors, as well as the social service providers.

The intersectional lens reveals how Islamophobia was not experienced in isolation but was compounded by race, gender, immigration status, and socioeconomic class. Muslim refugee mothers, for example, were not only targeted for their religious identity but also faced racialized and gendered assumptions that shaped how they were perceived and treated by institutions. Black Muslim refugee mothers experienced a convergence of anti-Black racism and anti-Muslim bias, which increases how much they are watched or judged by others, including neighbors and government actors (Alimahomed-Wilson, 2020; Ellis et al., 2020). Women are often seen through the lens of cultural stereotypes, which can lead to unfair treatment by child welfare systems (Mahmood, 2024). Intersectionality helps us see how different parts of a person's identity—like race, gender, and class—combine to shape their experiences with Islamophobia (Alimahomed-Wilson, 2020).

Intersectional practice requires that service providers recognize how multiple forms of oppression shape refugee women's experiences. Trauma-informed care must be paired with anti-racist, anti-Islamophobic, and culturally responsive frameworks that acknowledge the full complexity of Muslim women's lives (Alimahomed-Wilson, 2020). This includes recognizing how visibility, such as wearing a hijab or having a Muslim name, can increase vulnerability to discrimination and shape interactions with front-line service providers and law enforcement (Mahmood, 2024). Policies should be based on data that looks at all parts of a person's identity, as Yazdiha (2023) reminds us, people's backgrounds shape how they see their choices and risks, so we need to design programs that reflect that complexity.

For social workers supporting Muslim refugee communities, it is essential to understand how overlapping identities—such as race, gender, class, and immigration status—shape individuals' experiences with discrimination and access to services. Research shows that Muslim women, especially those who are Black, visibly Muslim, or immigrants, often face multiple forms of oppression, including gendered Islamophobia and racial profiling (Alimahomed-Wilson, 2020; Mahmood, 2024). These intersecting challenges can lead to deep mistrust of institutions like social services and law enforcement, which may discourage women from seeking help (Ellis et al., 2020; Saksena & McMorrow, 2021). To address this, social workers must go beyond basic cultural competence and adopt practices that are trauma-informed, anti-racist, and anti-Islamophobic. This includes advocating for inclusive policies, ensuring language access, and building trust through community engagement. As Yazdiha (2023) points out, understanding how a person's background influences their sense of safety and agency is key to creating effective and equitable support systems.

We concur with Critelli and Yalim (2021) that practicing with cultural sensitivity and empowering refugee families creates trust between providers and refugees and enhances help-seeking and service effectiveness. Structural interventions like improving communication and service accessibility for refugee women create a positive experience for refugee service users, engendering trust (Holtmann & Rickards, 2018). Emphasizing social connection and well-being, better community engagement, and fairer policing can enhance trust between institutions and refugee communities (Ellis et al., 2020; Saksena & McMorrow, 2021).

Building Trust and Cultural Sensitivity

There are several implications for social work practice with refugees. For instance, Muslim refugee populations could benefit from more culturally responsive support from social service providers for a longer period (Saksena & McMorrow, 2021). Enhancing cultural understanding among providers and revising protocols to include refugee and immigrant perspectives can improve institutional trust (Holtmann & Rickards, 2018). Implementing culturally sensitive and trauma-informed approaches is crucial for building trust with refugee women, and better training to include simulation-based trauma-informed care education can foster empathy and improve clinician practice with refugee and migrant populations (Critelli & Yalim, 2021; Palnati et al., 2024). Integrating peer support is a culturally responsive method that builds trust, empowers refugee domestic violence survivors, and better engages individuals and communities (Critelli

& Yalim, 2021). Police measures include having Muslim community members as partners and adhering to procedural justice principles (Ali et al., 2022).

Ensuring confidentiality and understanding refugees' unique concerns for discretion are essential for building trust (Haider et al., 2023). Refugee families require safety, support, and discretion when connecting to services and respect for their choices about involving law enforcement (Merken et al., 2023). Other cultural considerations that enhance trust include providing language support and culturally sensitive services and empowering immigrant women to lead their own care (Merken et al., 2023).

Epistemic Trust

Epistemic trust refers to how forced migrants are viewed, as knowers and knowledge producers affect their trust in institutions (Sundbäck, 2024). Epistemic notions of trust and distrust in institutional encounters emphasize the importance of recognizing refugees as knowledgeable individuals and supporting them in navigating complex systems (Sundbäck, 2024). Strategies for building epistemic trust include respecting the knowledge and backgrounds of refugees and their communities, empowering them with information and resources, and training them as community leaders (Critelli & Yalim, 2021). Service providers should adopt a humble attitude, recognize their knowledge limits, clearly explain institutional processes, and empower service users (Sundbäck, 2024). Additional recommendations for policy and program development include educational interventions to increase mental health literacy and reduce stigma (Byrow et al., 2020).

Policy and Program Development

This research also calls for more comprehensive and holistic approaches to supporting refugees beyond the initial resettlement period (Saksena & McMorrow, 2021). Emphasizing safety as an outcome of refugee resettlement can strengthen policy and guide community responses (Shaw et al., 2021). Other types of structural interventions that can enhance trust in service providers and government entities include improving support and collaboration and securing long-term funding for services (Holtmann & Rickards, 2018). Service providers may mitigate structural barriers to trust and help-seeking by providing clear information and assistance for financial support, language services, and stabilizing housing (Byrow et al., 2020). Adherence to procedural justice enhances legitimacy and cooperation with authorities (Ali et al., 2022).

Conclusion

This chapter demonstrates that because Muslim refugee women experience punishment instead of unequivocal support from police and social workers, they develop both fear and mistrust in the criminal legal and child welfare systems. Their experiences of surveillance and social control by these institutions are not isolated. As discussed in this chapter, both policing and social work institutions emerged from histories of slavery and settler colonialism in the United States (Duvenage, 2024; Mazo & Smith, 2018; Roberts, 2002; Ward, 2018). These histories involved the forced removal of children and family policing mechanisms that separated native/indigenous and Black mothers from their children (Ibid). Viewed in this context, Muslim refugee women's experiences reflect the (re)production of these dynamics in the context of different forms of systemic racism: xenophobia and islamophobia. Taking an intersectional approach allows us to better apprehend the multiple vulnerabilities Muslim refugee women face as women (who, in some cases, have also experienced intimate partner violence) and as mothers. A historical approach also requires us to consider questions about when care and protection can bleed into systems of control and the potential harm caused in such cases.

Future research in this area should center on the systemic and socio-structural factors that contribute to engendering mistrust in state institutions (Tekeste, 2022). Trust is critical to therapeutic and case management services; addressing cultural and structural barriers to building trust through culturally sensitive practices and supportive policies is important to help-seeking behavior and overall well-being among refugee families. Future research should continue to explore these themes and develop strategies to foster trust and cooperation with service providers for this vulnerable population.

References

Alang, S., McAlpine, D. D., & Hardeman, R. (2020). Police brutality and mistrust in medical institutions. *Journal of Racial and Ethnic Health Disparities, 7*, 760–768.

Ali, M. M., Murphy, K., & Cherney, A. (2022). Counter-terrorism measures and perceptions of police legitimacy: The importance Muslims place on procedural justice, representative bureaucracy, and bounded-authority concerns. *Journal of Criminology, 55*(1), 3–22.

Alimahomed-Wilson, S. (2020). The matrix of gendered Islamophobia: Muslim women's repression and resistance. *Gender & Society, 34*(4), 648–678.

Alsaidi, S., Velez, B. L., Smith, L., Jacob, A., & Salem, N. (2023). "Arab, brown, and other": Voices of Muslim Arab American women on identity, discrimination, and well-being. *Cultural Diversity and Ethnic Minority Psychology, 29*(2), 163.

Al-Shdayfat, N., & Hatamleh, R. (2017). Syrian refugee women's reasons for not reporting violence: An exploratory study. *International Journal of Nursing Education, 9*(4). https://doi.org/10.5958/0974-9357.2017.00103.9

Ansari, S. N., & Patel, T. G. (2024). Islamophobia as intersectional phenomenon. In A. Easat-Daas & I. Zempi (Eds.), *The Palgrave handbook of gendered islamophobia*. Palgrave Macmillan.

Ashai, S. K. (2021). *Investigating Islamophobia: Identifying risk and protective factors in the Muslim American community* [Master's thesis, University of Maryland, College Park]. https://www.proquest.com/dissertations-theses/investigating-islamophobia-identifying-risk/docview/2693509897/se-2?accountid=14606

Bach, W. A. (2022). *Prosecuting poverty, criminalizing care*. Cambridge University Press.

Bezusko, A. (2013). Criminalizing Black motherhood: How the war on welfare was won. *Souls, 15*(1–2), 39–55.

Byrow, Y., Pajak, R., Specker, P., & Nickerson, A. (2020). Perceptions of mental health and perceived barriers to mental health help-seeking amongst refugees: A systematic review. *Clinical Psychology Review, 75*, 101812.

Chaudhry, A., Hebert-Beirne, J., Hanneke, R., Alessi, E. J., Mitchell, U., Molina, Y., Abboud, S., et al. (2024). The health needs of sexual and gender minority migrant women in the United States: A scoping review. *LGBT Health, 11*(1), 1–19.

Chenane, J. L., & Pryce, D. K. (2024). The antecedents of obligation to obey and cooperation with police: The views of African immigrant women in the United States. *American Behavioral Scientist*, 0(0). https://doi.org/10.1177/00027642241300923

Collins, P. H. (2000). *Black feminist thought: Knowledge, consciousness, and the politics of empowerment* (2nd ed.). Routledge.

Collins, P. H. (2009). *Black feminist thought: Knowledge, consciousness, and the politics of empowerment* (1st ed.). Routledge.

Collins, P. H. (2015). Intersectionality's definitional dilemmas. *Annual Review of Sociology, 41*(1), 1–20.

Crenshaw, K. (1989). Demarginalizing the intersection of race and sex: A Black feminist critique of antidiscrimination doctrine, feminist theory and antiracist politics. *University of Chicago Legal Forum, 1*(8), 139–167.

Critelli, F., & Yalim, A. C. (2021). Improving access to domestic violence services for women of immigrant and refugee status: a trauma-informed perspective. In *Immigrant and refugee youth and families* (pp. 97–115). Routledge. https://doi.org/10.1080/15313204.2019.1700863

Di Giuseppe, K. (2021). You are not alone! Experiences of LGBTQ+ migrants in the UK during Covid-19 lockdown. A minority stress perspective. *Migration and Diasporas: An Interdisciplinary Journal, 3*(1), 32–71.

Duvenage, A. (2024). *Black feminist thought and intersectionality* (1st ed.). Routledge.

Ellis, B. H., Lincoln, A. K., Abdi, S. M., Nimmons, E. A., Issa, O., & Decker, S. H. (2020). "We all have stories": Black Muslim immigrants' experience with the police. *Race and Justice, 10*(3), 341–362.

Fineran, S., & Kohli, H. K. (2020). Muslim refugee women's perspectives on intimate partner violence. *Journal of Family Social Work, 23*(3), 199–213.

Goodwin, M. (2020). *Policing the womb: Invisible women and the criminalization of motherhood.* Cambridge University Press.

Hagan, R. (2021). *Hatred of the Hijab: Islamophobia and Muslim Women in America.* [Honors Thesis, Florida Southern College]. http://hdl.handle.net/11416/551

Haider, S., Maheen, A., Ansari, M., & Stolley, M. (2023). Health beliefs and barriers to healthcare of Rohingya refugees. *Journal of Racial and Ethnic Health Disparities, 10*(4), 1560–1568.

Holtmann, C., & Rickards, T. (2018). Domestic/intimate partner violence in the lives of immigrant women: a New Brunswick response. *Canadian Journal of Public Health, 109*, 294–302.

Jiménez-Ivars, A., & León-Pinilla, R. (2018). Interpreting in refugee contexts. A descriptive and qualitative study. *Language & Communication, 60*, 28–43.

Khan, A. A. (2023). Not a monolith: Influence of race and religiosity on Muslim perceptions of police. Available from *ProQuest Dissertations & Theses Global.* (2808430514). Retrieved from https://www.proquest.com/dissertations-theses/not-monolith-influence-race-religiosity-on-muslim/docview/2808430514/se-2

Kohli, H. K., & Fineran, S. (2020a). "The rain grows plants, the thunder does not": Refugee and asylee women's narratives on child abuse and neglect. *Journal of Immigrant and Refugee Studies, 18*(2), 224–238.

Kohli, H. K., & Fineran, S. (2020b). "If they misbehaved, we took a stick to discipline them": Refugee mothers' struggles raising children in the United States. *Journal of Child and Family Social Work, 25*(2), 488–495.

Langlois, J. R. (2025). *The lingering wound: Examining the interplay of cultural mistrust, help-seeking attitudes, and race-based counseling preferences among Black Americans.* [Dissertation, Liberty University]. https://digitalcommons.liberty.edu/cgi/viewcontent.cgi?article=7833&context=doctoral

Lorde, A. G. (1984). *Sister outsider: Essays and speeches.* Crossing Press.

Mahadevan, J., & Mayer, C.-H. (Eds.). (2017). *Muslim minorities, workplace diversity and reflexive HRM* (1st ed.). Routledge.

Mahmood, M. (2024). *Living in a society that 'Doesn't Want Us': Examining the experiences of Muslim youth in post-9/11 America through intersectionality.* [Master's thesis, Tufts University].

Malik, S. (2023). Reviving the legacy: Addressing Muslim mental health. *Academic Psychiatry, 47*(6), 620–621.

Mazo, A., & Smith, B. (Directors). (2018). *Dawnland* [Film]. Upstander Project.

Merken, S., Slakoff, D. C., Aujla, W., & Moton, L. (2023). Navigating biases and distrust of systems: American and Canadian intimate partner violence service providers' experiences with trans and immigrant women clients. *Victims & Offenders, 18*(1), 141–168.

Meyer, I. H. (2003). Prejudice, social stress, and mental health in lesbian, gay, and bisexual populations: Conceptual issues and research evidence. *Psychological Bulletin, 129*(5), 674.

Miller, M. H. (Ed.). (2024). *Criminalizing motherhood and reproduction.* Taylor & Francis.

Mirza, H. S. (2013). Embodying the veil: Muslim women and gendered Islamophobia in 'New Times'. In Z. Gross, L. Davies, & A. K. Diab (Eds.), *Gender, religion and education in a chaotic postmodern world.* Springer.

Mohammadifirouzeh, M., Oh, K. M., Basnyat, I., & Gimm, G. (2023). Factors associated with professional mental help-seeking among U.S. immigrants: A systematic review. *Journal of Immigrant and Minority Health, 25*(5), 1118–1136.

Monish, B. (2020). The permission to be cruel: Street-level bureaucrats and harms against people seeking asylum. *Critical Criminology, 28*(2), 277–292.

O'Neill, M., & Harindranath, R. (2006). Theorizing narratives of exile and belonging: the importance of biography and ethno-mimesis in "understanding" asylum. *Qualitative Sociology Review, 2*, 39–53.

Palnati, M., Martinez, A. E., Audil, A., Tovar, E., Macfarlane, P., Gerber, M., & Wagner, K. (2024). Simulation-based trauma-informed care education instills empathy and improves clinician practices towards refugee and migrant populations. *MedEdPORTAL, 20*, 11475.

Roberts, D. E. (2002). *Shattered bonds: The color of child welfare*. Basic Books.

Roberts, D. (2014). *Killing the black body: Race, reproduction, and the meaning of liberty*. Vintage Books.

Roberts, D. E. (2021). Keynote: How I became a family policing abolitionist. *Columbia Journal of Race and Law, 11*(3), 455.

Sadek, K., & Hashem, H. M. (2024). Teasing apart the role of identity and help-seeking intentions among Arab/MENA and South Asian Muslim Americans. *Social Sciences & Humanities Open, 9*, 100789.

Saksena, J., & McMorrow, S. (2021). At the intersection of gender and discrimination: Experiences of Congolese refugee women with social and cultural integration in the United States. *Women's Studies International Forum, 88*, 102517.

Saleh, N., Clark, N., Bruce, A., & Moosa-Mitha, M. (2022). Using narrative inquiry to understand anti-Muslim racism in Canadian nursing. *Canadian Journal of Nursing Research, 55*(3), 292–304.

Schofield, N., & Yap, A. (2024). *2023 Refugees annual flow report*. Office of Homeland Security Statistics. https://ohss.dhs.gov/topics/immigration/refugees-and-asylees/rfa-annual-flow-report

Shaw, S. A., Rodgers, G., Poulin, P., Olive, M., & Allen, A. (2021). Safety among newly resettled refugees in the USA. *Journal of International Migration and Integration, 22*(3), 1045–1062.

Smith, K. (2015). Stories told by, for, and about women refugees: Engendering resistance. *ACME: An International E-Journal for Critical Geographies, 14*(2), 461–469.

Sundbäck, L. (2024). Epistemic notions of trust and distrust in institutional encounters with forced migrants in Finland and Sweden. *Journal of Ethnic and Migration Studies*, 1–18. https://doi.org/10.1080/1369183X.2024.2404224

Tekeste, M. (2022). Ethiopian immigrants in the US: The implications of perceived public mental illness stigma and mistrust of mental health providers for mental health help-seeking intentions (Order No. 29061524). *ProQuest Dissertations & Theses Global. (2713477208)*. https://www.proquest.com/dissertations-theses/ethiopian-immigrants-us-implications-perceived/docview/2713477208/se-2

Terrell, F. (1984). Race of counselor, client sex, cultural mistrust level, and premature termination from counseling among Black clients. *Journal of Counseling Psychology, 31*(3), 371.

United Nations High Commissioner for Refugees. (2024a). *Refugee Data Finder*. UNHCR. https://www.unhcr.org/refugee-statistics/

United Nations High Commissioner for Refugees. (2024b). *Global Trends Report 2023*. UNHCR. https://www.unhcr.org/refugee-statistics/

Ward, G. (2018). Living histories of white supremacist policing: Towards transformative justice. *Du Bois Review: Social Science Research on Race, 15*(1), 167–184.
Yazdiha, H. (2023). The relational dynamics of racialised policing: Community policing for counterterrorism, suspect communities, and Muslim Americans' provisional belonging. *Journal of Ethnic and Migration Studies, 49*(11), 2676–2697.

CHAPTER 12

Trauma and Punishment: Detaining and Deporting Young Migrants During the Crimmigration Era

Luis A. Romero

Introduction

Migrants are often met with carceral systems, surveillance, and punishment, making their daily existence in the USA precarious. Living full and free lives requires not only incorporating migrants within the social institutions that provide groups of people with jobs (Friedberg & Hunt, 1998) but also having family, community, health, financial freedom, the autonomy to pursue their goals, and freedom from punishment regimes (Byrd, 2023). This is especially important for migrant youth, given their vulnerable status within the USA (e.g., Abrego, 2006; Zayas, 2015). However, living in the USA is perilous for Central American migrant youth as the USA has built upon restrictionist and punishment regimes that began in the 1980s.

L. A. Romero (✉)
Department of Sociology & Anthropology, Texas Christian University, Fort Worth, TX, USA
e-mail: LUIS.ROMERO@tcu.edu

J. S. Hong et al. (eds.), *Violence and Trauma Without Borders*,
https://doi.org/10.1007/978-3-032-29221-6_12

Not all migrant groups have had equal access to opportunities and freedom in the USA. Rather, there exist carceral and punishment regimes for migrants from non-European countries. This punishment has grown in contemporary times, as criminal enforcement and immigration enforcement have merged into what is commonly referred to as "crimmigration" (Stumpf, 2006). The dawn of the crimmigration era, which began in the 1980s, has introduced an exponential growth within immigration detention and deportation, which are difficult obstacles for migrant youth to remain in the USA. This has been evident in the number of immigrant youth who have been apprehended by the US Border Patrol in the previous decade. During fiscal year (FY) 2010, 18,622 children were apprehended by the US Border Patrol (U.S. Border Patrol, 2019). That number grew significantly to 76,136 during FY 2019 (U.S. Border Patrol, 2019). Since then, we have seen a further increase in the number of child apprehensions, with 145,474 in FY 2023 and 116,578 in FY 2024 (U.S. Border Patrol, 2025).

This chapter aims to analyze how the crimmigration regime impacts the lives of Central American migrant youth in the United States. With the rise of immigration detention and deportation, the crimmigration regime has become a crucial regime that young migrants arriving in the USA contend with upon arrival. I argue that opportunities to live full lives are blocked and erased for many Central American migrant youth in the crimmigration era and are replaced with "administrative punishment" that carries with it the entire carceral system. Various data are used, such as governmental and nongovernmental reports, data from immigrant rights organizations, the Transactional Records Access Clearinghouse (TRAC) at Syracuse University, newspaper accounts, and secondary sources. Using these various sources of data, I assess the ways in which migrant youth from Central America are treated in detention and during deportation proceedings, two of the prominent arms of the crimmigration regime. This paper conceptualizes Central American youth as minors (up to age 17) from Guatemala, Honduras, and El Salvador. I explore how these Central American youth have experienced the immigration detention system and deportation proceedings in the USA.

Detention sites are spaces where immigrants are held in custody and serve to keep them away from their families and support networks as they await their hearing in immigration court. Deportation proceedings in immigration court work to remove immigrants, eliminating an opportunity for life in the USA. As a result, migrant youth must find a way to navigate the prison-like conditions and abuses found in detention, while having minimal protections against deportation, as seen in the lack of representation they are afforded in court, while also being separated from their families and loved ones. Thus, the crimmigration regime uses punishment as a form of deterrence to manage immigrant youth. As more young migrants from Central America enter detention and are deported, punishment becomes more integrated into the immigration system, as noted in the increasing numbers within both types of punishment. In the sections that follow, the rise of the crimmigration era in the United States will be discussed, followed by two sections discussing the experiences of young migrants in detention and deportation. These efforts to criminalize migrants have contributed to the policy efforts to justify the punishment of all migrants, including migrant youth from Central America.

The Rise of Crimmigration

The development of a complex immigration enforcement system since the 1980s has been attributed to the creation of various punitive immigrant programs and policies that have enabled the rise of what Juliet Stumpf (2006) termed "crimmigration," the merging of the criminal incarceration and immigration enforcement systems. Detention provides one of the most direct connections between these two enforcement regimes, due to their shared resources and approaches. This has led to an increase in the number of immigration officers and in the number of detention sites, creating the modern immigration detention infrastructure that began in the 1980s (García Hernández, 2014).

While detention has taken many different forms throughout US history (Hernandez, 2008), the expansion of the detention system into its modern iteration can be in part attributed to several restrictionist migration policies. According to García Hernández (2014), the rise of the modern detention system can be traced back to the Anti-Drug Abuse Acts of 1986 and 1988 and other policies enacted between 1986 and 1996. These policies enabled immigration enforcement entities to utilize the new antidrug policies to expand the mandatory detention of immigrants, important tools in the contemporary detention era (Sayed, 2011). Throughout the 1980s and half of the 1990s, the average daily population remained under 10,000 people. However, by the year 2000, the average daily population was around 20,000 (Kassie, 2019).

Moreover, the post-9/11 era and the subsequent policies that followed also created a higher demand for detention bed space. Part of this demand can be attributed to rhetoric and policies that conveyed fear of a subsequent attack on US territory (Romero & Zarrugh, 2018; Zarrugh, 2019). Also responsible for this demand are policies such as the start of "catch and remove" and the Expedited Removal provisions in 2004 and 2005. New policies and infrastructure created after 9/11 increased the number of immigrants slated for mandatory detention and are part of the reason that the average daily population increased into the 30,000 range between 2000 and 2010.

Deportation has followed an exponential growth as well. While the current president's political regimes are known for their harsh, anti-immigrant policies, deportations have been rising in the USA and reached new highs during the Obama administration, earning him the nickname of the "deporter-in-chief" by many activists and pro-immigrant supporters. According to an analysis of ICE data, there were 863,958 people deported during the Clinton years, approximately 2 million people deported during the Bush administration, and approximately 3 million people deported during the Obama presidency (Pérez, 2025). We have seen the current president declare that his second presidential term will be marked as the largest deportation operation in US history. The increasing reliance on deportations to handle migration cases has retaken an important role in the twenty-first century and is one that has continued during the crimmigration era, especially as the second administration of the current president focuses on mass deportation and detention. These efforts have led crimmigration scholars to conclude that "[c]rime control and migration control have become so intertwined that they have ceased to be distinct processes or to target distinct acts, for both noncitizens and individuals suspected of being noncitizens." (García Hernández, 2014: 1459).

Migrant Youth in Detention

The crimmigration regime has made immigration detention a violent experience for immigrant youth attempting to enter and live in the USA. Inside detention, young migrants are faced with a system that is like the criminal incarceration context, whether unaccompanied or within a family context. Namely, they have dealt with abusive guards, been placed under inhumane conditions, and been separated from their families. This treatment of immigrant minors flies in the face of protections that migrant youth are afforded through the Flores Settlement Agreement (FSA). The FSA has determined that immigrant minors should be placed in the "least restrictive setting" to provide the necessary services while detained in the USA. In this section, I outline the lived experiences of migrant youth in detention, its similarities to US criminal incarceration, the games that are played within detention, and the abuses that have been reported on by investigative reporters and news outlets.

Detention for migrant youth takes many different forms. For example, when children are detained with their families, they can be under the custody of ICE and held in family detention sites that often resemble or were former prisons. When migrant youth, particularly those classified as "unaccompanied," are detained under the custody of the Office of Refugee Resettlement (ORR), which is under the Department of Human and Health Services (HHS), they are held in custody in various types of facilities, such as shelters, group homes, long-term foster care, and transitional foster care programs (Ramos, 2022). While the location and duration of unaccompanied children's detention change across presidential administrations, as was the case from the first presidency of the current president to the Biden presidency (Doering-White et al., 2025), one consistent aspect is the government's framing of children in ORR and ICE detention under the framework of "care." As migration scholars have noted, though, the "care" framework of migrant youth in ORR and ICE custody should be scrutinized, given the treatment and lived experiences of the children who must navigate the complexities and violence found inside these detention sites (Heidbrink, 2014; Ramos, 2022).

The everyday experiences of immigrant youth in detention often resemble prison-like living conditions. For example, detention sites across the USA are known for their regimented lifestyles, with prison guards monitoring and controlling everyday aspects of detained migrants. Additionally, there are punishments put in place for detained migrants who do not abide by the rules. Recreational time and visitations from the outside world are often limited or do not exist in certain contexts. Detention sites are also marked by the lack of space, with cramped living quarters. Lastly, there is the uncertainty that comes with being in detention: not knowing how long one will be detained or what the outcome of being detained will be.

One of the most infamous cases of maltreatment faced by immigrant youth was at the T. Don Hutto Detention Center during its first iteration as the Hutto Family Detention Center. During this time period, Hutto was one of only two detention sites that held immigrant families along with the Berks detention site in Pennsylvania (Talbot, 2008). Family detention sites like Hutto faced many controversies. In 2007, the American Civil Liberties Union (ACLU) won a lawsuit it filed for 26 children detained at Hutto against ICE. This lawsuit claimed that Hutto was in violation of the Flores Settlement Agreement due to the prison-like treatment of children inside the detention site (ACLU, 2007; Castillo, 2008; Garay, 2007). Among these violations against the migrant children were the limitation of recreational time outdoors, receiving threats from the detention guards, wearing prison uniforms, a lack of privacy in the restrooms, and a lack of nutritional food (ACLU, 2007). This should not have been a surprising revelation because Hutto, much like other detention sites, is operated by a private prison company. According to a report, Hutto used “prison guards to watch over the immigrant adults and children” and had “little or no experience” running a family-based site because it had only operated adult prisons (Hawkes, 2008, p. 173). In other words, ICE utilized a space initially intended for criminal incarceration and repurposed it for the detainment of children and families without making changes to the way it operated (Libal et al., 2012; Romero, 2023).

The carceral and restrictive nature of it is not only found in former prisons like Hutto, but also in ORR facilities for unaccompanied minors. For example, Terrio (2015) notes how children are impacted by detention and how the USA manages unaccompanied child migrants by historicizing and describing the stories of immigrant children in ORR custody. Terrio traces the stages of the detention system that children face and how behavioral problems are met with punishment, not sympathy or mental health considerations. Overall, Terrio points out that while children should be placed in the “least restrictive setting” given the Flores case, immigration detention is not an appropriate setting, and children should not be detained. Part of the reason for this is that she finds that immigrant youth must jump through various hoops and participate in arbitrary games, which serve as a form of psychological abuse, in order to gain favor with the detention guards. These games are like those found within the prison context. In a study on unaccompanied children in ORR custody, Heidbrink and Diaz (2024) find numerous concerns inside ORR facilities. For example, they note that about 85% of children are held in congregate care facilities, that care is inconsistent across facilities, that vulnerable populations (e.g., LGBTQIA+, Indigenous, pregnant and parenting teens, and children with disabilities) do not consistently receive appropriate care, and that there is a lack of transparency and accountability. As this research finds, migrant youth are still subjected to substandard care in a carceral context, even under ORR custody.

In addition to the prison-like conditions of detention, sexual abuse is also an issue found within detention sites across the USA. One investigative report noted that between 2010 and 2017, only 43 cases of sexual abuse out of over 1200 (3.58%) that occurred within immigrant detention were investigated (Speri, 2018). Other data obtained by immigrant rights activists found that only 570 instances of sexual abuse out of 33,126 (1.72%) that occurred within the entire Department of Homeland Security (DHS), the parent organization of ICE, between 2010 and 2016 were investigated, with ICE and Customs and Border Protection (CBP) ranking first and second in the number of complaints (Merton & Fialho, 2017). Combined, they accounted for three-fourths of all complaints.

The culture of sexual abuse that occurs within detention is also found in detention sites where children are detained. For example, there have also been reports of sexual abuse found within detention sites. The US Justice Department reported in 2019 that there were 4500 complaints of sexual abuse against detained immigration children over a four-year period (Haag, 2019). According to a *New York Times* report on the sexual abuse during this time period, records provided by the federal government revealed "allegations that adult staff members had harassed and assaulted children, including fondling and kissing minors, watching them as they showered and raping them" (Haag, 2019). That immigrant children are subjected to an institution with rampant sexual abuse shows the limits of the "least restrictive setting." Instead of "caring" for them, migrant youth are faced with abuse and violence during their "administrative detention."

Migrant Youth and Deportation

In addition to the harsh detention context, migrant youth from Central America are also subjected to unfair deportation proceedings and suffer the consequences of being separated from their families when their parents or other relatives are deported. If the criminal incarceration system is analogous to immigrant detention within the crimmigration regime, then the courts, judges, and attorneys should be the comparison to deportation proceedings for migrants, including Central American migrant youth. However, unlike the court system for criminal proceedings, deportation proceedings do not provide migrants with the right to an attorney. Part of this reason is the legal distinction made between the stated punitive nature of criminal court and the "administrative" nature of immigration cases. Because of this distinction, migrants are not afforded the right to an attorney as people who are faced with criminal charges would be in the criminal court context.

The lack of an established right to legal counsel within immigration cases and deportation proceedings has serious and negative consequences for migrants. According to data obtained by the TRAC, of the over 63,000 pending cases in immigration court involving unaccompanied juveniles, only 20,691 had an attorney, less than one-third of all juveniles (TRAC, 2014). More recent data show that this has not improved, with only about a fourth of immigrant children being represented by an attorney (TRAC, 2017). The consequences for not having legal representation in deportation proceedings are stark. According to the same TRAC data, being represented by an attorney has a dramatic impact on the decision to deport or stay in the United States. For example, over 80% of unaccompanied juveniles who do not have an attorney are deported, while less than 20% of them stayed in the USA (TRAC, 2014). Conversely, almost 80% of unaccompanied juveniles with an attorney stayed in the USA, while just over 20% of them were deported. The stark contrast in outcomes shows the importance of attorneys during deportation proceedings.

However, due to the lack of a government-appointed attorney for migrants and migrant youth, they are left with the likelihood of deportation. This is unlikely to change, given the civil nature of immigration cases under the law, but also due to the apathy of government officials. As one senior immigration judge told the ACLU in 2016, "I've taught immigration law literally to 3- and 4-year-olds…They get it" (ACLU, 2016). This shows how migrant youth are left to defend themselves in immigration court without the proper support and without any real changes occurring soon.

The legal advocacy that does exist for migrant youth is vital but also complicated for both migrants and lawyers. While it is impossible for immigrant children to gain access to any semblance of due process without legal representation, the lack of legal resources and available representation creates a "triage model" that assigns "humanitarian capital" to the cases of immigrant youth (Galli, 2023). This leads to assigning value to immigrant children's cases based on their suffering, which legal brokers determine based on the likelihood that immigration judges and officers are likely to grant a legal stay and avoid deportation. Complicating matters is that legal brokers often base humanitarian capital on how an immigrant youth is willing to share their traumatic story, both to the brokers and in legal proceedings. As Ramos (2022) notes, this is difficult for children to do because they have a distrust of service providers, whom they are meeting for the first time, and may be unable to communicate traumatic experiences on command. Additionally, many children may have to terminate their parents' rights over them and be unable to petition for their parents to stay in the USA in order to be granted a protected status, such as the Special Immigrant Juvenile Status (SIJS).

In addition to the lack of protection for immigrant youth in deportation proceedings, the lives of migrant youth are further disrupted, even when they are not the focus of the deportation. For example, Zayas (2015) focuses his research on migrant children, and his research examines how these children are impacted by the deportation of their parents. He argues that by deporting the migrant parents of children, they either become exiled or they become orphans. As a result, these children become exiled when they are forced to leave the USA with their parents because of their deportation. Alternatively, these children can become orphans when they are left behind after their parents are deported. Becoming exiled or an orphan for a child results in depression and trauma and becomes the "collateral damage" of US immigration policy and the crimmigration regime.

Furthermore, the research conducted by Zayas has found how much psychological damage deportation has on children who are left behind. For example, he determines that in the case of two sisters who witnessed both of their parents' arrests (and were subsequently detained), the two young children suffered from depression and separation anxiety disorder. Zayas notes that one of the sisters, Maricela, scored very low on psychological tests on self-worth and sense of self-efficacy. Based on this, he concludes that her "background story, clinical findings, interview impressions, and academic records reflect that Maricela was a child who was suffering a significant level of depression and trauma-related stress." (Zayas, 2015, p. 118). Research like this is essential to contextualize how people are affected by detention and deportations and the impact it has on children, even if they are not the target of the crimmigration regime.

For migrant youth who are deported, the deportation experience is also very confusing and troubling. These deportation experiences are varied in that some migrant youth are deported with family while others are deported before reaching the United States. As reports indicate, deported youth face the possibility of taking multiple flights by themselves, without knowing where they are at any given moment and without knowing where they will end up (Dickerson, 2020). Many of these migrant youth must return to their home counties, back to the humanitarian crises that were responsible for their migration in the first place. As noted by Heidbrink (2020), the post-deportation experience is taxing, including for those who never made it to the USA, as is the case for Guatemalan migrant youth who are deported from Mexico to Guatemala. Heidbrink finds that deportation has led to parent disappointment in deported children, especially in cases where debt was accrued to enable the initial migration, depression, and death. By being deported, Central American migrant youth are denied the opportunity to stay in the USA. As with detention, deportation has eliminated any chance of living in the USA and serves as a punishment for Central American migrant youth attempting to find a safer place to live.

Conclusion

Over the last four decades in the USA, migration has become increasingly difficult with the introduction of the crimmigration system. This chapter contributes to this conversation through its discussion of the impacts that crimmigration has on migrant youth—namely, analyzing the role of two prominent forms of crimmigration, detention and deportation, and how Central American youth are exposed to both punishment regimes.

Migrant youth have been of concern to immigration officials since the beginnings of the crimmigration era in the 1980s. For example, one of the most ethically problematic actions that the Immigration and Naturalization Service (INS), the immigration enforcement agency during the beginnings of the crimmigration era and preceding agency to ICE, undertook was using the children of immigrants to ensnare their undocumented parents. News stories revolving around the use of this method circulated in various news outlets. For instance, two Salvadoran teenagers were released from an INS detention site after refugee advocates protested INS' use as "lures" against these children. The General Counsel for the National Center for Immigrants' Rights declared that "[INS] are just trying to force the parents to come in" (Mathews, 1985). A similar story reported by the *Los Angeles Times* stated that a class-action lawsuit was filed against the INS, charging it with detaining "The children of thousands of illegal aliens… and used as 'bait' to capture parents" (Los Angeles Times, 1985). Aside from being used as bait by immigration enforcement, children were also subject to the same forms of punishment as adults.

In the detention context, migrant youth are exposed to a prison-like space in which detention guards surveil and routinize their daily interactions. Despite the FSA, which is meant to protect minors and provide the "least-restrictive setting," immigrant youth are still victims of abuses and being treated like prisoners within various spaces, some of which are former prisons. When entering deportation proceedings, Central American migrant youth are not afforded any kind of legal counsel and must represent themselves in court or rely on legal brokers who are weighing the humanitarian capital of their cases. This leads to a high rate of deportation for those youth who do not have an attorney. Data also shows that most migrant youth do not have legal representation, which exacerbates this problem. The lives of migrant youth are also damaged when their relatives are deported, as they become orphans or exiles, as coined by Zayas (2015). When migrant youth face deportation itself, they are often left confused and without recourse when they are sent back to their home countries. Thus, in both crimmigration institutions, migrant youth are blocked from being able to live full lives and are instead given trauma and punishment.

References

Abrego, L. J. (2006). '"I Can't go to College Because I Don't Have Papers"': Incorporation Patterns of Latino Undocumented Youth. Latino Studies, 4(3), 212–231.

Ackerman, A. R., & Furman, R. (2013). The criminalization of immigration and the privatization of immigration detention: Implications for justice. *Contemporary Justice Review, 16*(2), 251–263.

ACLU. (2007, March 6). Lawsuits Ask That Children and Their Families be Released From Texas Facility Under Appropriate and Humane Supervision. American Civil Liberties Union. https://www.aclu.org/press-releases/aclu-challenges-illegal-detention-immigrant-children-held-prison-conditions?redirect=cpredirect/28865

ACLU. (2016). Shutting Down the Profiteers: Why and How the Department of Homeland Security Should Stop Using Private Prisons. ACLU. https://www.aclu.org/sites/default/files/field_document/white_paper_09-30-16_released_for_web-v1-opt.pdf

Bever, L. (2014, July 2). Protesters in California block busloads of immigrant children and families. *The Washington Post*. https://www.washingtonpost.com/news/morning-mix/wp/2014/07/02/protesters-in-california-block-busloads-of-immigrant-children-and-families/

Bruck, S. (2011). The impact of constitutional liability and private contracting on health care services for immigrants in civil detention. *Georgetown Immigration Law Journal, 25*, 487.

Byrd, K. (2023). Charting a path to full and free lives: An abolitionist vision for reentry. *Abolitionist Perspectives in Social Work, 1*(1), 1–19.

Cano, R. (2014, July 1). Protesters turn back busloads of immigrants in Murrieta. *The Desert Sun*. https://www.desertsun.com/story/news/2014/07/01/protesters-turn-back-busloads-immigrants-murrieta/11945751/

Castillo, J. (2008, January 12). Standards set for detainees at immigration. Austin American-Statesman.

Coleman, M., & Kocher, A. (2019). Rethinking the 'gold standard' of racial profiling: §287(g), Secure Communities, and racially discrepant police power. *American Behavioral Scientist, 63*(9), 1185–1220.

Collingwood, L., Morin, J. L., & El-Khatib, S. O. (2018). Expanding carceral markets: Detention facilities, ICE contracts, and the financial interests of punitive immigration policy. *Race and Social Problems, 10*(4), 275–292.

Conlon, D., & Hiemstra, N. (Eds.). (2017). *Intimate economies of immigration detention: Critical perspectives*. Routledge.

Coon, M. (2017). Local immigration enforcement and arrests of the Hispanic population. *Journal on Migration and Human Security, 5*(3), 645–666.

Dart, T. (2014, July 19). Communities polarised by influx of unaccompanied child migrants. *The Guardian*. https://www.theguardian.com/world/2014/jul/19/communities-polarised-unaccompanied-child-migrants

DHS. (2016). *Annual flow report: DHS immigration enforcement: 2016*. https://www.dhs.gov/sites/default/files/publications/DHS%20Immigration%20Enforcement%202016.pdf

Dickerson, C. (2020, May 20). 10 Years Old, Tearful and Confused After a Sudden Deportation. The New York Times. https://www.nytimes.com/2020/05/20/us/coronavirus-migrant-children-unaccompanied-minors.html

Doering-White, J., Darrow, J., Grace, B., Roth, B., Herring, A., & Liew, S. (2025). Care under pressure: Policy contradictions of speedy release, safety, and placement suitability in ORR-contracted programs for unaccompanied migrant children. *Children and Youth Services Review, 169*, 108093.

Elliot, R. (2014, August 11). Obama vow to speed deportation of children at odds with public opinion. *Reuters*. https://www.reuters.com/article/us-usa-immigration-children/obama-vow-to-speed-deportation-of-children-at-odds-with-public-opinion-idUSKBN0GB0AJ20140811

Feagin, J. (2013). *Systemic racism: A theory of oppression*. Routledge.

Fernandez, M. (2014, July 16). Towns fight to avoid taking in migrant minors. *The New York Times*. https://www.nytimes.com/2014/07/17/us/towns-fight-to-avoid-taking-in-migrant-minors.html

Fishman, J. M. (2017). *Death makes the news: How the media censor and display the dead*. NYU Press.

Fox News. (n.d.). Border kids battle invasion of America: Maryland site nixed for unaccompanied minors. *Fox News.*

Friedberg, R., & Hunt, J. (1998). Immigration and the receiving economy. Brown University, Population Studies and Training Center.

Galli, C. (2023). *Precarious protections: Unaccompanied minors seeking asylum in the United States.* University of California Press.

Garay, A. (2007, May 2). Demonstrators call for immigration reform. Lubbock Avalanche-Journal.

García Hernández, C. C. (2014). Immigration detention as punishment. *Immigration and Nationality Law Review, 35,* 385.

Gilman, D., & Romero, L. A. (2018). Immigration detention, inc. *Journal on Migration and Human Security, 6*(2), 145–160.

Granski, M., Keller, A., & Venters, H. (2015). Death rates among detained immigrants in the United States. *International Journal of Environmental Research and Public Health, 12*(11), 14414–14419.

Haag, M. (2019, February 27). Thousands of Immigrant Children Said They Were Sexually Abused in U.S. Detention Centers, Report Says. The New York Times. https://www.nytimes.com/2019/02/27/us/immigrant-children-sexual-abuse.html

Hansen, M., & Boster, M. (2014, July 1). Protesters in Murrieta block detainees' buses in tense standoff. *Los Angeles Times.* https://www.latimes.com/local/lanow/la-me-ln-immigrants-murrieta-20140701-story.html

Hawkes, D. (2008). Locking Up Children: Lessons from the T. Don Hutto Family Detention Center. *Journal of Law & Family Studies, 11,* 171–181.

Heidbrink, L. (2014). *Migrant youth, transnational families, and the state: Care and contested interests.* University of Pennsylvania Press.

Heidbrink, L. (2020). *Migranthood: Youth in a new era of deportation.* Stanford University Press.

Heidbrink, L., & Diaz, S. (2024). *Kids in care: Unaccompanied children in federal government custody.* Loyola University Chicago. https://ecommons.luc.edu/chrc/36/

Hernández, D. M. (2008). Pursuant to deportation: Latinos and immigrant detention. *Latino Studies, 6*(1–2), 35–63.

Jaafari, S., & Kulkarni, S. S. (2014, July 15). Arizona residents came out for and against a bus of migrants reportedly heading to their town. *The World.* https://www.pri.org/stories/2014-07-15/fierce-debate-over-migrant-children-spurs-rival-protests-small-arizona-town

Jefferis, D. C. (2014, July 19). Hundreds of protests set this weekend against illegal immigration, Obama's policies. *Fox News.* https://www.foxnews.com/politics/hundreds-of-protests-set-this-weekend-against-illegal-immigration-obamas-policies

Jefferis, D. C. (2019). Private prisons, private governance: Essay on developments in private-sector resistance to privatized immigration detention. *Northwestern Journal of Law and Social Policy, 15*, 82.

John, A. (2014, July 2). Protestors block buses full of migrant children in California. *The Atlantic*. https://www.theatlantic.com/politics/archive/2014/07/protestors-block-buses-full-of-migrant-children-in-california/373854/

Johnson, J. (2014a, July 14). Graffiti on proposed shelter for immigrant children in Maryland: 'No illeagles here.' *The Washington Post*. https://www.washingtonpost.com/local/md-politics/graffiti-on-proposed-shelter-for-immigrant-children-in-maryland-no-illeagles-here/2014/07/14/cc89610a-0b89-11e4-b8e5-d0de80767fc2_story.html

Johnson, M. A. (2014b, July 14). Protests to greet undocumented immigrants' arrival at Arizona camp. *NBC News*. https://www.nbcnews.com/storyline/immigration-border-crisis/protests-greet-undocumented-immigrants-arrival-arizona-camp-n155886

Johnson, K. (2016, December 1). DHS panel raises concerns about privately-run detention centers. *USA Today*. https://www.usatoday.com/story/news/politics/2016/12/01/dhs-panel-raises-concerns-privately-run-detention-centers/94727944/

Jonsson, P. (2014, July 19). Border kids protests build amid calls for troops on the border, even secession. *The Christian Science Monitor*. https://www.csmonitor.com/USA/Politics/2014/0719/Border-kids-protests-build-amid-calls-for-troops-on-the-border-even-secession

Kassie, E. (2019, September 24). Detained: How the US built the world's largest immigrant detention system. The Guardian. https://www.theguardian.com/us-news/2019/sep/24/detained-us-largest-immigrant-detention-trump

Libal, B., Martin, L., & Porter, N. (2012). "A Prison Is Not a Home": Notes from the Campaign to End Immigrant Family Detention. In Beyond Walls and Cages: Prisons, Borders, and Global Crisis (pp. 253–265). The University of Georgia Press.

Lind, D. (2014, July 1). Anti-immigrant protests are back. And they're targeting detainee families. *Vox*. https://www.vox.com/2014/7/1/5862432/anti-immigrant-protest-murrieta-detainee-family-buses-turned-around

Litwin, M. B. (2011). The decentralization of immigration law: The mischief of 287(g). *Seton Hall Law Review, 41*, 399.

Lopez, I. F. H. (1994). The social construction of race: Some observations on illusion, fabrication, and choice. *Harvard Civil Rights-Civil Liberties Law Review, 29*, 1.

Los Angeles Times. (1985, July 11). INS Uses Children as "Bait" to Capture Parents, Suit Says. Los Angeles Times. https://www.latimes.com/archives/la-xpm-1985-07-11-mn-8432-story.html

Margolis, J. (2014, July 21). Protests are spreading across the US against unaccompanied migrant children coming over the US-Mexico border and being relocated to detention centers. *The World*. https://www.pri.org/stories/2014-07-21/protests-spread-north-over-unaccompanied-migrant-children-coming-our-town

Markel, H. (2014, October 15). Before Ebola, Ellis Island's terrifying medical inspections. *PBS NewsHour*. https://www.pbs.org/newshour/health/october-15-1965-remembering-ellis-island

Martin, L. (2011). The geopolitics of vulnerability: Children's legal subjectivity, immigrant family detention and US immigration law and enforcement policy. *Gender, Place & Culture, 18*(4), 477–498.

Martin, L. (2017). Discretion, contracting, and commodification: Privatization of US immigration detention as a technology of government. In D. Conlon & N. Hiemstra (Eds.), *Intimate economies of immigration detention: Critical perspectives*. Routledge.

Martinez, M., Yan, H., & Shoichet, C. E. (2014, July 16). Growing protests over immigrant children hits Arizona. *CNN*. https://www.cnn.com/2014/07/15/us/arizona-immigrant-children/index.html

Mathews, J. (1985, July 20). Group Says INS Uses Children as Lures for Illegal Alien Parents: Salvadoran Youths Ordered Released. The Washington Post, A8.

Mehta, S., & Megerian, C. (2014, July 3). Murrieta protests return immigration issue to forefront of state politics. *Los Angeles Times*. https://www.latimes.com/local/la-me-pol-immigration-politics-20140703-story.html

Menjívar, C. (2014). Immigration law beyond borders: Externalizing and internalizing border controls in an era of securitization. *Annual Review of Law and Social Science, 10*(1), 353–369. https://doi.org/10.1146/annurev-lawsocsci-110413-030842

Merton, R., & Fialho, C. (2017, April 11). Re: Sexual Abuse, Assault, and Harassment in U.S. Immigration Detention Facilities. CIVIC. http://www.endisolation.org/wp-content/uploads/2017/05/CIVIC_SexualAssault_Complaint.pdf

Moinester, M. (2019). A look to the interior: Trends in U.S. immigration removals by criminal conviction type, gender, and region of origin, fiscal years 2003–2015. *American Behavioral Scientist, 63*(9), 1276–1298. https://doi.org/10.1177/0002764219835276

Molina, N. (2006). *Fit to be citizens?: Public health and race in Los Angeles, 1879–1939* (Vol. 20). University of California Press.

NBC News. (2014, July 15). Arizona residents protest arrival of undocumented immigrant children. *NBC News*. https://www.nbcnews.com/storyline/immigration-border-crisis/arizona-residents-protest-arrival-undocumented-immigrant-children-n155941

Neeley, S. (2008). Immigration detention: The inaction of the Bureau of Immigration and Customs Enforcement. *Administrative Law Review, 60*, 729.

Ngai, M. M. (2014). *Impossible subjects: Illegal aliens and the making of modern America*. Princeton University Press.

O'Donnell, N. (2014, July 18). Underpants and overpasses: Immigration protest organizers include longtime Obama critics. *NBC 7 San Diego*. https://www.nbcsandiego.com/news/local/immigration-protest-border-crisis-obama/98503/

Olson, L. (2014, July 18). Tea Party to protest influx of unaccompanied foreign children. *The Morning Call*. https://www.mcall.com/news/local/mc-xpm-2014-07-18-mc-kidspeace-immigration-children-protest-20140718-story.html

Omi, M., & Winant, H. (2014). *Racial formation in the United States*. Routledge.

Park, H. (2014, October 21). Children at the border. *The New York Times*. https://www.nytimes.com/interactive/2014/07/15/us/questions-about-the-border-kids.html

Pérez, W. S. (2025, August 29). What 30+ Years of Deportations Show Across 5 Presidents. Latino News Network. https://latinonewsnetwork.com/community/who-deported-more-migrants-obama-or-trump-we-checked-the-numbers/

Ramos, E. S. (2022). *Acompañando niños migrantes "no acompañados": A feminist geopolitical perspective on Central American unaccompanied minors in U.S. long term foster care (LTFC)* [Master's thesis, University of Texas at Austin]. https://repositories.lib.utexas.edu/server/api/core/bitstreams/8276f8c9-3b77-4c02-94ad-7527b499ee80/content

Romero, L. A. (2023). Malleable detention: The restructuring of carceral space within U.S. immigration detention. *Punishment & Society, 25*(4), 848–866.

Romero, L. A., & Zarrugh, A. (2018). Islamophobia and the making of Latinos/as into terrorist threats. Ethnic and Racial Studies, 41(12), Article 12. https://doi.org/10.1080/01419870.2017.1349919

Ruiz, O. (2018). Immigrants or children? The expulsion of unaccompanied minors from two California towns. *International Journal of Migration and Border Studies, 4*(1/2), 89.

Ryo, E. (2017). Legal attitudes of immigrant detainees. *Law & Society Review, 51*(1), 99–131.

Ryo, E. (2019). Understanding immigration detention: Causes, conditions, and consequences. *Annual Review of Law and Social Science, 15*(1), 97–115.

Ryo, E., & Peacock, I. (2020). Jailing immigrant detainees: A national study of county participation in immigration detention, 1983–2013. *Law & Society Review, 54*(1), 66–101.

Samsel, E. (2014, July 19). *Immigration protests staged around the country*. MSNBC. https://www.msnbc.com/msnbc/immigration-protests-staged-around-the-country-msna372916

Sanchez, T. (2014, June 30). SoCal region to get young migrant border crossers. *The Desert Sun*. https://www.desertsun.com/story/news/2014/07/01/socal-young-migrant-border-crossers-el-centro-murrieta/11833669/

Sayed, F. W. (2011). Challenging detention: Why immigrant detainees receive less process than enemy combatants and why they deserve more. *Columbia Law Review, 111*(8), 1833–1877.

Shafer, J. (2019, June 26). Whose deaths aren't we seeing? *POLITICO Magazine*. https://politi.co/2Yisgku

Smith, J. S. (2014, July 18). Pro-immigration protesters call opposition racists cowards as emotions boil over in Lansing. *MLive*. https://www.mlive.com/lansing-news/2014/07/immigration_protesters_state_c.html

Speri, A. (2018, April 11). Detained, Then Violated: 1,224 Complaints Reveal a Staggering Pattern of Sexual Abuse in Immigration Detention. Half of Those Accused Worked for ICE. The Intercept. https://theintercept.com/2018/04/11/immigration-detention-sexual-abuse-ice-dhs/

Stickney, R., & Fleming, O. (2014, July 1). Protestors block buses of undocumented immigrants in Murrieta. *NBC 7 San Diego*. https://www.nbcsandiego.com/news/local/immigrant-children-san-diego-plane-murrieta-minors-deport/60604/

Stickney, R., & McVicker, L. (2014, July 2). Murrieta immigration protest, police criticized. *NBC 7 San Diego*. https://www.nbcsandiego.com/news/local/murrieta-police-protest-immigration-controversy-bus-children-san-diego/1977411/

Stickney, R., Tevrizian, M., & Guevara, D. (2014, July 8). Third plane of undocumented immigrants lands in San Diego. *NBC 7 San Diego*. https://www.nbcsandiego.com/news/local/third-plane-of-undocumented-immigrants-lands-in-san-diego/1977710/

Stumpf, J. (2006). The crimmigration crisis: Immigrants, crime, and sovereign. *American University Law Review, 56*, 367–419.

Talbot, M. (2008, February 24). The Lost Children. The New Yorker. https://www.newyorker.com/magazine/2008/03/03/the-lost-children

Terrio, S. J. (2015). *Whose child am I?: Unaccompanied, undocumented children in U.S. immigration custody*. University of California Press.

TRAC. (2014). *Representation for unaccompanied children in immigration court*. https://trac.syr.edu/immigration/reports/371/

TRAC. (2017). Children: Amid a Growing Court Backlog Many Still Unrepresented. https://tracreports.org/immigration/reports/482/

U.S. Border Patrol. (2019). *BP total monthly UACs by sector FY10-19*. U.S. Border Patrol. https://www.cbp.gov/sites/default/files/assets/documents/2020-Jan/U.S.%20Border%20Patrol%20Total%20Monthly%20UAC%20Apprehensions%20by%20Sector%20%28FY%202010%20-%20FY%202019%29_0.pdf

U.S. Border Patrol. (2025). *Nationwide encounters | U.S. Customs and Border protection*. Nationwide encounters. https://www.cbp.gov/newsroom/stats/nationwide-encounters

U.S. News and World Report. (2017, April 13). *Texas getting first immigrant center built under President Trump*. U.S. News and World Report. https://www.usnews.com/news/best-states/texas/articles/2017-04-13/texas-getting-first-immigrant-lockup-built-under-trump

Warner, A. (2014, July 8). Kids crossing the border: What to know about the immigration crisis. *NBC 7 San Diego*. https://www.nbcsandiego.com/news/national-international/border-kids-what-to-know-immigration-crisis-border-central-america

Warren, R. (2016). US undocumented population drops below 11 million in 2014, with continued declines in the Mexican undocumented population. *Journal on Migration and Human Security*, *4*(1), 1–15. https://doi.org/10.1177/233150241600400101

Wilson, R. (2014, June 14). Arizona Republicans threaten action over immigration. *The Washington Post*. https://www.washingtonpost.com/blogs/govbeat/wp/2014/06/14/arizona-republicans-threaten-action-over-immigration/

Zarrugh, A. (2019). The development of US regimes of disappearance: The war on terror, mass incarceration, and immigrant deportation. *Critical Sociology*, 1–15. https://doi.org/10.1177/0896920519826640

Zayas, L. H. (2015). Forgotten Citizens: Deportation, Children, and the Making of American Exiles and Orphans. Oxford University Press.

CHAPTER 13

Domestic Violence in Immigrant Families

Bushra Sabri and Karime Jiménez-Limas

Introduction

Definition

Domestic violence is a concept that varies widely across cultures, differing not only in terminology but also in the behaviors and victims included within its scope. Cultural understandings of these behaviors and their motivations, shaped by distinct social norms and linguistic nuances, make it challenging to establish a universally standardized definition (Barocas et al., 2016; Fernández, 2006; Huecker et al., 2023; Kalokhe et al., 2015). Among immigrant families, these understandings are further influenced by the complexities of migration, where the intersection of cultural norms from their home countries and host societies creates additional layers of nuance (Park et al., 2021; Sabri et al., 2018a). These cultural and

B. Sabri (✉)
School of Nursing, Johns Hopkins University, Baltimore, MD, USA
e-mail: bsabri1@jhu.edu

K. Jiménez-Limas
School of Nursing, Johns Hopkins University,
Baltimore, MD, USA
e-mail: kjimene7@jh.edu

J. S. Hong et al. (eds.), *Violence and Trauma Without Borders*,
https://doi.org/10.1007/978-3-032-29221-6_13

linguistic differences pose unique challenges in defining domestic violence in a way that fully addresses the experiences of immigrant families. In some cultures, the vocabulary for domestic violence is limited or nonexistent, complicating efforts to fully understand or address the issue. For instance, in Russia, domestic violence is referred to as "home violence" (Fernandez, 2006; Horne, 1999; Pisklakova, 1995), a term not universally recognized, whereas in South Africa, the term "woman abuse" is more commonly used (Bograd, 1990; Boonzaier & De la Rey, 2003; Fernández, 2006).

Potential victims of domestic violence also differ widely across contexts. Some definitions extend beyond women to include children, elders, and even men as potential victims (Barocas et al., 2016; Huecker et al., 2023). For example, in some African countries, domestic violence has traditionally been understood as the beating of children, with the wife beating only recently entering public discourse (Fernandez, 2006). This shift is often framed within notions of discipline, where wife-beating is recognized as abuse only when it exceeds certain cultural norms or is perceived as the husband's right (Fernández, 2006; Ofei-Aboagye, 1994; Sabri et al., 2018a). Similarly, in Chile, "private violence" primarily refers to harm inflicted on both women and children (Fernández, 2006; McWhirter, 1999). Cultural nuances further shape the understanding of domestic violence in Japan and India (Fernández, 2006; Kalokhe et al., 2015; Kozu, 1999). For example, some Japanese women perceive culturally specific acts, such as overturning a dining table or being doused with liquid, as more severe than physical assault (Fernández, 2006; Sokoloff & Dupont, 2005). In Japan and India, relationships such as those between mothers-in-law and daughters-in-law are often sources of abuse (Fernández, 2006; Kalokhe et al., 2015; Kozu, 1999).

This diversity underscores the importance of considering cultural differences in how domestic violence is defined, understood, and experienced worldwide, particularly among immigrant families. Migration often brings unique challenges as individuals navigate the intersection of cultural norms from their home countries and those of their host societies, which can influence perceptions of acceptable behavior and the recognition of abuse (Park et al., 2021; Sabri et al., 2018a). In this chapter, we will primarily adopt the United Nations' definition of domestic violence, which characterizes it as a pattern of behavior used to gain or maintain power and control over an intimate partner. It includes physical, sexual, emotional, economic, or psychological abuse (United Nations, 2020). Nevertheless, we will also explore broader interpretations that encompass more than just intimate partner violence, recognizing that domestic violence can occur in various types of relationships (e.g., children or other relatives or any other household members) and cultural contexts (United Nations, 2020), including those shaped by the experiences of immigrant families.

Prevalence, Gender Disparities, and Impact on Immigrant Women

Domestic violence is a pervasive public health crisis that significantly affects individuals, families, and communities across the United States. According to the Centers for Disease Control and Prevention, nearly half of all women (47.3%) and over 44% of men in the United States report experiencing stalking, sexual violence, and/or physical violence by an intimate partner at some point in their lives, with 7.3% of women and 6.8% of men reporting such violence in the past year (Leemis et al., 2022). When broken down further, the data reveal troubling trends: Physical violence affects over two in five individuals, sexual violence is reported by nearly one in five women and one in 13 men, and stalking impacts approximately one in seven women and one in 20 men in the United States. Psychological aggression is equally widespread, affecting nearly half of both women (49.4%) and men (45.1%) (Leemis et al., 2022).

While both men and women experience domestic violence, women are disproportionately affected, both in prevalence and severity. The impact of violence in the United States population further highlights this disparity: about two in five (41%) women report consequences of domestic violence compared to one in four men (26.3%) (Leemis et al., 2022). Gender disparities are further evident in the severity of violence: In 2023, an estimated 51,100 women and girls were killed by intimate partners or family members worldwide—an average of 140 female homicides per day (UNWomen, 2023). Moreover, 60% of female homicides are committed by intimate partners or family members, compared to just 12% of male homicides occurring within the household (UNWomen, 2023). Unfortunately, the United States lacks a comprehensive surveillance system that captures and disaggregates femicide data in the way that many global systems do. However, existing evidence shows that women are disproportionately affected by homicide, especially in cases involving intimate partners (Lewis et al., 2024). Among the most vulnerable in the United States are immigrant women: Foreign-born women victims of homicide are more likely than United States–born victims to have died as a result of intimate partner violence (Sabri et al., 2021a). Given these stark disparities, this chapter focuses specifically on domestic violence perpetrated against women, with particular attention to immigrant women in the United States. This population often faces compounded challenges—including cultural differences, language barriers, immigration status vulnerabilities, and limited access to resources, all of which can exacerbate their risk of experiencing and addressing domestic violence (El-Moslemany et al., 2020; Kim, 2019; Morrison et al., 2023; Njie-Carr et al., 2021; Park et al., 2021; Sabri et al., 2018a; Sasseville et al., 2022).

Migration Trends and Immigrant Women's Vulnerability

As of 2020, the most recent global estimate, there were approximately 281 million international migrants, representing 3.6% of the world population (McAuliffe & Oucho, 2024). Of these, approximately 135 million were women, constituting 3.5% of the global female population (McAuliffe & Oucho, 2024). These global migration trends set the stage for understanding the demographic composition of immigrant populations in specific host countries, such as the United States, which has been the leading destination for international migrants since 1970 (International Organization for Migration, 2024). As of 2023, immigrants comprised 14.3% of the United States population—approximately 47.8 million individuals (Migration Policy Institute, 2023)—with women accounting for about 51% of this group (US Census Bureau, 2022).

The majority of international migrants come from regions such as Asia and Latin America (International Organization for Migration, 2024)—regions with documented higher lifetime prevalence rates of domestic violence against women (Sardinha et al., 2022; World Health Organization, 2021). This is particularly relevant in the United States context, where many immigrant women come from these same regions, including countries such as Mexico, India, China, and the Philippines (International Organization for Migration, 2024). Understanding the cultural and structural vulnerabilities these women may bring with them is critical for developing effective domestic violence prevention and intervention strategies.

Immigrant women in the United States face heightened risks of domestic violence due to intersecting factors such as immigration policies, language barriers, social isolation, and limited financial resources (El-Moslemany et al., 2020; Kim, 2019; Morrison et al., 2023; Njie-Carr et al., 2021; Park et al., 2021; Sabri et al., 2018a; Sasseville et al., 2022).

These vulnerabilities are often weaponized by abusers, who may use a woman's immigration status to exert power and control—employing tactics such as threats of deportation, intimidation, and obstruction of access to support services (Njie-Carr et al., 2021; Sabri et al., 2018a). These challenges are particularly concerning in the context of the growing global immigrant population (Sabri et al., 2018a).

Prevalence, Risk, and Protective Factors Across Socio-Ecological Levels

Rates of domestic violence victimization among immigrant populations in the United States vary widely. Most studies on domestic violence within immigrant populations have been limited to specific ethnic groups or have failed to consider ethnicity altogether (Morrison et al., 2023). A systematic review of research on domestic violence in single-ethnic immigrant groups in the United States, which included both men and women, revealed a wide range of lifetime victimization rates, spanning from 13.9% to 93% (Barkho et al., 2011; Morrison et al., 2023; Shibusawa & Yick, 2007). The past-year domestic violence victimization rates among immigrant individuals in the United States varied from 3.8% to 46.9% (Kimber et al., 2015; Morrison et al., 2023). However, the review did not provide gender-stratified prevalence rates (Morrison et al., 2023). These variations in domestic violence victimization highlight the urgent need for tailored interventions and support systems that address the unique challenges faced by immigrants in domestic violence situations in the United States.

Given the complex and variable rates of domestic violence victimization among immigrant women, understanding the underlying risk and protective factors is essential for addressing this issue. Domestic violence is influenced by various risk and protective factors that operate at different levels—individual, interpersonal, community, and societal levels (Sabri et al., 2018a). Risk factors elevate the chances of survivors facing safety threats. In contrast, protective factors help mitigate the risk of IPV and strengthen women's ability to respond to violence and its associated health and safety concerns (World Health Organization/London School of Hygiene and Tropical Medicine, 2010; Sabri et al., 2018a). Understanding these factors is critical for developing effective prevention and intervention strategies that meet the unique needs of immigrant women experiencing domestic violence. To systematically explore these multifaceted influences, the socio-ecological model offers a comprehensive framework that highlights how risk and protective factors operate and interact across different levels of society.

The Socio-Ecological Model

The socio-ecological model provides a useful framework for understanding how various factors at multiple levels—societal, community, interpersonal, and individual—interact to influence behaviors and outcomes (Bronfenbrenner, 1979). This model is particularly relevant for examining domestic violence because it recognizes that no single factor fully explains domestic violence; rather, it is the interplay of influences across different levels that shapes the risk and resilience of women. By applying the socio-ecological model, we can systematically explore the risk and protective factors affecting immigrant women's experiences with domestic violence and develop comprehensive interventions that target these interconnected levels.

Risk Factors for Domestic Violence Victimization in Immigrant Women

Societal Level Risk Factors

The societal level encompasses broader norms, institutional structures, and policy-related factors that influence the prevalence and dynamics of domestic violence. Societal norms, legal frameworks, and systemic inequalities collectively contribute to the risks of domestic violence, particularly among immigrant women, where cultural and structural vulnerabilities intersect.

Patriarchal Norms Deeply ingrained patriarchal norms are significant drivers of domestic violence among immigrant women (Morrison et al., 2023; Park et al., 2021; Sabri et al., 2018a). Across various cultural contexts, while specific practices differ, the pervasive influence of patriarchy remains consistent, shaping attitudes toward gender roles and justifying male dominance. These norms often assign women a subordinate social status, impose rigid expectations around gender roles, and normalize violence as a mechanism to enforce male control (Morrison et al., 2023; Park et al., 2021; Sabri et al., 2018a). Women bear the burden of keeping the family together, so they are blamed for any marital conflict (Sabri et al., 2018a). Such cultural conditioning creates an environment where domestic violence is more likely to occur and less likely to be challenged, perpetuating cycles of abuse.

Cultural Norms Related to Marriage and Divorce Cultural norms that perpetuate gender inequality, reinforce rigid gender roles, and uphold the low status of women significantly increase the risk of domestic violence. In many societies, marriage is viewed as a cornerstone of a woman's identity, and strict gender roles within marriage create expectations of submission and obedience. Women who challenge these roles may be perceived as defying cultural norms, which can provoke abusive behaviors. Abusers frequently exploit these beliefs, leveraging societal values such as family honor and female chastity to exert control. For example, abusive partners may threaten to humiliate women by spreading damaging rumors, accusing them of infidelity, or sharing false claims of mental illness or illness like AIDS (Sabri et al., 2018a). Cultural beliefs that tie family honor to women's behavior can place undue pressure on women to maintain submissive roles, leaving them vulnerable to violence. This can also discourage women from seeking help, as domestic violence is often considered a private family matter. Practices such as dowries, bride prices, and forced or arranged marriages reflect a consistent pattern of subordinating women, often reducing them to financial transactions. Insufficient dowries or the perception of bride prices as ownership can exacerbate abuse within marriages, sometimes involving extended family members, such as mothers-in-law (Sabri et al., 2018a). The stigma surrounding divorce further traps women in abusive relationships, as leaving a marriage may bring social disgrace or economic hardship. Immigrant women, particularly those from cultures with these practices, face heightened risks due to unfamiliarity with local systems or legal protections and may feel additional pressure to conform to cultural norms (Sasseville et al., 2022). These dynamics collectively reinforce a system where women's autonomy is curtailed, increasing their vulnerability to domestic violence.

Religious Doctrines Religious beliefs and practices can also exacerbate the risk of domestic violence by normalizing male authority through religious teachings, imposing restrictions on divorce and annulment, and discouraging women from seeking help or leaving harmful relationships (Sabri et al., 2018a; Westenberg, 2017). For example, in the Hmong culture, when a husband transforms into a full Shaman—gaining mastery over spirits and influencing the spiritual world—violent behavior toward a partner might be accepted as part of this transition. Additionally, fear of leaving an abusive relationship is common among Hmong women due to beliefs surrounding reincarnation. In Hmong culture, it is believed that if her husband or his family abandons a woman, she may not receive a proper burial, which in turn prevents her from being reincarnated. Without reincarnation, her spirit is believed to be condemned to hell (Sabri et al., 2018a). While this example illustrates specific beliefs, many religions have doctrines or practices that, intentionally or unintentionally, sustain environments where domestic violence is rationalized, abuse is normalized, and leaving an abusive partner is stigmatized (Westenberg, 2017).

Community-Level Risk Factors

At the community level, the broader social environment in which women live plays a critical role in either reinforcing or challenging the prevalence of domestic violence among immigrant women. Community norms, support systems, and local resources interact to shape women's experiences of abuse, influencing their ability to seek safety and justice (Sabri et al., 2018a). Key factors include the availability of culturally responsive protection services, prevailing community attitudes toward violence and divorce, and the presence of networks that may revictimize survivors.

Community Attitudes and Norms Community attitudes and norms surrounding marriage, divorce, and family honor further compound immigrant women's challenges in escaping abuse. For many, deeply ingrained beliefs about lifetime marital commitments and the stigma of divorce create significant barriers to leaving abusive relationships and risk factors for domestic violence victimization (Park et al., 2021; Sabri et al., 2018a). For some immigrant women, preserving family honor and upholding the appearance of marital happiness outweigh personal safety and well-being. For instance, in a study, it was found that among Indian women, maintaining family honor and projecting marital happiness often take precedence over addressing violence, as exemplified by one woman's statement: "I have three daughters, if it [domestic violence accusations and divorce rumors] goes out in society, nobody will marry my daughters" (Sabri et al., 2018a). Such attitudes discourage women from seeking help out of fear of ostracism and reputational damage while fostering environments where abuse is normalized or minimized. Some domestic violence survivors face community shaming and isolation for leaving abusive relationships or seeking a divorce (Sabri et al., 2018a). By stigmatizing survivors and prioritizing family honor over individual safety, these entrenched beliefs reinforce cycles of abuse, leaving immigrant women isolated and vulnerable.

Lack of Culturally Responsive Protection Services The lack of cultural competence of service providers places immigrant women at increased risk for continued exposure to domestic violence. Immigrant women often face unique threats shaped by cultural and spiritual practices that may not be recognized or adequately addressed by Western legal systems. For example, practices such as black magic or rituals of reincarnation are sometimes weaponized by male partners to intimidate or harm women, creating significant emotional and spiritual risks (Sabri et al., 2018a). Western legal systems, however, often fail to grasp the cultural dimensions of these threats, leaving women without appropriate support or legal recourse (Sabri et al., 2018a). This lack of understanding exacerbates immigrant women's vulnerability, as they may feel isolated in a foreign culture where their experiences are misunderstood or dismissed. Developing culturally competent services that acknowledge and address these unique challenges is critical to providing adequate support and protection to immigrant survivors of domestic violence.

Interpersonal Level Risk Factors

The interpersonal level examines the dynamics within relationships and social interactions. Here, the focus is on how relationships with partners, family members, and peers can contribute to the risk of domestic violence in immigrant women (Park et al., 2021; Sabri et al., 2018a). Power dynamics, communication patterns, and relational conflicts are critical in understanding how interpersonal factors can exacerbate this risk (Morrison et al., 2023; Park et al., 2021; Sabri et al., 2018a).

Partner Behaviors and Contextual Risks in Intimate Relationships Studies indicate that specific partner behaviors—such as threats to harm the survivor or their family, threats to take custody of children, threats of self-harm, control over immigration documents, jealousy, suspicion, coercion, isolation, physical violence, sexual assault, choking, verbal and psychological abuse, and financial control—significantly heighten the risk of severe intimate partner violence or intimate partner homicide (Campbell et al., 2003; Messing et al., 2013; Sabri et al., 2016, 2018a). These abusive behaviors often create barriers that prevent survivors from seeking help (Sabri et al., 2018a).

In addition to these partner behaviors, certain contextual factors in intimate relationships can further exacerbate risks for domestic violence or domestic violence homicide, particularly for immigrant women. Immigrant women often face unique vulnerabilities tied to navigating cultural and systemic differences in unfamiliar environments (El-Moslemany et al., 2020; Kim, 2019; Morrison et al., 2023; Njie-Carr et al., 2021; Park et al., 2021; Sabri et al., 2018a; Sasseville et al., 2022). For instance, some Asian survivors have reported that being in a relationship with a partner from a different racial or ethnic background, particularly from a White majority culture, may increase their risk of severe IPV or IPH. This increased risk is often linked to dynamics of power, privilege, and systemic inequalities (Sabri et al., 2018a). Moreover, immigrant women partnered with a US-born individual may experience additional challenges due to their partners' greater familiarity with legal and social systems (Sabri et al., 2018a). This disparity often disadvantages immigrant women, limiting their access to resources and support systems necessary for safety and well-being.

In-Law Abuse Residing with abusive in-laws was identified as a risk factor for domestic violence and domestic violence homicide among immigrant women from diverse backgrounds (Sabri et al., 2018a). In such cases, in-laws may instigate or reinforce violent behaviors by an abusive partner, often exerting control through cultural norms or familial expectations. Moreover, they may act as direct perpetrators of violence themselves, using psychological, verbal, or physical abuse to dominate and marginalize the survivor (Choi, 2022; Erez & Harper, 2018; Ragavan & Iyengar, 2020; Sabri et al., 2018a). For example, in-laws may leverage economic dependency as tools of control or exploit dowry practices as tools for control and abuse, exacerbating survivors' vulnerability (Erez & Harper, 2018; Sabri et al., 2018a). This dual role of in-laws—as instigators and perpetrators—not only intensifies the risk of harm but also complicates survivors' ability to seek help, particularly in culturally isolated or tightly knit immigrant communities.

Role of Children in the Family While children can serve as a strong motivator for immigrant survivors to leave an abusive relationship, they also introduce challenges. Concerns about financial stability and the capacity to provide for their children independently often complicate the decision to leave (Herrero-Arias et al., 2019; Sabri et al., 2018a). Additionally, children may inadvertently become a tool for manipulation by the abusive partner, as threats of custody battles, alienation, or harm to the children can be used to exert control and prevent the survivor from leaving (Erez & Harper, 2018; Sabri et al., 2018a). The responsibility of protecting children from the trauma of exposure to violence further heightens the emotional and logistical burden on survivors.

Individual-Level Risk Factors

At the individual level, personal characteristics and life experiences intersect to shape immigrant women's vulnerability to domestic violence. Factors such as childbearing status, past trauma, socioeconomic instability, and disabilities can increase the likelihood of experiencing abuse (Sabri et al., 2018a; Sasseville et al., 2022). Additional vulnerabilities include being on a dependent or temporary visa, lacking financial independence or formal education, undocumented immigration status, and isolation due to the absence of family or support networks in the United States (Morrison et al., 2023; Park et al., 2021; Sabri et al., 2018a). In a study, survivors cited challenges such as having no safe place to go and fears of legal consequences for the abuser as barriers to seeking help. Further, survivors often rationalized abuse or internalized self-blame, believing they were responsible for the violence rather than their partners. This mindset hindered help-seeking behaviors and perpetuated their vulnerability (Sabri et al., 2018b). Acculturation-related factors, such as tensions arising from women's independence or empowerment, were also identified as triggers for violence when they challenged traditional gender roles and threatened male partners' perceived authority (Sabri et al., 2018a, 2018b).

Disabilities Women with disabilities are at higher risk of victimization by domestic violence (García-Cuéllar et al., 2023). Physical and psychological health issues, including disabilities, are also significant risk factors for domestic violence among immigrant women (Sasseville et al., 2022). Studies show that women with disabilities are two to five times more likely to experience domestic violence over their lifetime and nearly twice as likely as nondisabled women to have faced domestic violence in the last five years (Sasseville et al., 2022; Schröttle & Glammeier, 2013; Sinha, 2013). Some forms of domestic violence are unique to women with disabilities and do not occur in the same way among women without disabilities. For instance, abusers may exploit a woman's disability to degrade her or fail to fulfill familial responsibilities (García-Cuéllar et al., 2023; Plummer & Findley, 2012; Ruiz-Pérez et al., 2018). Additionally, experiencing domestic violence can significantly hinder access to support services. Women with disabilities facing domestic violence deal with a dual sense of fear, concerned not only about the stigma of partner violence but also about how professionals' misconceptions about disability may impact their care (Bradbury-Jones et al., 2015; García-Cuéllar et al., 2023). Immigrant women with disabilities facing domestic violence often face multiple layers of vulnerability, such as language barriers and cultural stigma surrounding both domestic violence and disability. These factors create additional obstacles, making it even more difficult for them to access the support they need or to escape abusive situations.

Length of Stay in the Host Country Recent immigration from a developing country has been identified as a risk factor for domestic violence among immigrant women (Brownridge & Hali, 2002; Sasseville et al., 2022). Women who have recently migrated to a new country often face challenges with acculturation, which can place them at a disadvantage compared to their partners, who may be more familiar with the country's systems and have stronger support networks from family and community (Sabri et al., 2018a; Sasseville et al., 2022). This can put immigrant women at a disadvantage, as they often have limited support networks, lack knowledge of local systems, and experience social isolation (Sabri et al., 2018a). However, in a study of Chinese immigrant women in the United States, it was found that those with a longer duration of stay had an increased risk of experiencing domestic violence (Li et al., 2020). This may be due to a power dynamic issue, such as when a domestic violence survivor's increased independence or empowerment leads to backlash from an abusive partner (Sabri et al., 2018a).

Low Education and Income Low education and low income are well-known risk factors for experiencing domestic violence (Morrison et al., 2023; Sabri et al., 2018a). Women with lower levels of education and income often face greater economic dependence and limited access to resources, which can exacerbate their vulnerability to being abused (Morrison et al., 2023). However, having a master's degree has also been linked to a higher risk of past-year IPV among a sample of Chinese immigrant women in the United States (Li et al., 2020). This may stem from the increased independence and socioeconomic power these women acquire post-immigration, which can disrupt traditional relationship dynamics and lead to conflicts with partners who perceive their patriarchal authority as being undermined (Li et al., 2020).

Childbearing and Preference for a Male Child In many cultures, childbearing and the preference for male children are highly valued (Ardabily et al., 2011; Rahebi et al., 2019). In the context of these dynamics, which are not exclusive to immigrant populations, women are often held solely responsible for a couple's infertility and the sex of the baby, exposing them to a heightened risk of domestic abuse (Rahebi et al., 2019; Sabri et al., 2018a). Marital conflict frequently stems from difficulties in conceiving or bearing male children, leading to social, physical, emotional, and economic consequences. For instance, in a study, immigrant survivors specifically cited infertility and the inability to have a male child as key risk factors for abuse (Sabri et al., 2018a).

Protective Factors Against Domestic Violence Among Immigrant Women

Societal-Level Protective Factors

Law and Regulations in the Host Country Laws in some countries, such as the United States, can protect immigrant women facing domestic violence, offering more freedom and legal recourse than in their home countries (Njie-Carr et al., 2021; Sabri et al., 2018a; Sasseville et al., 2022). In a study, survivors noted that the United States has strong legal measures against intimate partner violence and greater access to resources (Njie-Carr et al., 2021). Divorce laws, for example, give women more freedom and hope for independence, and the legal system's enforcement of consequences for abusers helps empower survivors about their rights and protections not available in their countries of origin (Njie-Carr et al., 2021; Sabri et al., 2018a).

Religion While religion was also described as a risk factor for domestic violence, it can also serve as a protective factor (Njie-Carr et al., 2021; Sabri et al., 2018a). In a study, immigrant survivors of domestic violence and practitioners serving immigrant women shared instances where women received crucial support from their religion. For example, women have sought guidance from priests, religious leaders, or fellow congregants, leading to safety planning and intervention (Njie-Carr et al., 2021). In some cases, religious leaders reminded abusive partners of their responsibilities toward their spouses, reinforcing the need for respectful treatment (Sabri et al., 2018a).

Community-Level Protective Factors

The Role of Social Networks in the Community While community involvement is often seen as a risk factor for violence against immigrant women due to its reinforcement of traditional gender norms, it can, in certain circumstances, act as a protective factor (Sabri et al., 2018a). In a study, immigrant women survivors of domestic violence often shared experiences of receiving support from their communities, including help from friends, co-workers, and neighbors—ranging from emotional support to assistance with contacting authorities, offering shelter, or helping them reach a safe place (Njie-Carr et al., 2021; Sabri et al., 2018a). Formal sources of support, such as healthcare providers and the police, can also play a protective role. Healthcare professionals often recognize signs of abuse and connect women to resources, while the police may help survivors find safety and offer information about further assistance. These informal and formal community supports contribute significantly to protecting women from ongoing violence; however, it is important to note that for some survivors, differential treatment by the police and the court system may also be a barrier to reporting and addressing the abuse (Sabri et al., 2018a).

Culturally Appropriate Services Access to culturally relevant resources serves as a protective factor for immigrant women facing domestic violence (Sabri et al., 2018a; Tavrow et al., 2022). When support services, such as shelters, align with the cultural needs and preferences of the community, women are more likely to feel safe and supported to disclose domestic violence experiences (Rai et al., 2023; Sabri et al., 2018a; Tavrow et al., 2022). Culturally tailored services and activities can make women feel less demeaned and more understood than generic shelters that may not meet their specific needs (Rai et al., 2023; Sabri et al., 2018a). Overcoming barriers to accessing help can improve access to these resources, reducing survivors' risk of being returned to inadequate options like general homeless shelters (Sabri et al., 2018a). Thus, culturally appropriate support services play a crucial role in protecting women from domestic violence.

Interpersonal Level

Family Support Having support from family members serves as a protective factor and empowers survivors by facilitating their path to safety and helping them leave their abusive situation (Howell et al., 2018; Mughal & Saint Arnault, 2024; Sabri et al., 2018a). Survivors often rely on family members for various forms of assistance, including emotional support that helps them avoid despair and suicidal thoughts. Families may also provide financial help, offer a safe place to stay, and assist with legal actions such as filing restraining orders. Additionally, family members might intervene directly with the abuser or encourage the survivor to have the confidence to leave the abusive relationship (Mughal & Saint Arnault, 2024; Sabri et al., 2018a).

Having Children For many domestic violence survivors, having children can be a source of immense strength and resilience (Njie-Carr et al., 2021; Sabri et al., 2018a). Children often serve as a motivating force and provide emotional support, as survivors may choose to stay alive and cope with the abuse for their children's sake, avoiding suicidal thoughts (Sabri et al., 2018a). In some cases, children take protective actions themselves, such as disclosing the abuse to teachers in their school or neighbors or calling the authorities, which can lead to immediate intervention (Sabri et al., 2018a). Although it was previously described how the presence of children could also complicate the women's decision to leave abusive situations, it has been repeatedly described by immigrant survivors as a fuel to seek safety and build a better future (Herrero-Arias et al., 2019; Sabri et al., 2018a).

Individual Level

The Role of Acculturation, Knowledge, and Resources: Key Elements in Protecting Women from Domestic Violence Acculturation can act as a protective factor for domestic violence among immigrant women by enhancing their understanding of the legal system and available resources in their new country (Sabri et al., 2018a). Survivors who become more integrated and fluent in the local language are better equipped to advocate for themselves, access support services, and navigate legal protections, reducing their risk of violence (Morrison et al., 2023; Sabri et al., 2018a; Sasseville et al., 2022). However, as previously mentioned, it is important to recognize that acculturation can also introduce risks, such as when a survivor's increased independence or empowerment leads to backlash from an abusive partner (Sabri et al., 2018a).

Internal Sources of Strength Immigrant survivors of domestic violence have described internal sources of strength as vital protective factors (Njie-Carr et al., 2021; Sabri et al., 2018a). Survivors often draw upon their qualities, such as resilience, determination, and optimism, which help them navigate and overcome abusive situations. Attributes like patience, a proactive willingness to seek help, and the ability to remain calm under pressure serve as coping mechanisms and motivators, enabling them to take decisive steps toward achieving safety (Sabri et al., 2018a).

Use of Safety Strategies Immigrant women's use of safety strategies plays a crucial protective role in safeguarding them from their abusers. For example, in a study, immigrant women and practitioners serving immigrant women reported women's use of protective strategies such as creating safety circles with family, friends, and community members and seeking assistance from authorities, healthcare providers, or shelters (Sabri et al., 2018a). Effective strategies for survivors include keeping a phone with emergency numbers accessible, developing escape plans, filing restraining orders, minimizing interactions with the abuser, avoiding going out alone at night, relocating if necessary, and employing practical measures such as changing locks, installing motion lights, or using code words to signal emergencies (Sabri et al., 2018a). Additionally, strategies such as maintaining silence to avoid provoking the abuser or leaving temporarily when tensions rise can offer short-term protection (Sabri et al., 2018a). By actively utilizing these safety strategies, survivors can better manage their circumstances and enhance their overall security.

Interventions Addressing Domestic Violence Among Immigrant Women Using the Socio-Ecological Framework

Interventions addressing domestic violence among immigrant women require a comprehensive, culturally responsive, and multilevel approach that aligns with the socio-ecological framework (Bronfenbrenner, 1979). Prior work on domestic violence interventions among immigrant populations has varied in approach, target populations, and outcomes (Greene et al., 2021; Li et al., 2022, 2023; Rai et al., 2023; Tiwari et al., 2020). Interventions grounded in a socio-ecological framework recognize that domestic violence is shaped by interactions across multiple levels—individual, interpersonal, community, and societal—and, therefore, demand interventions that operate at and across these levels. Some key strategies to enhance support for domestic violence survivors among immigrant populations at different levels include the following.

Societal-Level Interventions: Integrating Public Awareness and Educational Interventions to Address Domestic Violence

Societal-level interventions can be used to shift gender inequitable cultural norms, raise awareness, and improve survivors' systemic access to safety and support. Public awareness campaigns, mainly through media outlets, can help reach a broad audience and disseminate vital information about available resources for domestic violence and legal rights (Carlyle et al., 2019; Yoshihama & Hammock, 2023). By leveraging ethnic media, social media platforms, and community networks, these campaigns can create a more informed public, reduce stigma, and empower immigrant women to seek help (Carlyle et al., 2019; Yoshihama & Hammock, 2023). In tandem with these campaigns, workshops and educational interventions can play a critical role in deepening understanding of domestic violence, building awareness of legal protections, and teaching practical skills to address violence (Sabri et al., 2018a; Yoshihama & Hammock, 2023). These initiatives often incorporate culturally tailored curricula and community-based resources, which help foster empowerment, develop crucial life skills, and improve access to support systems (Sabri et al., 2018a). Additionally, immigrant survivors and practitioners serving immigrant women have identified key areas that educational programs should address, including food and financial assistance (especially emergency loans without requiring identification), legal support, pathways to sustainable employment and education, English or driving classes, affordable housing, and resources to help women return to their home country for safety (Sabri et al., 2018a). These programs help address critical social determinants of health and support women in rebuilding their independence.

Educational initiatives can also target families and community norms. For instance, domestic violence curricula integrated into workshops have been shown to increase knowledge of legal rights, healthy relationship dynamics, and available community resources (Yoshihama & Hammock, 2023). Such efforts not only empower individuals but also shift collective understanding and community responses to abuse. In this way, public awareness campaigns and targeted educational programs serve a dual function—enhancing individual agency while promoting broader cultural change and practical engagement within immigrant communities.

Community-Level Interventions: Culturally Grounded, Localized Support

Community-based interventions for domestic violence can provide a localized, culturally sensitive support system through outreach in trusted spaces, such as ethnic community centers, religious organizations, and immigrant-owned businesses (Bacchus et al., 2024; Choi et al., 2017, 2019; Trabold et al., 2018). These interventions also involve training community leaders and activists to recognize signs of abuse and offer direct assistance, ensuring that resources are accessible and survivors feel safe and supported (Choi et al., 2017, 2019; Sabri et al., 2018a). For example, a scoping review on domestic violence interventions for immigrant communities found that programs for East Asian and Latinx communities empowered clergy as confidants for women experiencing domestic violence, connecting them to resources while reframing cultural views on abuse (Choi et al., 2017, 2019; Rai et al., 2023). Similarly, broader interventions promoted healthy relationships by challenging traditional gender roles, dismantling patriarchal norms, and addressing power imbalances. These efforts emphasized rethinking masculinity and authority, fostering mutual respect, and overcoming cultural barriers that perpetuate abuse. Despite cultural differences, all interventions aimed to eliminate oppression, promote equality, and prevent domestic violence through education and community engagement (Rai et al., 2023). For instance, in a review, two interventions for South Asian immigrants utilized the community mobilization model to address domestic violence. This approach included educating the community, fostering support from key stakeholders, creating programs to strengthen social networks, and organizing groups to challenge societal norms that perpetuate violence (Tripathi & Azhar, 2022; Yoshihama et al., 2012; Yoshihama & Tolman, 2015).

Home visiting programs are a powerful community-level intervention strategy that provides survivors of domestic violence with direct, in-home support (Prosman et al., 2015). A culturally adapted home visiting program, enhanced with a curriculum focused on domestic violence, incorporated relationship education, violence screening, and referrals to improve the identification of domestic violence among Latina women in the United States (Li et al., 2022). This approach proved effective in increasing both empowerment and detection rates. However, cultural and structural barriers, such as language differences and the fear of deportation, hindered its overall effectiveness, particularly in increasing reports of abuse and preventing domestic violence within the Latinx community (Li et al., 2022).

Interpersonal-Level Interventions: Strengthening Family and Peer Relationships

At the interpersonal level, interventions could focus on improving survivors' relationships with people with whom they regularly interact (Sabri et al., 2022a, b), including intimate partners, in-laws, extended family members, children, and peers. These efforts focus on reducing interpersonal conflict, strengthening supportive connections, and promoting safer family dynamics. For example, a parenting workshop for Chinese immigrant women emphasized nonviolent parenting strategies and not only helped enhance participants' parenting skills but also successfully reduced parenting stress in the context of domestic violence (Tiwari et al., 2020). Such interventions can enhance not only parenting skills but also the overall family environment, thereby improving the emotional well-being of both survivors and their children. Additional interpersonal-level strategies may involve engaging couples and extended family members in educational programs that address the dynamics of domestic violence. These interventions can focus on increasing awareness about the impact of inequitable gender norms on health and relationship outcomes while fostering skills for equitable negotiation of gender roles, effective partner communication, nonviolent conflict resolution, and the establishment of personal boundaries. Educational sessions may also help participants distinguish between healthy and unhealthy relationship patterns, ultimately promoting more respectful and supportive interactions within families (Sabri et al., 2022a, b).

Individual-Level Interventions: Culturally Responsive, Survivor-Centered, and Intersectional Approaches to Safety Planning and Mental Health Support

At the individual level, interventions for supporting immigrant survivors of domestic violence can emphasize survivors' autonomy, safety, and psychological well-being. Effective strategies must consider cultural backgrounds and intersectional factors shaping women's abuse experiences (Rai et al., 2023), as well as their unique safety needs. Research highlights that survivors of domestic violence emphasize the importance of a survivor-centered and culturally sensitive approach when working with immigrant communities. A survivor-centered model prioritizes autonomy and informed decision-making, while culturally sensitive strategies ensure that service providers understand survivors' backgrounds, languages, and unique challenges (Sabri et al., 2018a). Building on these principles, safety planning is a crucial intervention that provides immigrant survivors with strategies to recognize risks and protect themselves from further harm (Sabri et al., 2022a, b; Wood et al., 2019). A comprehensive, culturally responsive, and intersectional approach to safety planning could ensure that interventions address the multiple and overlapping barriers immigrant survivors face, including legal, financial, mental, and social constraints (Sabri et al., 2024a). These interventions adopt individualized approaches that address immigrant women's unique cultural, legal, mental, and community-specific challenges. By considering these factors, these interventions empower women to protect themselves and their families while navigating abusive environments (Sabri et al., 2024b).

Strategies may include practical safety measures, such as altering daily routines, changing locks, or installing security systems, as well as emotional and logistical support, like identifying safe places and securing emergency contacts (National Domestic Violence Hotline, n.d.; Parker et al., 2015). In addition to these immediate measures, women are encouraged to develop personalized safety plans, which might involve preparing an emergency bag containing essential items such as money, identification, medication, and important documents (e.g., birth certificates and social security cards) (National Domestic Violence Hotline, n.d.; Parker et al., 2015). These plans also emphasize the importance of protecting children, knowing when and how to reach out to hotlines or crisis centers, and ensuring access to resources supporting immediate safety needs (National Domestic Violence Hotline, n.d.; Parker et al., 2015). Importantly, safety planning should be an ongoing process, addressing both immediate and long-term concerns. Survivors require continuous support beyond initial interventions to ensure sustained safety and well-being (Sabri et al., 2018a).

Safety planning interventions are often complemented by educational and mental health programs to enhance survivors' empowerment and well-being (Tiwari et al., 2020; Li et al., 2023). In a qualitative study, practitioners and survivors emphasized the importance of integrative programs for immigrant women facing domestic violence, incorporating legal, financial, career planning, food access, and mental health resources. These programs also include securing safe housing and transportation and ensuring accommodations for children (Sabri et al., 2018a). One example of an integrative approach is the BSHAPE intervention, designed for immigrant women with cumulative exposure to violence, including domestic violence. This program incorporates psychoeducation, mindfulness-based stress reduction, and tailored safety planning. Preliminary evaluations of BSHAPE showed women's significant improvements in stress management, mental health, and safety-related empowerment, supporting survivors in their healing process (Sabri et al., 2021a, b, 2024c). A 12-week integrated domestic violence intervention for Chinese immigrant women provided practical safety strategies alongside education on the cycle of violence, legal protections, and community resources. This comprehensive approach effectively enhanced participants' safety behaviors and empowered them to navigate their situations with greater confidence for at least six months post-intervention (Tiwari et al., 2020). Similarly, another integrated domestic violence intervention integrated self-compassion and mindfulness training with safety planning, demonstrating the potential of mobile health platforms to support survivors in implementing safety measures.

Evidence shows the benefits of an integrated approach to safety planning that incorporates a mental health component by addressing the psychological impacts of domestic violence, particularly for immigrant women. Effective interventions combine therapy, advocacy, and peer support to enhance resilience. For example, cognitive processing therapy paired with advocacy counseling helped Congolese refugee women manage PTSD, depression, and anxiety despite retention challenges (Greene et al., 2021). Mobile health technology incorporating elements such as self-compassion training and mindfulness exercises improved mental health outcomes among immigrant women (Sabri et al., 2021a, b, 2024c). Similarly, telephone support from social workers and peer volunteers reduced isolation and fostered emotional resilience (Tiwari et al., 2020). These approaches highlight the value of integrating mental health into safety planning.

Recommendations

Addressing domestic violence among immigrant women requires a multifaceted and culturally responsive approach that prioritizes both immediate safety and long-term mental and physical well-being (Li et al., 2023; Rai et al., 2023; Sabri et al., 2018a; Tiwari et al., 2020). Effective interventions must recognize the intersection of trauma, cultural barriers, and systemic challenges, ensuring survivors receive comprehensive support (Rai et al., 2023; Sabri et al., 2018a). Our key recommendations for addressing domestic violence in immigrant communities include the following:

1. At the societal/policy level, there is a need to expand protections for immigrant survivors through programs such as the Violence Against Women Act and U visas for victims of crime and reduce barriers that prevent immigrant women from reporting abuse, such as fear of deportation (Bacchus et al., 2024; Choi et al., 2017, 2019; Trabold et al., 2018). There is also a need for increased funding for programs serving immigrant women (Modi et al., 2013). Moreover, mandating that law enforcement, social service, and healthcare providers receive training on cultural competence, trauma-informed care, and immigration-related challenges can be beneficial (Rai et al., 2023; Sabri et al., 2018a).
2. At the community level, there is a need to engage community leaders, religious leaders, and local organizations to challenge harmful

gender norms and promote awareness about domestic violence resources (Bacchus et al., 2024; Choi et al., 2017, 2019; Trabold et al., 2018). Also, multilingual campaigns should be developed to educate women about their rights and available services while reducing the stigma around seeking help (Cardenas et al., 2024). Further, there is a need to strengthen informal support networks through religious and social groups via training to recognize signs of domestic violence and provide appropriate support to survivors (Choi et al., 2017, 2019). Moreover, multi-sector collaborations that integrate healthcare, law enforcement, social services, and legal aid to provide holistic support to immigrant survivors can be strengthened (Sabri et al., 2018a).

3. At the interpersonal level, interventions should focus on strengthening immigrant survivors' relationships with partners and family members. The strategies may include family education programs that promote healthy communication, nonviolent conflict resolution, and shared decision-making within households (Sabri et al., 2022a, b). Parenting workshops and couple-based interventions can be used to address gender norms, enhance parenting skills, and reduce household stress, all of which contribute to the emotional well-being of both survivors and their children (Tiwari et al., 2020). Training for partners and family members can include topics such as recognizing abusive behaviors, setting healthy boundaries, and understanding the effects of domestic violence on all family members (Sabri et al., 2022a, b).
3. At the individual level, there is a need for culturally tailored trauma-informed empowerment-focused interventions that use a holistic approach in working with immigrant survivors of domestic violence (Rai et al., 2023; Sabri et al., 2024a, b, c). This includes prioritizing safety and connecting survivors to appropriate resources that address basic needs and other threats to safety.

By strengthening systemic policy reforms, community-based solutions, and individual-level interventions, a comprehensive support framework can be developed for addressing domestic violence among immigrant communities.

References

Ardabily, H. E., Moghadam, Z. B., Salsali, M., Ramezanzadeh, F., & Nedjat, S. (2011). Prevalence and risk factors for domestic violence against infertile women in an Iranian setting. *International Journal of Gynaecology and Obstetrics: The Official Organ of the International Federation of Gynaecology and Obstetrics, 112*(1), 15–17. https://doi.org/10.1016/j.ijgo.2010.07.030

Bacchus, L. J., Colombini, M., Pearson, I., Gevers, A., Stöckl, H., & Guedes, A. C. (2024). Interventions that prevent or respond to intimate partner violence against women and violence against children: A systematic review. *The Lancet Public Health, 9*(5), e326–e338. https://doi.org/10.1016/s2468-2667(24)00048-3

Barkho, E., Fakhouri, M., & Arnetz, J. E. (2011). Intimate partner violence among Iraqi immigrant women in Metro Detroit: A pilot study. *Journal of Immigrant and Minority Health, 13*(4), 725–731. https://doi.org/10.1007/s10903-010-9399-4

Barocas, B., Emery, D., & Mills, L. G. (2016). Changing the domestic violence narrative: Aligning definitions and standards. *Journal of Family Violence, 31*(8), 941–947.

Bograd, M. (1990). Feminist perspectives on wife abuse: An introduction. In K. Yllö & M. Bograd (Eds.), *Feminist perspectives on wife abuse* (pp. 11–26).

Boonzaier, F., & De La Rey, C. (2003). "He's a man and I'm a woman": Cultural constructions of masculinity and femininity in South African women's narratives of violence. *Violence Against Women, 9*(8), 1003–1029.

Bradbury-Jones, C., Breckenridge, J. P., Devaney, J., Duncan, F., Kroll, T., Lazenbatt, A., & Taylor, J. (2015). Priorities and strategies for improving disabled women's access to maternity services when they are affected by domestic abuse: A multi-method study using concept maps. *BMC Pregnancy and Childbirth, 15*, 350. https://doi.org/10.1186/s12884-015-0786-7

Bronfenbrenner, U. (1979). *The ecology of human development: Experiments by nature and design*. Harvard University Press. https://doi.org/10.2307/j.ctv26071r6

Brownridge D. A., & Hali S. (2002). Double jeopardy? Violence against immigrant women in Canada. *Violence and Victims, 17*(4), 455–471.

Campbell, J. C., Webster, D., Koziol-McLain, J., Block, C., Campbell, D., Curry, M. A., Gary, F., Glass, N., McFarlane, J., Sachs, C., Sharps, P., Ulrich, Y., Wilt, S. A., Manganello, J., Xu, X., Schollenberger, J., Frye, V., & Laughon, K. (2003). Risk factors for femicide in abusive relationships: Results from a multisite case control study. *American Journal of Public Health, 93*(7), 1089–1097.

Cardenas, I., Fraga Rizo, C., Ward, M., & Jiwatram-Negrón, T. (2024). Systematic review of intimate partner violence interventions for Latinas in the U.S. *Trauma,*

Violence, & Abuse, 25(5), 3473–3487. https://doi.org/10.1177/15248380241253037

Carlyle, K. E., Guidry, J. P. D., Dougherty, S. A., & Burton, C. W. (2019). Intimate partner violence on Instagram: Visualizing a public health approach to prevention. *Health Education & Behavior, 46*(2), 90S–96S. https://doi.org/10.1177/1090198119873917

Choi, A. W. (2022). In-law psychological aggression and its impacts on women's health. *Aggressive Behavior, 48*(2), 163–172. https://doi.org/10.1002/ab.22015

Choi, J., Phua, J., Armstrong, K. J., & An, S. (2017). Negotiating the cultural steps in developing an online intervention for Korean American intimate partner violence. *Journal of Aggression, Maltreatment & Trauma, 26*(8), 920–936. https://doi.org/10.1080/10926771.2017.1327911

Choi, Y. J., Orpinas, P., Kim, I., & Ko, K. S. (2019). Korean clergy for healthy families: Online intervention for preventing intimate partner violence. *Global Health Promotion, 26*(4), 25–32. https://doi.org/10.1177/1757975917747878

El-Moslemany, R., Mellon, L., Tully, L., & McConkey, S. J. (2020). Factors associated with intimate partner violence perpetration and victimization in asylum seeking and refugee populations: A systematic review. *Trauma, Violence, & Abuse, 23*(3), 827–839. https://doi.org/10.1177/1524838020977147

Erez, E., & Harper, S. (2018). Intersectionality, immigration, and domestic violence. In R. Martínez, M. E. Hollis, & J. I. Stowell (Eds.), *The handbook of race, ethnicity, crime, and justice*. https://doi.org/10.1002/9781119113799.ch20

Fernández, M. (2006). Cultural beliefs and domestic violence. *Annals of the New York Academy of Sciences, 1087*, 250–260. https://doi.org/10.1196/annals.1385.005

García-Cuéllar, M. M., Pastor-Moreno, G., Ruiz-Pérez, I., & Henares-Montiel, J. (2023). The prevalence of intimate partner violence against women with disabilities: A systematic review of the literature. *Disability and Rehabilitation, 45*(1), 1–8. https://doi.org/10.1080/09638288.2022.2025927

Greene, M. C., Likindikoki, S., Rees, S., Bonz, A., Kaysen, D., Misinzo, L., Njau, T., Kiluwa, S., Turner, R., Ventevogel, P., Mbwambo, J. K. K., & Tol, W. A. (2021). Evaluation of an integrated intervention to reduce psychological distress and intimate partner violence in refugees: Results from the Nguvu cluster randomized feasibility trial. *PLoS One, 16*(6), e0252982. https://doi.org/10.1371/journal.pone.0252982

Herrero-Arias, R., Ortiz-Barreda, G., Hollekim, R., Briones-Vozmediano, E., & Vives-Cases, C. (2019). The position of the child in the life experiences of immigrant survivors of intimate partner violence: A study of service providers' perspectives in Spain. *Journal of Interpersonal Violence, 36*(21–22). https://doi.org/10.1177/0886260519889931

Horne, S. (1999). Domestic violence in Russia. *American Psychologist, 54*, 55–61.

Howell, K. H., Thurston, I. B., Schwartz, L. E., Jamison, L. E., & Hasselle, A. J. (2018). Protective factors associated with resilience in women exposed to intimate partner violence. *Psychology of Violence, 8*(4), 438–447. https://doi.org/10.1037/vio0000147

Huecker, M. R., King, K. C., Jordan, G. A., & Smock, W. (2023). *Domestic violence.* StatPearls Publishing. https://www.ncbi.nlm.nih.gov/books/NBK499891/

International Organization for Migration. (2024). *Interactive world migration report.* https://worldmigrationreport.iom.int/msite/wmr-2024-interactive/

Kalokhe, A. S., Potdar, R. R., Stephenson, R., Dunkle, K. L., Paranjape, A., del Rio, C., & Sahay, S. (2015). How well does the World Health Organization definition of domestic violence work for India? *PLoS One, 10*(3), e0120909.

Kim, C. (2019). Social isolation, acculturative stress and intimate partner violence (IPV) victimization among Korean immigrant women. *International Journal of Intercultural Relations: IJIR, 72*, 87–95.

Kimber, M., Henriksen, C. A., Davidov, D. M., Goldstein, A. L., Pitre, N. Y., Tonmyr, L., & Afifi, T. O. (2015). The association between immigrant generational status, child maltreatment history and intimate partner violence (IPV): Evidence from a nationally representative survey. *Social Psychiatry and Psychiatric Epidemiology, 50*(7), 1135–1144. https://doi.org/10.1007/s00127-014-1002-1

Kozu, J. (1999). Domestic violence in Japan. *American Psychologist, 54*, 50–54.

Leemis, R. W., Jr., Friar, N., Khatiwada, S., Chen, M. S., Kresnow, M., Smith, S. G., Caslin, S., Basile, K. C., & Centers for Disease Control and Prevention. (2022). *The National Intimate Partner and sexual violence survey: 2016/2017 report on intimate partner violence.* National Center for Injury Prevention and Control, Centers for Disease Control and Prevention. https://www.cdc.gov/violenceprevention/pdf/nisvs/nisvsreportonipv_2022.pdf

Lewis, P. C., Kaslow, N. J., Cheong, Y. F., Evans, D. P., & Yount, K. M. (2024). Femicide in the United States: A call for legal codification and national surveillance. *Frontiers in Public Health, 12*, 1338548. https://doi.org/10.3389/fpubh.2024.1338548

Li, Y., Bloom, T., Herbell, K., & Bullock, L. F. C. (2020). Prevalence and risk factors of intimate partner violence among Chinese immigrant women. *Journal of Advanced Nursing, 76*(10), 2559–2571. https://doi.org/10.1111/jan.14458

Li, Q., Riosmena, F., Valverde, P. A., Zhou, S., Amura, C., Peterson, K. A., Palusci, V. J., & Feder, L. (2022). Preventing intimate partner violence among foreign-born Latinx mothers through relationship education during nurse home visiting. *Journal of Nursing Management, 30*(6), 1639–1647. https://doi.org/10.1111/jonm.13565

Li, Y., Rhee, H., Bullock, L. F. C., McCaw, B., & Bloom, T. (2023). Self-compassion, health, and empowerment: A pilot randomized controlled trial for Chinese immigrant women experiencing intimate partner violence. *Journal of*

Interpersonal Violence, 39(7–8), 1571–1595. https://doi.org/10.1177/08862605231207624

McAuliffe, M., & Oucho, L. A. (2024). *World migration report 2024.* International Organization for Migration. https://publications.iom.int/books/world-migration-report-2024

McWhirter, P. T. (1999). La violencia privada: Domestic violence in Chile. *American Psychologist, 54*, 37–40.

Messing, J. T., Amanor-Boadu, Y., Cavanaugh, C. E., Glass, N. E., & Campbell, J. C. (2013). Culturally competent intimate partner violence risk assessment: Adapting the danger assessment for immigrant women. *Social Work Research, 37*(3), 263–275. https://doi.org/10.1093/swr/svt019

Migration Policy Institute. (2023). *U.S. immigrant population and share over time, 1850-Present.* https://www.migrationpolicy.org/programs/data-hub/charts/immigrant-population-over-time

Modi, M. N., Palmer, S., & Armstrong, A. (2013). The role of violence against women act in addressing intimate partner violence: A public health issue. *Journal of Womens Health, 23*(3), 253–259. https://doi.org/10.1089/jwh.2013.4387

Morrison, A. M., Campbell, J. K., Sharpless, L., & Martin, S. L. (2023). Intimate partner violence and immigration in the United States: A systematic review. *Trauma, Violence & Abuse, 25*(1), 846.

Mughal, F. B., & Saint Arnault, D. (2024). Protective factors affecting trauma recovery among female South Asian immigrant intimate partner violence survivors: A scoping review. *Trauma, Violence, & Abuse, 25*(4), 2927–2941. https://doi.org/10.1177/15248380241231602

National Domestic Violence Hotline. (n.d.). *What is a safety plan?* The Hotline. https://www.thehotline.org/what-is-a-safety-plan/

Njie-Carr, V. P. S., Sabri, B., Messing, J. T., Suarez, C., Ward-Lasher, A., Wachter, K., Marea, C. X., & Campbell, J. (2021). Understanding intimate partner violence among immigrant and refugee women: A grounded theory analysis. *Journal of Aggression, Maltreatment & Trauma, 30*(6), 792.

Ofei-Aboagye, R. O. (1994). Altering the strands of the fabric: A preliminary look at domestic violence in Ghana. *Journal of Women in Culture and Society, 19*, 924–936.

Park, T., Mullins, A., Zahir, N., Salami, B., Lasiuk, G., & Hegadoren, K. (2021). Domestic violence and immigrant women: A glimpse behind a veiled door. *Violence Against Women, 27*(15–16), 2910.

Parker, E. M., Gielen, A. C., Castillo, R., & Webster, D. (2015). Safety strategy use among women seeking temporary protective orders: The relationship between violence experienced, strategy effectiveness, and risk perception. *Violence and Victims, 30*(4), 614–635. https://doi.org/10.1891/0886-6708.VV-D-14-00003

Pisklakova, M. (1995). *The crisis center for women and the first results of its operation*. Moscow.

Plummer, S. B., & Findley, P. A. (2012). Women with disabilities' experience with physical and sexual abuse: A review of the literature and implications for the field. *Trauma, Violence, and Abuse, 13*(1), 15–29. https://doi.org/10.1177/1524838011426014

Prosman, G.-J., Lo Fo Wong, S. H., van der Wouden, J. C., & Lagro-Janssen, A. L. M. (2015). Effectiveness of home visiting in reducing partner violence for families experiencing abuse: A systematic review. *Family Practice, 32*(3), 247–256. https://doi.org/10.1093/fampra/cmu091

Ragavan, M., & Iyengar, K. (2020). Violence perpetrated by mothers-in-law in northern India: Perceived frequency, acceptability, and options for survivors. *Journal of Interpersonal Violence, 35*(17–18), 3308–3330. https://doi.org/10.1177/0886260517708759

Rahebi, S. M., Rahnavardi, M., Chamani, S. R., Nazari, M., & Sabetghadam, S. (2019). Relationship between domestic violence and infertility. *Eastern Mediterranean Health Journal, 25*(08), 537–542. https://doi.org/10.26719/emhj.19.001

Rai, A., Ravi, K., Shrestha, N., & Alvarez-Hernandez, L. R. (2023). Culturally responsive domestic violence interventions for immigrant communities in the United States: A scoping review. *Journal of Social Work in the Global Community, 8*, 1–29. https://doi.org/10.5590/JSWGC.2023.8.1.01

Ruiz-Pérez, I., Pastor-Moreno, G., Escribà-Agüir, V., & Maroto-Navarro, G. (2018). Intimate partner violence in women with disabilities: Perception of healthcare and attitudes of health professionals. *Disability and Rehabilitation, 40*(9), 1059–1065. https://doi.org/10.1080/09638288.2017.1288273

Sabri, B., Campbell, J. C., & Dabby, F. C. (2016). Gender differences in intimate partner homicides among ethnic subgroups of Asians. *Violence Against Women, 22*(4), 432–453.

Sabri, B., Nnawulezi, N., Njie-Carr, V. P. S., Messing, J., Ward-Lasher, A., Alvarez, C., & Campbell, J. C. (2018a). Multilevel risk and protective factors for intimate partner violence among African, Asian, and Latina immigrant and refugee women: Perceptions of effective safety planning interventions. *Race and Social Problems, 10*(4), 348–365.

Sabri, B., Simonet, M., & Campbell, J. C. (2018b). Risk and protective factors of intimate partner violence among south Asian immigrant women and perceived need for services. *Cultural Diversity & Ethnic Minority Psychology, 24*(3), 442–452. https://doi.org/10.1037/cdp0000189

Sabri, B., Campbell, J. C., & Messing, J. T. (2021a). Intimate partner homicides in the United States, 2003–2013: A comparison of immigrants and nonimmigrant victims. *Journal of Interpersonal Violence, 36*(9–10), 4735–4757. https://doi.org/10.1177/0886260518792249

Sabri, B., Vroegindewey, A., & Hagos, M. (2021b). Development, feasibility, acceptability and preliminary evaluation of the internet and mobile phone-based BSHAPE intervention for immigrant survivors of cumulative trauma. *Contemporary Clinical Trials, 110*, 106591. https://doi.org/10.1016/j.cct.2021.106591

Sabri, B., Sellke, R., Smudde, M., Bourey, C., & McIvor Murray, S. (2022a). Gender-based violence interventions in low- and middle-income countries: A systematic review of interventions at structural, community, interpersonal, individual, and multiple levels. *Trauma, Violence, & Abuse, 24*(5), 3170–3186. https://doi.org/10.1177/15248380221126181

Sabri, B., Tharmarajah, S., Njie-Carr, V. P. S., Messing, J. T., Loerzel, E., Arscott, J., & Campbell, J. C. (2022b). Safety planning with marginalized survivors of intimate partner violence: Challenges of conducting safety planning intervention research with marginalized women. *Trauma, Violence, & Abuse, 23*(5), 1728–1751. https://doi.org/10.1177/15248380211013136

Sabri, B., Hanson, G., Patch, M., Wilson, P., Alexander, K. A., Njie-Carr, V., & Campbell, J. C. (2024a). Characteristics of abusive relationships with presence of firearms: Impact of partners' firearm ownership on immigrant women's mental health and safety-related empowerment. *Journal of Family Trauma, Child Custody & Child Development*, (1), –24. https://doi.org/10.1080/26904586.2024.2423401

Sabri, B., Mata, T., Li, J., Butter, S., Campbell, J. C., & Chakra Budhathoki. (2024b). The digital MySteps for abused women at risk for firearm-related injuries and homicides: Findings from the feasibility, acceptability and preliminary efficacy trial. *Contemporary Clinical Trials Communications, 41*, 101357–101357. https://doi.org/10.1016/j.conctc.2024.101357

Sabri, B., Perrin, N., & Hagos, M. (2024c). The being safe, health and positively empowered pilot randomized controlled trial: A digital multicomponent intervention for immigrant women with cumulative exposures to violence. *Cultural Diversity & Ethnic Minority Psychology*. Advance online publication. https://doi.org/10.1037/cdp0000635

Sardinha, L., Maheu-Giroux, M., Stöckl, H., Meyer, S. R., & García-Moreno, C. (2022). Global, regional, and national prevalence estimates of physical or sexual, or both, intimate partner violence against women in 2018. *Lancet, 399*(10327), 803.

Sasseville, N., Maurice, P., Montminy, L., Hassan, G., & St-Pierre, É. (2022). Cumulative contexts of vulnerability to intimate partner violence among women with disabilities, elderly women, and immigrant women: Prevalence, risk factors, explanatory theories, and prevention. *Trauma, Violence, & Abuse, 23*(1), 88–100. https://doi.org/10.1177/1524838020925773

Schröttle, M., & Glammeier, S. (2013). Intimate partner violence against disabled women as a part of widespread victimization and discrimination over the lifetime: Evidence from a German representative study. *International Journal of Conflict and Violence, 7*(2), 232–248. https://doi.org/10.4119/ijcv-3021

Shibusawa, T., & Yick, A. (2007). Experiences and perceptions of intimate partner violence among older Chinese immigrants. *Journal of Elder Abuse & Neglect, 19*(3–4), 1–17. https://doi.org/10.1300/J084v19n03_01

Sinha, M. (2013). *Measuring violence against women: Statistical trends* (Statistics Canada Catalogue No. 85-002-X). Statistics Canada.

Sokoloff, N. J., & Dupont, I. (2005). Domestic violence at the intersections of race, class, and gender. *Violence Against Women, 11*, 38–64.

Tavrow, P., Azucar, D., Huynh, D., Yoo, C., Liang, D., Pathomrit, W., & Withers, M. (2022). Encouraging Asian immigrant women to disclose intimate partner violence in primary care settings. *Journal of Interpersonal Violence, 37*(7–8), NP5626–NP5648. https://doi.org/10.1177/0886260520959642

Tiwari, A., Fong, D. Y. T., Yuen, F. K. H., Fung, H. Y. K., Pang, P. O. Y., & Wong, J. Y. H. (2020). Purpose-built intervention for mental health of Mainland Chinese immigrant women survivors of intimate partner violence: A randomized controlled trial (abridged secondary publication). *Hong Kong Medical Journal, 8*(6), 7–9.

Trabold, N., McMahon, J., Alsobrooks, S., Whitney, S., & Mittal, M. (2018). A systematic review of intimate partner violence interventions: State of the field and implications for practitioners. *Trauma Violence & Abuse, 21*(2), 311–325. https://doi.org/10.1177/1524838018767934

Tripathi, S., & Azhar, S. (2022). A systematic review of intimate partner violence interventions impacting south Asian women in the United States. *Trauma, Violence, & Abuse, 23*(2), 523–540. https://doi.org/10.1177/1524838020957987

U.S. Census Bureau. (2022). *Explore census data.* https://data.census.gov/table?t=Native%20and%20Foreign-Born&g=010XX00US

United Nations. (2020). *Domestic abuse.* United Nations. https://www.un.org/en/coronavirus/what-is-domestic-abuse

UNWomen. (2023). *Facts and figures: Ending violence against women.* UN Women – Headquarters. https://www.unwomen.org/en/what-we-do/ending-violence-against-women/facts-and-figures

Westenberg, L. (2017). 'When she calls for help'—Domestic violence in Christian families. *Social Sciences, 6*(3), 71. https://doi.org/10.3390/socsci6030071

Wood, S. N., Glass, N., & Decker, M. R. (2019). An integrative review of safety strategies for women experiencing intimate partner violence in low-and middle-income countries. *Trauma, Violence, & Abuse, 22*, 68–82.

World Health Organization. (2021). *Violence against women prevalence estimates, 2018.* World Health Organization. https://www.who.int/publications/i/item/9789240022256

World Health Organization/London School of Hygiene and Tropical Medicine. (2010). *Preventing intimate partner and sexual violence against women: Taking action and generating evidence.* World Health Organization.

Yoshihama, M., & Hammock, A. C. (2023). Assessing community readiness to develop a socioculturally relevant intimate partner violence prevention program. *Prevention Science, 24*(8), 1340–1351. https://doi.org/10.1007/s11121-023-01567-5

Yoshihama, M., & Tolman, R. (2015). Using interactive theater to create socioculturally relevant community-based intimate partner violence prevention. *American Journal of Community Psychology, 55*(1–2), 136–147.

Yoshihama, M., Ramakrishnan, A., Hammock, A. C., & Khaliq, M. (2012). Intimate partner violence prevention program in an Asian immigrant community: Integrating theories, data, and community. *Violence Against Women, 18*(7), 763–783.

Afterword

Violence and Trauma Without Borders: Perspectives of Immigrants, Migrants, and Refugees examines the experiences of diverse immigrant communities in the United States, most of which belong to marginalized or racialized groups that experienced voluntary migration or forced displacement. The conditions, reasons, and motivations for leaving one's country of birth are as varied and diverse as the backgrounds of immigrants themselves, as are the contexts of reception immigrants experience upon arrival in the United States. As such, it is difficult to generalize regarding the typical immigrant experience in this country. Nevertheless, examining diverse groups across different stages of the life course, the contributors to this volume clearly illustrate that violence and trauma are recurring, prevalent themes in the lives of many immigrants and their family members. Yet much of this violence and trauma could be mitigated by state interventions aimed at creating and fostering favorable socio-ecological and socio-legal contexts of reception. Anti-immigrant discourse, including what Leo Chavez (2013) has described as the Latino Threat Narrative, routinely contends that immigrants, particularly Latino immigrants, are unable and unwilling to integrate into American society. Nevertheless, as several chapters throughout this volume have noted, an immigrant group's ability to adapt to a given society in a pro-social direction, which I believe includes being free from violence, crime

J. S. Hong et al. (eds.), *Violence and Trauma Without Borders*,
https://doi.org/10.1007/978-3-032-29221-6

victimization, bullying, mistreatment and abuse, and racial discrimination, is just as contingent upon society's willingness to accept that group. While immigrant characteristics, such as socioeconomic status and access to various forms of capital, are crucial to the integration process, so too are the national and local contexts of reception (Portes & Rumbaut, 2001, 2024).

As of June 2025, nearly 51.9 million foreign-born individuals resided in the United States, accounting for 15.4% of the total US population (Kramer & Passel, 2025). Though these numbers dropped from all-time highs in January of the same year, a point to which I return below, immigrants and the immigrant experience represent important aspects of the US mainstream (Alba & Nee, 2003). After all, a prevailing societal ethos has long espoused the United States as a nation of immigrants. This is by no means a recent phenomenon. Though the share of the foreign-born population has increased decade-over-decade since the implementation of the 1965 Immigration and Nationality Act (INA), which effectively eliminated national quotas and discriminatory anti-Asian immigration policies set forth in the 1924 National Origins Act, it was in fact lower between 1970 and 2010 than it had been throughout most of the nineteenth century into the first two decades of the twentieth century. Between the mid-1800s and the early 1900s, the foreign-born population accounted for between 13.3% and 14.8% of the total population (Grieco, 2014). Thus, the notion that the United States is a nation of immigrants predates the post-1965 growth of the foreign-born population, with some sources attributing the phrase to then-US Senator John F. Kennedy's 1958 book titled *A Nation of Immigrants*. Yet several notable contextual factors differentiate pre- and post-1965 immigration, including globalization and racialization. In turn, I contend that these processes have contributed to many of the structural, socio-legal, and socioeconomic conditions resulting in the various forms of violence and trauma described throughout the volume.

Political, economic, and technological transformations throughout the second half of the twentieth century, particularly during the 1990s, contributed to increased rates of globalization, which can generally be described as the growing interconnectedness of societies worldwide (Held, 2000; Franko, 2020). Globalization has led to what geographer and anthropologist David Harvey (1990) described as time-space compression, perhaps best exemplified by the increased ease of international travel, trade, and human mobility. The increased visibility of non-White immigrants, refugees, and asylum seekers in the so-called Global North has led to a sense of ontological insecurity and a resurgence of nativism among a notable segment of the native-born population, who perceive immigrants as a threat (Franko, 2020). In turn, countries such as the United States have responded by implementing increasingly draconian immigration policies, expanding interior immigration enforcement, and militarizing their borders (Franko, 2020). These changes have had implications for the integration of immigrants and their families into society, especially irregular immigrants, as they undermine various forms of institutional support for this population. In the case of the United States, recent estimates placed the undocumented population at roughly 14 million individuals in 2023, including those with some form of protective status that could change quickly (e.g., DACA recipients, asylum applicants, individuals with Temporary Protected Status, parolees) (Passel & Krogstad, 2024). Slightly more dated estimates note that undocumented immigrants reside in more than 6 million households that comprise 22 million individuals, with half of these individuals being US-born or lawful immigrants (Passel & Krogstad, 2024). Given the current political context, many of these individuals will have to cautiously navigate various forms of regulatory and service-oriented institutional surveillance or risk deportation and family separation (Asad, 2023). Most relevant to the present volume, this could include decreased willingness to collaborate with local law enforcement in the investigation of crimes, report crime victimization, meet with one's children's teachers, or interact with social workers or doctors. These deteriorating conditions of reception will undoubtedly affect immigrants' integration into US society, ultimately undermining public safety. Yet it is not just irregular migrants and their loved ones who are affected by this worsening social context. During the first half of 2025, the US federal government began targeting legal permanent residents and student visa holders for immigration enforcement. Perhaps we should not be surprised that between January 2025 and June of the same year, more than one million foreign-born individuals left the United States—either forcibly or voluntarily (Kramer & Passel, 2025).

Another important difference between pre- and post-1965 immigration lies in the dominant regions of the world from which immigrants have originated (Waters & Ueda, 2007; Portes & Rumbaut, 2001). Prior to the implementation of the 1965 INA, immigration to the United States primarily originated from various European regions. Conversely, post-1965 immigrants have largely consisted of immigrants from Latin America and the Caribbean, Asia, and, to a lesser extent, Africa. In other words, immigrants today are more likely to be racialized as non-White in the United States, which is a racially stratified society in which non-Hispanic Whites experience comparatively better measures of well-being relative to other groups (Bonilla Silva, 1997). Prior research has found that race can have profound effects on shaping immigrant youth's life chances and affecting their integration patterns (Portes & Rumbaut, 2001; Portes & Rumbaut, 2024), which was also evident in several chapters throughout this volume.

This experience of racialization was not as pronounced among pre-1965 immigrants. While Southern and Eastern European immigrants in the early twentieth century did experience notable discrimination and were often treated as distinct "races" (i.e., nationalities and ethnicities) from Northern and Western Europeans, Fox and Guglielmo (2012) demonstrated that the social boundaries between these groups, both institutionally and socially, were virtually nonexistent, especially when compared to those of racialized groups such as Black Americans, Mexican Americans, Asian Americans, and Native Americans. It is precisely this historical social construction of race and these racialization processes with which post-1965 immigrants are confronted today.

In sum, globalization—or perhaps more precisely, the reactions of native-born residents and nation-states to globalization—coupled with the racialization of post-1965 immigrants, has contributed to alarming rises in anti-immigrant sentiment, punitive immigration policies, interior immigration enforcement, and border militarization over the past few decades, especially in recent years. In turn, these changes have resulted in unfavorable contexts of reception that make the prospect of integrating into US society daunting. Importantly, it is these contexts that further risk exacerbating the various forms of violence and trauma the contributors discussed throughout this volume. For many immigrants, the United States has represented hope and opportunity, inspiring forward-looking and optimistic aspirations to achieve the American Dream. For others, the contexts of reception they encounter upon arrival are more akin to a nightmare than a dream.

To me, it is evident that favorable contexts of reception are not simply about immigration and who does or does not have the right to be present in the United States; it is also about race and racialization. The racialization of post-1965 immigrants and their perceived "otherness" in particular raises serious questions regarding what it means to be a "real American" to an emboldened segment of the US population. Related, it is curious that the ethos regarding the United States being "a nation of immigrants" emerged at a time when the (1) children and grandchildren of European immigrants had largely integrated into US society, (2) rates of immigration had been steadily decreasing since the early 1920s, and (3) the little immigration that had persisted was largely dominated by Northern and Western Europeans.

For decades, the United States has touted itself as a nation of immigrants. Yet the current political context is not particularly welcoming. This presents a compelling paradox. How can we, on the one hand, claim to celebrate this country's history of immigration, but on the other, permit the contemporary social and political conditions that are harming so many immigrant families? Again, I think this speaks to notions of what it means to be a "real American," with White supremacy playing a central role in addressing this question.

University of Arizona
Tucson, AZ, USA

Daniel E. Martínez

References

Alba, R., & Nee, V. (2003). *Remaking the American mainstream: Assimilation and contemporary immigration*. Harvard University Press.

Asad, A. (2023). *Engage and evade: How Latino immigrant families manage surveillance in everyday life*. Princeton University Press.

Bonilla-Silva, E. (1997). Rethinking racism: Toward a structural interpretation. *American Sociological Review, 62*(3), 465–480.

Chavez, L. (2013). *The Latino threat: Constructing immigrants, citizens and the nation*. Stanford University Press.

Fox, C., & Guglielmo, T. A. (2012). Defining America's racial boundaries: Blacks, Mexicans, and European immigrants, 1890–1945. *American Journal of Sociology, 118*(2), 327–379.

Franko, K. (2020). *Globalization & crime*. Sage.

Grieco, E. M. (2014). *The 'second great wave' of immigration: Growth of the foreign-born population since 1970*. US Census Bureau. https://www.census.gov/newsroom/blogs/random-samplings/2014/02/the-second-great-wave-of-immigration-growth-of-the-foreign-born-population-since-1970.html

Harvey, D. (1990). The condition of postmodernity: An enquiry into the origins of cultural change. .

Held, D. (2000). *Democracy and the global order*. Polity Press.

Kramer, S., & Passel, J. S. (2025). *What the data says about immigrants in the U.S.* Pew Research Center. https://www.pewresearch.org/short-reads/2025/08/21/key-findings-about-us-immigrants/

Passel, J. S., & Krogstad, J. M. (2024). What we know about unauthorized immigrants living in the U.S. Pew Research Center. https://www.pewresearch.org/short-reads/2024/07/22/what-we-know-about-unauthorized-immigrants-living-in-the-us/

Portes, A., & Rumbaut, R. (2001). *Legacies: The story of the immigrant second generation*. University of California Press.

Portes, A., & Rumbaut, R. G. (2024). *Immigrant America: A portrait*. University of California Press.

Waters, M. C., & Ueda, R. (2007). *The new Americans: A guide to immigration since 1965*. Harvard University Press.

Index

J. S. Hong et al. (eds.), *Violence and Trauma Without Borders*,
https://doi.org/10.1007/978-3-032-29221-6

W

FSC
www.fsc.org
MIX
Papier | Fördert
gute Waldnutzung
FSC® C083411

Kolibri 360 GmbH
Ferdinand-Jühlke-Straße 7
99095 Erfurt, Deutschland
produktsicherheit@kolibri360.de